Bloom's Modern Critical Interpretations

Bloom's Modern Critical Interpretations

William Golding's
Lord of the Flies
New Edition

Edited and with an introduction by
Harold Bloom
Sterling Professor of the Humanities
Yale University

BLOOM'S
LITERARY CRITICISM
An imprint of Infobase Publishing

Bloom's Modern Critical Interpretations: Lord of the Flies—New Edition

Copyright © 2008 Infobase Publishing

Introduction © 2008 by Harold Bloom

Bloom's Literary Criticism
An imprint of Infobase Publishing
132 West 31st Street
New York NY 10001

Library of Congress Cataloging-in-Publication Data
William Golding's Lord of the flies / edited and with an introduction by Harold Bloom. — New ed.
    p. cm. — (Bloom's modern critical interpretations)
  Includes bibliographical references (p.   ) and index.
   ISBN 978-0-7910-9826-4 (acid-free paper) 1. Golding, William, 1911–1993. Lord of the flies. I. Bloom, Harold. II. Title: Lord of the flies. III. Series.

PR6013.O35L649 2008
823'.914—dc22

                                       2008002451

Bloom's Literary Criticism books are available at special discounts when purchased in bulk quantities for businesses, associations, institutions, or sales promotions. Please call our Special Sales Department in New York at (212) 967-8800 or (800) 322-8755.

You can find Bloom's Literary Criticism on the World Wide Web at
http://www.chelseahouse.com

Contributing Editor: Pamela Loos
Cover designed by Ben Peterson
Cover photo Mark William Perry and Chad Littlejohn/Shutterstock.com

Printed in the United States of America
IBT EJB 10 9 8 7 6 5 4

This book is printed on acid-free paper.

Contents

Editor's Note

My Introduction, regarding *Lord of the Flies* as a period piece, argues that British schoolboy savagery is not in itself an adequate emblem of universal evil.

K. Chellappan generously finds in the novel "the total fusion of form and meaning"; while James Ginden commends both *Lord of the Flies* and *The Inheritors* as presages of greater works to come.

Lord of the Flies is praised by S.J. Boyd with a dangerous comparison to *King Lear*, a contrast which sinks poor Golding's scholastic allegory without trace.

L.L. Dickson and Lawrence S. Friedman contribute to the chorus of overvaluation, after which Stefan Hawlin fashionably applies postcolonialism to the work.

The influence of Aldous Huxley upon Golding is James R. Baker's concern, while Paul Crawford goes so far as to connect *Lord of the Flies* to the Holocaust, and Virginia Tiger discovers an amazing richness in the novel's meanings.

HAROLD BLOOM

Introduction

Popular as it continues to be, *Lord of the Flies* essentially is a period piece.
Published in 1954, it is haunted by William Golding's service in the Royal
Navy (1940–45), during the Second World War. The hazards of the endless
battles of the North Atlantic against German submarines culminated in
Golding's participation in D-Day, the Normandy invasion of June 6, 1944.
Though *Lord of the Flies* is a moral parable in the form of a boys' adventure
story, in a deeper sense it is a war story. The book's central emblem is the dead
parachutist, mistaken by the boys for the Beast Beelzebub, diabolic Lord of
the Flies. For Golding, the true shape of Beelzebub is a pig's head on a stick,
and the horror of war is transmuted into the moral brutality implicit (in his
view) in most of us. The dead parachutist, in Golding's own interpretation,
represents History, one war after another, the dreadful gift adults keep
presenting to children. Golding's overt intention has some authority, but not
perhaps enough to warrant our acceptance of so simplistic a symbol.

Judging *Lord of the Flies* a period piece means that one doubts its long-
range survival, if only because it is scarcely a profound vision of evil. Golding's
first novel, *Lord of the Flies* does not sustain a critical comparison with his
best narratives: *The Inheritors, Pincher Martin* (his masterpiece), *Free Fall*
and the much later *Darkness Visible*. All these books rely upon nuance, irony,
intelligence, and do not reduce to a trite moral allegory. Golding acknowledged
the triteness, yet insisted upon his fable's truth:

Man is a fallen being. He is gripped by original sin. His nature is
sinful and his state perilous. I accept the theology and admit the
triteness; but what is trite is true; and a truism can become more
than a truism when it is a belief passionately held.

Passion is hardly a standard of measurement in regard to truth. *Lord of the
Flies* aspires to be a universal fable, but its appeal to American schoolchildren
partly inheres in its curious exoticism. Its characters are implausible because
they are humorless; even one ironist among them would explode the book.
The Christlike Simon is particularly unconvincing; Golding does not know
how to portray the psychology of a saint. Whether indeed, in his first novel,
he knew how to render anyone's psychology is disputable. His boys are indeed
British private school boys: regimented, subjected to vicious discipline, and
indoctrinated with narrow, restrictive views of human nature. Golding's long
career as a teacher at Bishop Wordsworth's School in Salisbury was a kind
of extension of his Naval service: a passage from one mode of indoctrination
and strict discipline to another. The regression to savagery that marks *Lord
of the Flies* is a peculiarly British scholastic phenomenon, and not a universal
allegory of moral depravity.

By indicating the severe limitations of Golding's first novel, I do not
intend to deny its continued cultural value. Any well-told tale of a reversion
to barbarism is a warning against tendencies in many groups that may become
violent, and such a warning remains sadly relevant in the early twenty-first
century. Golding's allegorical fable is no *Gulliver's Travels;* the formidable
Swiftian irony and savage intellectualism are well beyond Golding's powers.
Literary value has little sway in *Lord of the Flies.* Ralph, Piggy, Simon, and
Jack are ideograms, rather than achieved fictive characters. Compare them
to Kipling's Kim, and they are sadly diminished; invoke Huck Finn, and
they are reduced to names on a page. *Lord of the Flies* matters, not in or for
itself, but because of its popularity in an era that continues to find it a useful
admonition.

K. CHELLAPPAN

Vision and Structure in Lord of the Flies: *A Semiotic Approach*

It was Frank Kermode who said that "Golding's novels are simple in so far as they deal in the primordial patterns of human experience and in so far as they have skeletons of parable. On these simple bones the flesh of narrative can take extremely complex forms. This makes for difficulty, but of the most acceptable kind, the difficulty that attends the expression of what is profoundly simple."[1] Yes, the difficulty that attends the expression of what is profoundly simple is the essence of his art, just as the complexity of being simply human is his vision And the triumph of most of his novels, particularly, *Lord of the Flies*, is due to the total fusion of form and meaning. The novel seems to simply evoke the heart of darkness in every one of us, as all great myths do. To quote Isabel MacCaffrey, "Studied alive, myth is not symbolic, but a direct expression of its subject matter, it is not an explanation in satisfaction of a scientific interest, but a narrative resurrection of a primitive reality, told in satisfaction of deep religious wants."[2] Golding's novel is a modern myth on an ancient theme and the complex simplicity of the novel as a simple but profound tale of being and becoming human is a correlative to the myth of the mature children or the childish humanity. The mode of the novel is the mode of discovery of the children that is why we find reality itself becoming revelation. The elemental encounter with the cosmos is brought out by the primary mode of narration and ritual enactment. Events in their total simplicity and primeval freshness

---

From *William Golding: An Indian Response*, pp. 39–47. © 1987 by Taqi Ali Mirza.

are simply *shown* and that is why they become endlessly significant. In terms of narration, we find spatialisation of events based on symmetry and repetition and the linearity of events seems to be locked in the circularity of its overall structure. The events are stripped of time and become pictures absorbing time and the spatial form converts the human time into mythical time and the child-adult is the basic image of this static growth, or the fusion of being and becoming in the novel. In a sense the children are static symbols but they are capable of limitless growth. The theme of growth, parallels the structure of the novel growth, is only significant repetition, or existential enactment of an 'essential' condition and in this sense the novel attempts a Becket-like exploration of a no-exit situation—and the technique is one of reduction, but suggesting infinite possibilities of extension and therefore shall we say, revelation through reduction? The child is the basic reduction including all that is humanly possible, just as the island is the reduction of the universe, but also revelatory of the whole universe. In Lodge's terminology, metonymy itself becomes metaphor. On the one hand, there is the linearisation of the archetypal human condition, and on the other history is made to stand still.

Humanisation as a condition and as a process—'the essential illness'—that seems to be the central vision of the novel and this is brought out as a discovery of individuation and separateness. In the beginning, it is a discovery of the essence of things in their total newness, and the children first separate themselves from the physical and then from each other. And the discovery of the cosmos and the self is also a linguistic discovery, because now reality seems to create language, as much as they are creating reality through language. In the opening chapter we see a group of children thrown into being and togetherness on an island whose exploration and discovery is done as existentially as they discover each in relation to the other. Right in the beginning the human and the cosmic are juxtaposed. The Cry of the bird, a vision of red and yellow stirred by human intrusion is echoed by another cry. The 'meaningless cry' of the cosmos is juxtaposed with the human cry. Ralph's emergence is seen against the shimmering water—and "again to Ralph's left the perspectives of palm and beach and water drew to a point at infinite." And just as Ralph is distinguished from the cosmos, he (the fair boy) is also distinguished from Piggy (the fat boy).

The existential nature of Ralph is contrasted with the regression of the already-adult Piggy with his asthma and leaning on the adult world signified by the aunt. The discovery of the shell is the major event, in the beginning of the novel. Ralph's excitement at its otherness—pushed by the sapling—is to be contrasted with the approach of Piggy. The conch becomes the major sign from now onwards. Mark Kinkead-Weekes and Ian Gregor refer to the growing significance of the symbol—from physical noise to a civilising agency.[3] The most important thing is that it means different things to different people and also on different occasions though nothing but a shell in itself. Signification is a human act, and the shell, not in itself significant generates various meanings. The very sound is the result of human collaboration and when children and birds are disturbed, it is because of the meaning they attribute to it. It unites and divides people—as people desire it. But its intrinsic neutrality and otherness are equally emphasised. The major characters are differentiated with reference to it—to Ralph it has a communicative function, to Piggy it has a symbolic function and to Jack it has a pragmatic function. In fact the major conflict of the novel is between the symbolic and utilitarian attitudes and Ralph is torn between the two.

To both Piggy and Jack the external or adult significance of the noise as a means of power matters—though in different ways: to the regressive Piggy it is a protective device, to the aggressive Jack it is an expression of power. In fact both are anti-social, and there can be no communication without a shared code binding separate identities, and Ralph stands for this communicative function. To Jack the rationalising or the symbolic functions are primary—he thinks of smoke as a signal, whereas Jack wants the fire for hunting, and this urge for action involves him in crime. We might also say that Jack tries to impose an individual meaning, whereas Piggy is for the inherited one—and he always wants to 'retreat' to the adult world whereas Jack wants to exploit the present and Ralph the explorer is somewhere between the two. The allegoric mode is that of Piggy, whereas Simon's is that of identification. It is in Simon we find acceptance of the experience as it is neither the ritualistic signification of Piggy, nor the exploitation of Jack, but simple participation or communion. Mark Kinkead-Weekes and Ian Gregor refer to his function as a peace-maker between Jack and Piggy, between the visions of the utilitarian and the hunter.[4] We would make a slight distinction and say that Piggy is overcharging the signs with significance. He is not a utilitarian, he is a 'symbolist' whereas Jack is for aggressive action devoid of significance, but to the visionary Simon there is no dichotomy between the sign and the significance and what remains is the pure experience or the pure communion. "The candle-buds opened their wide white flowers glimmering under the light that pricked down from the first stars. Their scent spilled out into the air and took possession of the island." To quote Whitely, "Ralph wanted to light the candle-buds, Jack to cut and eat them but Simon just *sees* them."[5]

This variation in symbolisation or meaning-creation can be seen in their attitude to the fire also. Whereas to one it is only symbolic of possibility of the retreat to the adult world, Jack wants fire for destructive purposes, and Ralph wants it for purely pragmatic purposes. And both the images of the fire and the conch (both are 'things' and 'signs') are related to the central image of the beast which also acquires several identities, though basically, it seems to be unreal. There is an interesting juxtaposition of the island and the beast by Simon:

'As if it wasn't a good island.'

Astonished at the interruption, they looked up at Simon's serious face.

'As if', said Simon,

'the beastie, the beastie or the snake thing, was real.'

In fact the beast is already there—in themselves, in Piggy, to start with and in his case, there is the growth from the fictitious pigginess to an actual beastliness. In the case of Jack also, the descent into animality—or the discovery of the animal within is shown in different stages—from the frivolous attempt to hunt the piglet, he develops into a criminal hunter, and the ritualistic murder of the pig is only a release of the beast within; the hunter becomes also the hunted. His degeneration is linked with his mask, which signifies a separateness from this true being and a kinship with the beast. "The mask becomes a thing on its own, behind which Jack hid liberated from shame and self-consciousness." From now onwards he is associated with the ape which is later linked with the dead who seems to be "something like a great ape." The link between the ape and the essence is clear now.

In one sense Piggy is the essence, the static meaning and Jack the ape. In another sense Jack's real counterpart is Simon, the real nature and that is why he becomes the beast: the exterioration of evil or the scapegoat release for the human guilt. After the violent mime dance in which role playing explodes into reality and play becomes violent action, Simon's encounter with the Lord of the Flies shows his coming to grips with reality through acceptance of guilt and charity. The significance of the beast is widened to include the airman, and by an act of identification, Simon himself becomes the beast just as the hunters became the beast earlier.

> Symbolically, this may well be the central sign of the book, since it welds together other aspects of the beast. It is the beast, the head of the beast, the offering to the beast, left by the boys whose bestiality is marked by the head on a stick. The head becomes an external sign of Simon's recognition of his own state and that of the whole world.[6]

Here is a clear contrast between the beast hunting of Jack and the recognition of Simon—in one case, the collective action is itself an expression of ego; in the other, the individual identifies himself with all the beasts. The ritualistic death of Simon imparts meaning to the other ritual, and this is possible because of sympathy and identification, and again he fuses the sign with significance. In Jack action robbed the ritual itself of significance, which is restored by Simon by total identification with others. Whereas Jack is not able to communicate with others after the violence, Simon is still able to have communion.

Just as Jack and his group destroyed the significance of the mime by reducing it to action, Piggy robs the significance of everything by over-rationalisation. Action becomes the language of Jack, but to Piggy the sign is everything. But he too empties the conch of its significance as every one does in the later part; because the shell is a part of a system which is gone now. It is significant that the death of Piggy and the breaking of the conch are linked, and now the conflict between the social and the primitive instincts reaches its climax. "The rock struck Piggy a glancing blow from chin to knee, the conch exploded into a thousand white fragments and ceased to exist." Again the skull and the conch are put together.

> He walked slowly into the middle of the clearing and looked steadily and the skull that gleamed as white as ever the conch had done and seemed to jeer at him cynically.
>
> An inquisitive ant was busy in one of the eye sockets but otherwise the thing was lifeless. Or was it?
>
> Little prickles of sensation ran up and down his back. He stood, the skull about on a level with his face and held up his hair with two hands. The teeth grinned, the empty sockets seemed to hold his gaze masterfully and without effort.
>
> What was it?
>
> The skull regarded Ralph like one who knows all the answers and won't tell.

The essence of the shell is silence, which seems to be the essence of all life and all communication, as it is now glaring in death. The airman, Simon, and Piggy are united by the silence signified by death. The broken shell and the skull—they stand for the essence in a way without any extra signification, but the sign is its own significance. The shell which was speechless signified first, wonder, then fear and then hatred and now finally the silence of death—and all these emotions, ('The flames') are only the manifestations of the essence which is nothingness.

But we must make a distinction between two kinds of silence or nothingness; one is the ground all meaning—that is Simon's vision as well as death, and the other, the absurdity which all meaning points to, Piggy's rationalization as death. The contrasting way in which the deaths of Simon and Piggy are described is worth looking at.

> Somewhere over the darkened curve of the world the sun and moon were pulling; and the film of water on the earth planet was

held, bulging slightly on one side while the solid core turned. The great wave of the tide moved further along the island and the water lifted. Softly, surrounded by a fringe of inquisitive bright creatures, itself a silver shape beneath the steadfast constellations, Simon's dead body moved out towards the open sea.

Let us contrast this 'sea burial' with the unceremonial death of Piggy.

Piggy's arms and legs twitched a bit, like a pig's after it has been killed. Then the sea breathed again in a long, slow sigh, the water boiled white and pink, over the rock; and when it went, sucking back again, the body of Piggy was gone.

In one case, the death is part of cosmic orchestration—there is perfect rhythm and everything is seen in its relatedness. Throughout the novel we see things in relatedness—man near the rock, the lagoon etc. Now the total fusion of the cosmic and the human, Simon's dead body moving out towards the open sea. In the case of Piggy also, the death was part of the endless dance of the waves—but it was a real casualty—(without any causality)—the body of Piggy was gone, when water went back to its source, in a routine release, but reasserting an eternal pattern, in which life constantly seeks its source. When the signifier has just become an object, the sea, the source of significance, is fully humanised now—with verbs like "breathed." Halliday's analysis of the verb patterns in *The Inheritors* gives us a useful clue here.

Tracing the evolution of the theme in terms of transitivity, he says, "Transitivity is really the cornerstone of the semantic organization of experience; and it is at one level what *The Inheritors* is about. The theme of the entire novel, in a sense, is transitivity; man's interpretation of his experience of the world, his understanding of its processes and of his own participation in them."[7]

In *Lord of the Flies* personification plays a similar role throughout. Earlier, again in Simon's vision, "The creepers dripped their ropes like the rigging of foundered ships." And this kind of personification as well as the description of the death of Simon is different from that used to refer to the mechanical flow of the angry sea absorbing Piggy's body. This would make us believe that even though Golding seems to say that humanisation is evil, he is not postulating an absolutely indifferent cosmos. Earlier the warm salt water of the sea bathing pool brings humanity together, along with the shouting; and splashing and laughing. "Later; before these fantastically attractive flowers of violet and red and yellow, unkindness melted away."

The sea is the limit and the source of creativity, the beginning and the end of life. The dance of existence (as well as meaning) is enacted between its deep silence and its eternal roar. The sea is the final symbol parallel to the shell and this also manifests various emotions from wonder to acceptance, though in essence it has none of them. And if Simon and Piggy represent the silence and the roar, matter and energy, the mountain and the rock, Ralph is closer to the lagoon and the shore. And rightly we along with him come back to the shore, of course after his facing the angry forest (Jack?), again being hunted. The cycle is repeated, but completed in the larger movement and just as the sea receives Simon, civilisation receives Ralph, who represents the "full" humanity (through average)—having passed through all these phases. The heavenward movement is also the homeward movement, and after participating in the silence of the angry forest (p. 234, 235), and the endless pursuit of the other, Ralph stumbled on a root—the reality. "Then he was down, rolling over and over in the warm sand, crouching with arm up to ward off, trying to cry for mercy." We along with Ralph come again to the semicircle of boys, to the flame, to the smoke and then to the daylight reality of the naval officer—now alive. All reality (or shall we say the nightmare) dissolves as a fabric of vision, and we come back to reality in a different sense, with Ralph weeping for the end of innocence and wishing for his wise friend, Piggy, now deep down in the sea and the officer looking at the trim cruiser in the distance. The little island is caught between the silence in the depths of the sea and the cruiser, waiting to leave.

Deliberately the island is made unreal and real throughout. In the beginning it is said "Here at last was the imagined but never fully realized place leaping into real life." Finally, dream dissolves into reality in another sense. All the time the novel seems to be saying that it is all a fictitious world with deliberate references to other fictions and other children. But all the time it also seems to suggest—that it is nothing but reality. Was it a vision or a dream? Is it fiction or reality? It is this fundamental epistemological question of life that finds its aesthetic realisation (if not resolution) in *Lord of the Flies*. *Lord of the Flies* does not *mean*, in Piggies's sense, it *is* (like Simon). The novel in this sense becomes the Word—(or Christ) in which the sign is the significance.

Notes

1. Frank Kermode, "William Golding" in *On Contemporary Literature*, ed. Richard Kostelanetz (New York, 1969), pp. 378, 381.

2. Isabel Gamble MacCaffrey, *Paradise Lost as 'Myth'* (Harvard University Press, Cambridge, 1967), p. 23.

3. Mark Kinkead-Weekes, and Ian Gregor, *William Golding: A Critical Study* (London: Faber and Faber, 1975), p. 18.

4. *ibid.*, p. 29.

5. John S. Whitley, *Golding, Lord of the Flies* (Edward Arnold, London), p. 37.

6. *ibid.*, p. 48.

7. M.A.K. Halliday, "Linguistic function and literary style: An inquiry into the language of William Golding's *The Inheritors*," in *Explorations in the Functions of Language*, (London: Edward Arnold), p. 134.

JAMES GINDIN

The Fictional Explosion:
Lord of the Flies *and* The Inheritors

Given the complexity of Golding's thought, his need to express some fundamental statement about the nature of man in tangible terms, and his tendency to use sharply defined polarities to generate his ideas, his placement of his first two novels as intellectual responses to particular targets is not surprising. His religious impulse requires a heresy or an evil to excoriate; the pressure of his carefully shaped and internal fiction gains its force in reaction against some widely shared or familiar concept. Both the first two novels focus on their targets explicitly: *Lord of the Flies* on R. M. Ballantyne's 1857 novel *The Coral Island*, *The Inheritors* on H. G. Wells's *Outline of History*.

Ballantyne's *The Coral Island* represents, for Golding, an extremity of Victorian confidence and optimism in the civilised values of English schoolboy society. In Ballantyne's novel, the boys, shipwrecked on the island, organise their skills and exercise their imaginations to duplicate the comforts and the values of the society they have temporarily lost. Working with discipline, they build shelters and a boat, make various utensils for their convenience, and find a healthy and interesting variety of animal and vegetable food. With the same kind of devotion to higher powers that characterises the more adult survival in the earlier *Robinson Crusoe*, the boys in *The Coral Island* radiate a confidence in their sense of community and organisation which would seem rather smug were they not also genuinely pious and aware of their luck. Evil in the novel

From *William Golding*, pp. 20–37, 116. © 1988 by James Gindin.

is externalised, represented by cannibals on the island whom the English boys defeat because they work together and excel in both wit and virtue. Their rescue almost does not matter, for they have essentially recreated the world they came from. Ballantyne draws on a concept of the child that reaches back through the nineteenth century, at least as far as Rousseau and Locke, the child as inherently either good or neutral, manifesting his goodness if left alone and uncorrupted by the adult world or reflecting and recreating the healthy and civilised environment of his initial consciousness. This confidence in civilised Enlightenment, developed from a faith in human possibility in the eighteenth century to a particularly English social achievement in the nineteenth, is precisely what Golding, in *Lord of the Flies*, is determined to reverse. The locus of Golding's attention is the society of boys; the implication is an attack on the naïveté of Victorian confidence in English boys and in public schools, as well as on the whole Enlightenment doctrine about the progress and perfectibility of the human species. Golding's tone, however, is not that of triumphant response to a naïve and mistaken ideology. Rather, his shaping of events and experience on the island, his sense of the inherently predatory and evil characteristics his boys reveal, is dominated by the 'grief, sheer grief' he called the theme of the novel. The 'grief' compounds the presentation of 'sin', for, as Golding has said retrospectively as recently as December 1985, the novel was 'written at a time of great world grief' and that, in addition to the 'original sin' latent in the novel, 'what nobody's noticed is that it also has original virtue'.[32]

Golding's use of *The Coral Island* is direct and unambiguous. He refers to it explicitly several times: once, near the beginning of the novel, when the boys, in momentary agreement, decide they can have a 'good time on this island', like 'Treasure Island', and 'Coral Island'; later, on the last page of the novel, ironically, when they are rescued by the naval officer, who imperceptively comments, 'Jolly good show. Like the Coral Island'. Golding also derives the initial English types of some of his schoolboy characters from Ballantyne's novel. The narrator of *The Coral Island* is named Ralph, a sound and stable boy of 15 (his last name is Rover); the strongest, oldest, tallest boy is named Jack; the third member of Ballantyne's principal triumvirate is Peterkin Gay, a quick, sprite-like, imaginative boy of 14. Golding's Ralph comes closest to following the Ballantyne model, for Ralph, although not the narrator in Golding, is the centrally representative English schoolboy, simultaneously the one who both leads and accommodates to others in terms of the fondly cherished, moderate English tradition. Fair-haired, mild, neither the strongest nor the most discerning of the boys, Golding's Ralph is initially elected to govern the island and to organise building shelters and possible rescue. As the organisation increasingly breaks down, as the boys gradually succumb to dirt, ineptitude, laziness, cruelty and the predatory viciousness of the 'hunters',

Ralph reveals something of the same sense of inherent evil within himself (he willingly shares the spoils of the 'hunters' and, however reluctantly and unconsciously, joins in the ritualistic killing of Simon). Finally, hunted by the others, turned from leader into victim, his 'rescue' at the end is far from any reassertion of his moderation. At the end he 'weeps', his confidence shattered, recognising the failure and the irrelevance of the kind of human moderation and civilisation he had thought he embodied. Golding changes the Ballantyne version of the character of Jack, the powerful one outside the communal structure, more immediately and more markedly than that of Ralph. In the first place, Golding's Jack has his own community, his choir of 'hunters', each boy wearing 'a square black cap with a silver badge in it': 'Their bodies, from throat to ankle, were hidden by black cloaks which bore a long silver cross on the left breast and each neck was finished off with a hambone frill' (Chapter I). The physical description deliberately suggests the Nazis, the sense of inherent evil institutionalised and made visible in the chanting choir of the predatory. Ballantyne's Jack represented strength absorbed into the civilised community and displayed no sense of evil; Golding's Jack is the aggressive force of evil, acquiring more and more adherents as survival on the island becomes progressively more difficult. Jack imposes a sense of discipline on the others that Ralph can never manage.

The character of Piggy, Ralph's most loyal supporter, is entirely Golding's addition. Physically deficient (he is fat, asthmatic and has a weak bladder), Piggy is the voice of rationalism. He believes in the possibility of rescue by the adult society, in the values of civilisation, and in the possibility of directing human constructive effort. Normally less articulate than Ralph, attempting to endow the symbol of the conch shell, the parliamentary symbol, with silent power, Piggy, in his final scene, eventually poses, to the assembled boys on the pinnacle rock at the end of the island, a series of rhetorical questions that represent his values. He advocates that the boys 'be sensible like Ralph is', 'have rules and agree', and follow 'law and rescue', rather than follow Jack and 'hunt and kill' (Chapter XI). In response, Roger, Jack's most vicious lieutenant, high overhead, uses a boulder as a lever to hurl the rock that hits Piggy, casts him forty feet down to hit another rock that splatters his brains before he is washed out to sea. In his death 'Piggy's arms and legs twitched a bit, like a pig's after it has been killed', and Roger had leaned his weight on the lever in the same way he had earlier leaned his weight on his spear to kill the sow. Piggy is the human object, the victim, for the predators. Yet the rationalism and confidence in social organisation does not summarise the function of Piggy's character entirely. He is also *fearful*, not of the 'beast' the 'littluns' fear, for, unlike the 'littluns', who experience only chaos once they forget the superficial and carefully taught names, addresses and telephone numbers of identity, Piggy believes in scientific observation, in tracing patterns of cause and effect. Rather, Piggy is frightened of the 'beast' within the human being, of people themselves. When, at the end of the novel, Ralph weeps for 'the end of innocence, the darkness of man's heart, and the fall through the air of the true, wise friend called Piggy', the sense of Piggy's wisdom is not an endorsement of Piggy's rationalism or his science. Rather, Piggy's wisdom, despite all his manifest inadequacies, consisted in his knowing what to fear, in his accurate location of the human evil he attracts and can do nothing to prevent.

Piggy is not the only scapegoat for the human choir's evil, for both the rationalist and the visionary, both Piggy and Simon, are destroyed. Simon is considerably transformed from the model of Ballantyne's sprite-like Peterkin. In the 1959 interview with Frank Kermode, broadcast as 'The Meaning of it All', Golding directly indicated how he changed Peterkin into Simon (citing the New Testament transformation of 'Simon called Peter') and endowed the sensitive, isolated character, unlike the other boys, with insight into the unchanging nature of human beings and communities. Simon is mystic, unable to express what he always knows is man's essential illness. He is Golding's example of 'original virtue' in the novel. Yet he isolates himself, building his shelter hidden away within the jungle, gathering the leaves and fronds he finds as a natural protection against humanity. Simon, the only one of the boys to approach closely enough to understand what they fear, actually sees the 'beast' and recognises that the 'beast' is a dead man from the war outside and above the island, his corpse tangled in his failed parachute. His recognition, in a forcefully described scene, goes more deeply than the specific circumstances demand, for it is the 'ancient, inescapable recognition' that, with the 'white teeth and dim eyes, the blood' and that 'black blob of flies that buzzed like a saw' on the 'pile of guts', the 'beast' is humanity (Chapter VIII). Simon imagines the 'beast', 'The Lord of the Flies', as a schoolmaster. Running to proclaim his discovery to the others, Simon stumbles into the pig run down the mountainside while the others, led by the choir, are enacting a ritual of 'kill the pig'. In the rush of predatory emotion, identities are confused and the 'hunters', even Ralph and Piggy drawn to the fringes of the dark and crowded scene 'under the threat of the sky', kill Simon. Simon assumes something of the role of Christ, a Christian martyrdom, sacrifice of self for the truth that is generally unrecognised. Yet Golding's symbolism is suggestive rather than precise. Like the conch, the shell that cannot support the excessive reliance on it as a parliamentary symbol and becomes worn and bleached white like a skull, the Christian symbolism is pervasive and dramatic but does not cohere in the patterns of Christian parable or duplication of the story of Christ. Simon is his own sort of visionary religious martyr, sometimes seen as more Cassandra-like than Christian, sometimes perhaps as epileptic with his fainting fits, sometimes simply as the odd boy who does not fit the pattern of the school. Similarly complex, 'The Lord of the Flies' is a translation of Beelzebub, the Greek transliteration of the ancient Hebrew word for the Prince of the Devils, an incarnation of evil in both Judaism and Christianity. Yet the figure is also characterised as the 'Lord of Dung', of human refuse. The meanings do not contradict, and both reinforce the pervasive meaning of a symbolic dramatisation of inherent human evil. Yet the cluster of symbolic meanings, both humanly and religiously suggestive, coherent only in the force and tangibility of their metaphorical application to the human condition, make it difficult to push the novel into the total narrative and legendary coherence of parable.

A reading of *Lord of the Flies* as parable is also questionable because of the way in which Golding handles time, space and location. The particular setting, graphically described physically yet unconnected to any knowable geographical location, both invites parabolic or symbolic reading in its absence from specific location and limits or questions that reading in the absence of a consistent narrative of symbolic pattern. The island is described with immediate physical force, Golding providing a strongly visual and emotional sense of the beach, the lagoon, the jungle-like tracks to the mountain, and the splinters of precipitous rock at the end of the island opposite from the lagoon. The description of the island does not substantially change, and all the elements are used symbolically, yet a pattern of meaning never coheres from the details. The only coherence is in the implications of illusion or mistaken perception, as when Ralph initially describes the island 'like icing ... on a pink cake' (Chapter I). The geography is always physical and immediate as it simultaneously renders emotional states and ideas, but geography as a coherent entity does not serve to locate parabolic narrative, as would, for example, the desert or the sea in a Biblical parable. Similarly, although the novel describes events moving through time, attention to the fire lighted for rescue gradually subsiding, the claims of the instincts of the 'hunters' rising, and the fragile identities of the 'littluns' evaporating, Golding provides no clock sense, no particular indication of how many or how quickly days or weeks pass. Images of light and dark, day and night, suggest time both physically and symbolically, but the possibility of parabolic coherence through narrative is limited by the vagueness concerning any of our usual temporal increments of days or weeks. We find it difficult to apply any specific sense of change as gradual revelation through narrative. Anticipating *Pincher Martin* in a way, Golding has wrenched usual concepts of time and space away from familiar or conventional patterns.

The force of *Lord of the Flies* emerges less from any form, like parable, than from the strength, immediacy and suggestiveness of the prose Golding writes. He is always a strikingly visual writer, evoking physical sensation. The ritualistic killing of Simon, for example, is powerfully graphic, as the 'crowd

... leapt on to the beast, screamed, struck, bit, tore. There were no words, and no movements but the tearing of teeth and claws.' As Simon dies from the beating, Golding shifts his attention from the fiery 'hunters' to the victim: 'The line of his cheek silvered and the turn of his shoulder became sculptured marble ... The body lifted a fraction of an inch from the sand and a bubble of air escaped from the mouth with a wet plop.' A further shift transforms the scene to the cosmic:

> Somewhere over the darkened curve of the world the sun and moon were pulling; and the film of water on the earth planet was held, bulging slightly on one side while the solid core turned. The great wave of the tide moved further along the island and the water lifted. ... Simon's dead body moved out toward the open sea. (Chapter IX)

As this passage illustrates, Golding's prose is a remarkable blend of the abstract and the concrete, or, more accurately perhaps, a gesture toward the abstract and symbolic through a strongly visual use of the concrete, the water 'bulging slightly on one side while the solid core turned'. Such passages build structurally in *Lord of the Flies*, connecting the abstract with the concrete in developing, for example, the symbol of the 'beast' and moving it more and more into the centre of the human creature, or in paralleling the dissipation of the echoes of civilisation with the movement toward the human interior. The constancy of the concrete prose holds the variously symbolic novel together.

The linear movement of the novel, the progress of the narration, is symbolically directed toward the human interior, stripping away what Golding sees as the falsity of confidence in civilisation, the representative illusions of Ballantyne, as the novel moves toward its fictional conclusion. References from the very beginning indicate the point of view that sees the story as the process of the gradual erosion of meaning in the paraphernalia of civilisation. On the first page of the novel, before he is even named, Ralph is described in a way that signals a sharp juxtaposition between character and setting: 'The fair boy stopped and jerked his stockings with an automatic gesture that made the jungle seem for a moment like the Home Counties.' Questions about possible rescue are asked from the beginning, sometimes with an underlying confidence, sometimes with the fear that the atomic war has expunged all potential rescuers. Throughout most of the novel, Golding plays the intimations of rescue both ways. At times, the boys' inertia and incompetence seem to prevent rescue, as when they allow the signal fire to go out, see a passing ship that does not stop, and permit their cries for rescue to be drowned out by the ritualistic chant of the choir. At other times, especially when probing the nature of the human creature, the concept of rescue seems trivial and irrelevant. When Roger is first throwing stones near another boy and only 'the taboo of the old life' prevents him from aiming to hit the boy directly, a restraint that will soon disappear, Golding writes that 'Roger's arm was conditioned by a civilisation that knew nothing of him and was in ruins' (Chapter IV). The boys become increasingly dirty as the chants of the choir become louder and more atavistic. The feeble rationalist, Piggy, becomes more and more the butt, a link between the echoes of the only superficially civilised schoolboy's world where he 'was the centre of social derision so that everyone felt cheerful and normal' (Chapter IX) and the island world with none of the veneer of civilisation in which his spectacles are smashed as a dramatic prelude to his total destruction. The twins, 'Samneric', mutually redundant, the last holdouts against the choir apart from Piggy and Ralph, 'protested out of the heart of civilisation' (Chapter XI) just before they were forced to yield to Jack and his 'hunters'. The perspective is rather like that of Conrad's *Heart of Darkness*, a progressive stripping away of the faint echoes of civilisation as the narrative moves toward its conclusion in the centre of human darkness, although Golding refuses, in this novel, to defend Conrad's final palliative of the necessary 'lie'. Golding's perspective is also suffused with human guilt for all those intelligent and rational social constructions, all those various forms of spectacles, that have been unable to overcome or assuage the central darkness.

The directed perspective, moving through narrative time, and its symbolically conveyed moral implications have invited many readers and critics to see *Lord of the Flies* in terms of parable—or, rather, since parable suggests a Biblical or Christian orthodoxy that does not fit the novel, in terms of fable. Fable is also a more useful term than parable in that the religious sources of Golding's imagination are Greek as well as Christian, echoes of the conflict between the Dionysian and the Apollonian or of Euripidean tragedy that Golding has acknowledged. The term 'fable' was first introduced to account for Golding's fictions in an essay by John Peter in 1957, Peter defining fables as 'those narratives which leave the impression that their purpose was anterior, some initial thesis or contention which they are apparently concerned to embody and express in concrete terms.' Peter distinguished the fictional fable, like Orwell's *1984*, from the novel or non-fabulistic fiction like D. H. Lawrence's *The Rainbow*. For Peter, 'the coherence of the fable appears to us as a moral tool, and its patterns become precepts', and this quality distinguished Golding's work from the dearth of value in the fiction of his contemporaries in the 1950s.[33] Later critics, writing in the 1960s, such as Bernard Oldsey and Stanley Weintraub, and Mark Kinkead-Weekes and Ian Gregor, rightly saw 'fable' as too restrictive a term for what Golding was doing. They saw his fiction as too complex and various to be reducible to conclusive moral thesis or to yield to the connection of each important physical detail with a symbolic correlative. Yet 'fable', as a term that was frequently discussed and that still is useful as a means of initiating discussion about *Lord of the Flies*, cannot entirely be ignored.

Golding himself gave the term initial critical credibility by rather equivocally accepting it in so far as 'the fabulist is the moralist' and he always saw himself as the latter. He recognised that the term was not quite right for either the range or the structure of his fiction. In terms of range and suggestability, he said, he aimed for the larger and looser dimensions of 'myth', recognising how difficult and problematic it is to try to create comprehensive myths for one's own contemporaries. In terms of structure, he thought, somewhat humbly, that he reversed some of the implications of linear fable with 'gimmicks' at the ends of his novels. Critics initially often took him at his word: some elevated his work to 'myth', others complained that the 'gimmick' reversed, reduced or palliated the fiction. In perhaps the fullest account of 'fable' as it applies to *Lord of the Flies*, John S. Whitley quotes Golding as saying that where his fable 'splits at the seams' he would like to think the split is the result of a 'plentitude of imagination'.[34] But Whitley, in his careful analysis of the form and his recognition of all the possible adaptations of 'fable', points to all Golding's intrusions, his gestures toward establishing the form and withdrawing from it, realising that the question of 'plenitude' or paucity of imagination is less the point than is the fact that fabulistic form cannot really account for the range of Golding's coherence and appeal. Golding's proportions do not fit his ostensible structure.

The problem of the 'fable' is particularly acute at the end of *Lord of the Flies* in the 'rescue' that, in moral terms, is not really a rescue. A naval officer arrives on the island to pick up the boys and saves Ralph literally from the chanting choir of 'hunters' that destroyed Piggy. Yet the naval officer is as impercipient a representative of the civilised as is any voice of Ballantyne's, for he says, on the final page of the novel, 'I should have thought that a pack of British boys—you're all British aren't you?—would have been able to put up a better show than that', and he still thinks *The Coral Island* an appropriate parallel. Besides, the naval officer is part of the wider world involved in atomic war. The atomic war generated the novel in the first place, was the device to bring the evacuated schoolboys to the island (in this sense, the boys have only duplicated the adult world), and, in the ship and the dead parachutist who is the 'Lord of the Flies', the 'Lord of Dung', and Beelzebub, the war impinges at points throughout the whole novel. Ralph has come to understand something of this, to recognise the central evil of human experience, although he does survive, and Golding, in the final line of the novel, grants him a mysteriously equivocal stance in 'allowing his eyes to rest on the trim cruiser in the distance' without comment. In terms of meaning, symbol and morality, the implications of Golding's perspective are clear: the central darkness and evil the boys revealed reflects a larger human darkness and evil, not only a violation of confidence in what the English public school represents, but also a world at war violating the false confidence of progressive and civilised values. In terms of structure and plot, in terms that 'fable' as comprehensive form would satisfy, the conclusion of the novel (as well as some earlier intrusions) violates the structural expectation that the form should be able to carry all of the novel's meaning. As Whitley sees, this is less a matter of palliative 'gimmick', has fewer of the associations of undercutting or trickery than that term suggests, than the literarily conventional resolution of the plot through a 'deus ex machina'. The form adds a 'deus ex machina' to the fable; the meaning does not require one.

Suggestive as it is for provisional examination, the term 'fable' cannot account for the extraordinarily strong feeling of coherence in Golding's novel. Rather, the coherence is visible in the distinctive and effective language, the explosive pressure of the unique and constant connection between the abstract and concrete. Coherence is also visible in Golding's perspective, his constant probing of civilised illusion, his constant stripping away of facile assurance as he approaches the evil and details the 'grief' he finds central to human experience. These are strong and appealing matters of linguistic and thematic coherence, creations of a world in fiction. The concentrated pressure of Golding's prose also creates an expectation of or hope for formal coherence as well. If, ultimately, 'truth is single', a reader looks for the singular truth in Golding's form as well. And 'fable' is a good term for the kind of formal coherence closest to what Golding is doing. Yet because of Golding's complexity, 'plenitude' or paucity of imagination as it might be, 'fable' is too centred on plot and does not entirely carry the meaning. Golding's sense of formal achievement is not fully satisfied, as it is in some of the later novels. His form, in so far as it is entirely coherent, is conditioned still by the form against which he reacts, the model of Ballantyne's *The* Coral Island. The negative form, the target, provides the points of coherence that a reading as 'fable' cannot quite sustain.

Golding's next novel, *The Inheritors*, reveals a similar formal pattern, as well as a similar interest in exploring the inner nature of the human being. The intellectual target that generates Golding's imagination in this instance is H. G. Wells's *Outline of History*, a passage from which Golding quotes as an epigraph. Elaborating on Wells's prose by including that of someone else he quotes, Golding cites a passage describing Neanderthal man, the human being's evolutionary progenitor, as repulsively strange, short, inferior to man and ugly, 'gorilla-like monsters, with cunning brains, shambling gait, hairy bodies, strong teeth, and possibly cannibalistic tendencies', which 'may be the germ of the ogre in folklore'. This passage alone is, to some extent, a simplification of Wells's point of view, for the balance of *Outline of History* is not quite so confident of human superiority in every moral and aesthetic respect as the quotation itself might suggest. Wells recognised how little we know about Neanderthal man and emphasised evolutionary change and adaptation rather than intrinsic human superiority. Nevertheless, Golding uses Wells to reverse the implications of the epigraph, to show that, in his version of prehistory, the 'monsters' with 'cunning brains ... and possibly cannibalistic tendencies' are not the Neanderthals but the evolutionary subsequent *homo sapiens*. In framing most of the novel from the point of view of one of the Neanderthals, Lok, Golding tries carefully to duplicate the primitive perspective. The 'shambling gait', for example, is visible on the first page, when Lok is carrying the child, Liku, on his shoulders: 'His feet stabbed, he swerved and slowed.' At other times, he talks of his feet as 'no longer clever', or Golding adds that Lok's following the actions of others in his group is 'affectionate and unconscious parody'. The Neanderthals also flare nostrils grossly and are inhibited by their hairiness. They do not discriminate perceptions sharply and rationally, thinking in a kind of amalgamated metaphor as in describing 'lumps of smooth grey rock' as 'the bones of the land' (Chapter I). This perspective makes the Neanderthals appealing, although Golding could hardly do everything necessary to characterise them through their own eyes. Frequently, he breaks apart from the Neanderthal perspective to add an authorial voice. When Lok, having been hungry and eaten meat, is satisfied and 'became Lok's belly', Golding adds that 'his face shone with grease and serene happiness'. In the next sentence, Golding goes further to show what that is generally human Lok could not do: 'Tonight was colder than last night, though he made no comparisons' (Chapter IV). Occasionally, the authorial intrusions become more abstract, as in the confusion Lok shares with Fa, a female member of the group, when they first see a human being and Golding explains that 'There was nothing in life as a point of reference' (Chapter V).

Despite these probably necessary intrusions that interrupt the Neanderthal's point of view and despite what may be oversimplification of Wells, Golding does build a coherent, appealing and effective fictional portrait of the earlier species. The Neanderthals, or 'people', as they refer to themselves, are made amiable and attractive. Despite their perceptual limitations, the ingeniously conveyed strictures placed on their rational intelligence, the 'people' are warm and responsive. They have a deep and humble sense of their own limitations, as well as a faith in a female divine power (whom they call 'Oa') and in the goodness of the earth. Although we see a group of only eight 'people' (and one of these is a child, another an infant), they enjoy a family life free from fighting, guilt and emotional squabbling. Each has his or her function, carefully defined and limited, each a respect for the other members of the family. Their values are communal rather than individual, for they have no sense of private ownership or sole emotional claim. They all warm the Old Man with their bodies as he is dying. Their sexuality is also communal, for, although Lok and Fa sometimes seem to be mates, Liku is the daughter of Lok and Nil. Nil is the child-bearing woman and Ha the most intelligent man, although the four share sexual relationships, work and spontaneous concern and appreciation for the others. Their emotions centre on what is fundamental: food, shelter and closeness; birth, life and death. They keep and protect the image of Oa, the goddess that the Old Man tells them 'brought forth the earth from her belly. . . . The earth brought forth woman and the woman brought forth the first man out of her belly.' They share a vision of a previous paradise, unlike the colder and more difficult present, a time 'when there had been many people, the story that they all liked so much of the time when it was summer all year round and the flowers and fruit hung on the same branch.' They also have a strongly developed moral sense, not only toward each other but also toward other beings on the earth. When, at one point, out foraging for food, Lok and Fa bring back a deer, Fa assures him that 'A cat has killed the deer and sucked its blood, so there is no blame' (Chapter II).

The 'people' are, however, severely limited in conceptualising themselves. They sometimes split themselves literally into an inside and an outside, as if the two have no connection. Their conceptions of the exterior world are similarly blurred. On their annual migration with which the novel begins, they notice that a log they use to cross a deep stream is no longer there and they assume it has gone away. When the log they find to try to replace it does not hold, they assume the log swims as they assume the sun hides itself. They carry their fire with them, reverently, as if, like Prometheus, they had taken it from the Gods. Their fire is transported as a smouldering spark surrounded by wet clay that they open, blow to flame and feed. Although the fire seems to suit both their needs and their devotion to exterior power, they generally have little capacity as incipient engineers or organisers of the exterior world to maintain themselves. In the middle of a process that requires several consecutive steps, like building a bridge, they sometimes forget the first step before they have finished the second. Some, like Fa, are brighter than others, like Lok, in maintaining consecutive memory and in connecting cause and effect rationally. For all of them, however, language is a commitment that establishes unchangeable reality. Once something is spoken, it *is*, even when the words are those of the dying, hallucinatory Old Man who never recovers from the chill he caught by falling in the water during their inept attempt to reconstruct a bridge to replace the missing log. Imagination is not conveyed by speech; rather their imagination takes the form of 'pictures', images of the world that they dimly apprehend and try to sort out. When something happens outside their comprehension, they recognise that they have 'no pictures' and, therefore, no imagination, memory or words. They try, honestly and literally, to construct their world from those 'pictures' that they do observe and remember, and then to solidify, make permanent, that world through language.

Golding is most effective in describing the process, the way the minds of the 'people' try to sort out the 'pictures' of a changing exterior world. The 'people' are invariably direct, working out their perceptions honestly as far as they can (although they are capable of a warm humour, regarding Lok as the buffoon of the group when he nonsensically uses words for which he has no 'pictures'). Golding combines the moral respect and sympathy with the insistence on the intellectual limitation, the problems in connecting cause with effect or the difficulty in summoning a 'picture' and converting it into usable experience like speech. At times, Golding shows this process operating through a long scene, as in the one in which Lok and Fa fight off the hyenas and buzzards for the prize of the doe the cat has killed. Although Fa dimly understands, as Lok does not, that the feared cat will not return to a kill whose blood has been drained, she cannot convert her understanding into speech, although she can express the moral issue in asserting that there is no blame. The passage works in its compressed complexity, in the sense that understanding differently, intellectually or rationally separate although emotionally and morally congruent, one creature fearful, the other not, the two can work together to bring food home to the family. Golding creates a striking *tour de force*, a condensed prose metaphor that uses the 'people', with all their adequacies and inadequacies, to illustrate the qualities that he sees as simultaneously prior and fundamental to what we are able to regard only as human experience. The accuracy of Golding's version of Wells is irrelevant; we convert the moral and emotional implications of the metaphor into a statement about primal or basic human nature.

The Inheritors, however, does not rest in its metaphor of the mind of the 'people', as its action is not confined to the stasis of their decline and evolutionary replacement by *homo sapiens*. Rather, Golding introduces the new species, the human being, at first just as seen from the point of view of the 'people', then, in the short final chapter, with a switch to the human point of view. Human society is full of noise, fights and anger, of provocation, infidelity and betrayal. The individual, understanding and projecting more of his or her imagination, is capable of setting self against community, of trying to gain power or love at the expense of a fellow being. Lok and Fa, looking at the human beings from a distance, can see that they are predatory, that they have 'teeth that remembered wolf'. Lok and Fa are far from able to understand much that they see, although Fa is able to state the moral comment 'Oa did not bring them out of her belly' (Chapter IX). Only gradually is Lok able to realise that the long stick he sees from a distance that the human being holds is a bow and the tiny cross-stick that whizzes past his head into a tree is an arrow meant to harm him. He takes even longer to recognise that the human beings have captured Liku; when he does realise this, he thinks they wanted her only as a playmate for one of their children approximately her own age. He tries, at first, to throw food for her. The human beings, however, turn Liku into food, killing her in a ritual sacrifice when their hunt is a failure and devouring her remains. Worship is not respect or devotion but predatory propitiation. Liku, like Simon in *Lord of the Flies* (also like 'you', human beings generically), is the scapegoat, the sacrificial victim to predatory human evil. The 'people' will eat meat only when it is already dead, drained, and they can absolve themselves of 'blame'; human beings, more technologically skilful and rationally intelligent, will eat what they kill no matter how close the species is to themselves. The more intelligently individual and the more accurately self-conscious, the crueller and more evil the species. The 'people' had difficulty in separating themselves from the exterior world; the human being as a post-lapsarian creature, more intelligently divided, more conscious of what the individual self is, makes martyrs and victims out of his own species.

The moral and intellectual contrast between the 'people' and the human beings is not Golding's final statement in *The Inheritors*, for both species are capable of some amount of significant change through experience. The novel is about evolution, not only from one species to another, but of the capacities within each of the species themselves. Golding displays two senses of movement within the novel: from one species to the next; in a quicker, more impacted and interior way, from lesser to greater consciousness within each species. The final chapter shifts to the point of view of Tuami, one of the human beings. Although still the evil and individualistic human being, he is able to abandon his plot to kill his chief, recognising that the single action of his knife-blade would, at best, be only a sharp point against the overwhelming darkness of the world he would also exemplify. He can feel guilt and 'grief'; he can also recognise the possibilities of love and light. In short, Tuami's consciousness has expanded from a representation of man's essential evil to the suggestion of a more complex representation of fallible human possibility. Tuami, in the log he has made into a boat, ends the novel by looking at the light flashing on the water and 'he could not see if the line of darkness had an ending'. Toward the end of the novel, Lok also learns as he observes the human beings and tries to create 'pictures' of what they are. He begins to imagine similes, and, as Golding comments directly, 'Lok discovered "Like",' which he had 'used ... all his life without being aware of it'. Through his elementary understanding of simile, Lok begins to establish a prior condition for sorting out individuality, for understanding how creatures are both like and unlike each other. One of his similes seems crucially symbolic: 'They are like the river and the fall, they are a people of the fall; nothing stands against them' (Chapter X). In the final chapter, Tuami watches as Fa (always a few steps ahead of Lok) is precipitated over the falls to her death, a process the now diminished Lok, seen from a distance, is sure to follow. In the process of evolution, Golding symbolically suggests, the Neanderthals have fallen into humanity and attention shifts to the already explicitly human creature who can experience guilt and self-knowledge, just as he can adapt and master the log (suggestions of the 'Tree of Knowledge'), which defeated the 'people' in the initial episode of the novel. The fall into humanity is both a lost innocence and a 'fortunate' fall, fortunate in its recognition of human consciousness and the possibility, however dim, of redemption. The questions of likeness and difference, of one species against the other, have been transformed into a powerfully searching and traditionally religious statement about the nature of the human being.

As Golding's metaphorical statement deepens, the epigraph from Wells seems more a prod than an alternative, a propellant to the fictional explosion. Initially a response to what Golding regards as erroneous simplification in Wells's *Outline of History*, just as *Lord of the Flies* was a response to the confidence in civilisation in Ballantyne's fiction, *The Inheritors* becomes a more dense and searching statement about the human condition than any scientifically documentable polarity between Neanderthal and *homo sapiens* might suggest. Golding's account of evolution is simultaneously physical, rational, moral and religious, all conveyed in compact statements of similarity and difference in language that is both concrete and strikingly resonant, explosive prose. A description as 'fable' accounts for *The Inheritors* even less than it does for *Lord of the Flies*, for the pattern of matching action or the progress of narrative to meaning would imply a more simplified and linear process of evolution than that which Golding represents in the novel. The form of the 'fable', in its insistence on the significance of action, would restrict Golding's treatment of the human condition. Nor can one designate *The Inheritors* as 'myth' really achieved, for 'myth', at least in so far as one understands the Classical and Christian myths that echo so strongly through Golding's consciousness, requires an application to and assent from the general literature culture that is difficult to demonstrate in contemporary terms. Perhaps some future age will see Golding's original works as establishing 'myth' with twentieth-century referents (perhaps 'myth', on this level, can only be seen or applied retrospectively), but his powerful fiction seems too individual and idiosyncratic a version of the traditional to operate as the kind of 'myth' to which the literate culture assents. Rather, escaping from both the boundaries suggested by the form of 'fable' and the lines suggested by simple response to the prods and or propellants, the Ballantyne and the Wells, *Lord of the Flies* and *The Inheritors* evolve into distinctive and unique fictions. Without the propellants to set them in action, they might seem incoherent or mysterious, certainly difficult, and the simplified polarity is probably the best point of entrance into Golding's fictional world. But his own kind of form, his own incorporation of literary and religious tradition into an essential statement of the human condition, is not really achieved until his next novel, his next unique and symbolic literary explosion.

NOTES

32. William Golding, interview with Henry David Rosso, United Press International, published in *Ann Arbor News*, Ann Arbor Michigan, 5 December 1985.

33. John Peter, 'The Fables of William Golding', *Kenyon Review*, Autumn 1957. Reprinted in Nelson, *Golding's Lord of the Flies*, pp. 21–34.

34. John S. Whitley, *Golding: Lord of the Flies*, Studies in English Literature, no. 42, (London: Edward Arnold, 1970), pp. 3, 41.

S.J. BOYD

The Nature of the Beast:
Lord of the Flies

And Jesus called a little child unto him, and set him in the midst of them,

And said, Verily I say unto you, Except ye be converted,

and become as little children, ye shall not enter the kingdom of heaven.

—*St Matthew* 18. 2–3

As flies to wanton boys, are we to th' Gods;
They kill us for their sport.

—*King Lear*

Lord of the Flies has become almost compulsory reading for those enduring the painful process of growing up. One has the impression that *everyone* has studied and been impressed by this novel in the latter part of schooldays. It is not difficult to give reasons for this popularity: its protagonists are schoolboys, drawn with a remarkable awareness of the realities of the playground world, its unhappy theme 'the end of innocence' (LF p. 223). The loss of innocence for which Ralph weeps at the novel's close is not, however, a matter of transformation from childish goodness to adolescent depravity, is not a growing into wickedness. It is rather the coming of an awareness of darkness, of the evil in man's heart that was present in the children all along. To acknowledge

From *The Novels of William Golding*, pp. 1–23, 200. © 1988 by S. J. Boyd.

the presence of this darkness in one's own heart is a necessary but devastating condition of growing up, of becoming fully and yet flawedly human.

Golding's concern is to present us with a vision of human nature and also of the nature of the world which we inhabit through the experiences of a group of children cast away on a desert island. The two quotations above represent polar opposites of optimism and pessimism with regard to the nature of children (which we might take to be representative of essential or pristine human nature) and the nature of the universe in which we live. In the words of Jesus in St Matthew childhood is presented as a state of innocent goodness, a state which may be regarded as the kingdom of heaven on earth. As adults, fallen from this happy state, we may well hanker after a return to it and the possibility of such a conversion is held out to us in this passage by Jesus. There is room for optimism about human nature then, and there is considerable cause for optimism about the nature of our universe, for the speaker has traditionally been regarded as the creator and loving ruler of the universe, come down to earth to suffer and die so that we might be redeemed or rescued from our wickedness and restored to the original purity and happiness we see in children and remember, or think we remember, as our experience of childhood.

The tragic universe of *King Lear* is at its darkest in Gloucester's terrible words: we live in a cruel world which can only be governed by malevolent demons whose delight is to torture us; if we wish to see an image of these dark gods or devils we need look no further than children or our own childhood, need only examine 'the ghastly and ferocious play of children' (FF p. 150), where we see how little devils torture and kill insects for fun, playing god with flies. From within and without we are beset by evil, 'All dark and comfortless'.[1] *King Lear* is not everywhere so hopeless in outlook but it does seem to force us to accept that nature provides no evidence of beneficent paternal care for us and that in our human nature there is a terrifying propensity towards wanton cruelty which is evident even in children.

It scarcely needs to be said that the picture of childhood, of human nature, and of the nature of things, which emerges from *Lord of the Flies* is closer to that expressed by Gloucester than that in the passage from St Matthew, though in Golding's novel and in Shakespeare's play, as we shall see, some redeeming features are suggested which have much to do with the life of Jesus. The bleakness of the novel's vision has been eloquently encapsulated by Golding himself in a sentence which recalls the despair of Lear in its bludgeoning repetitions: 'The theme of *Lord of the Flies* is grief, sheer grief, grief, grief, grief' (MT p. 163). The grief which Golding expresses and powerfully elicits in the novel is grief at man's very nature and the nature of his world, grief that the boys, and we too, are 'suffering from the terrible disease of being human' (HG p. 87). Shakespeare's tragedy and Golding's novel both present us with a fearless and savage close-up of human nature, a stripping-down of man to what essentially he is. The effect is appalling and humiliating: we are, in Golding's words, a species that 'produces evil as a bee produces honey' (HG p. 87). As naturally as the humble insect produces sweetness, we produce the wickedness and violence which sour our lives. In *King Lear* the burgeoning evil of Lear's daughters and Cornwall finds extravagant expression in the blinding of Gloucester: in *Lord of the Flies* Jack and his gang with comparable callousness steal Piggy's glasses: '"That's them," said Piggy. "They blinded me. See? That's Jack Merridew."' (p. 187). Piggy has been blinded and his complaint indicates that this action of blinding was an expression of the essential nature of Jack Merridew and friends. The blinded Piggy has been granted insight. The darkness of Gloucester's experience leads to his despairing suicide attempt at the Dover cliff. He is, however, saved from death and despair by the loving care of his son: his heart, we are told, 'Twixt two extremes of passion, joy and grief, / Burst smilingly.'[2] Piggy too is led to the rocks at the island's tip—'"Is it safe? Ain't there a cliff? I can hear the sea"' (p. 193)[3]—but for him there is to be no comforting or consolation. The deathsman Roger wantonly knocks him over the cliff and his head bursts messily: 'His head opened and stuff came out and turned red' (p. 200). Piggy's experiences seem to recall those of Gloucester, but his end is more terrible. The crass prose that records his end matches the callousness of Cornwall in transforming Gloucester's eye to 'vile jelly',[4] which is exactly what Roger has done to Piggy's brain.

The evil of Cornwall and Roger transforms humanity into vileness. The compulsive viciousness of Roger might well provoke us to adapt Lear's exclamation concerning Cornwall's accomplice Regan: 'let them anatomise *Roger*; See what breeds about *his* heart.'[5] Roger's evil is inexplicable, in part because he is a shadowy character about whose background we know almost nothing, but Golding is determined, as was Shakespeare in *King Lear*, that we should confront the Roger or Regan within us, '"the reason why it's no go"' (LF p. 158). He has himself spoken of this characteristic determination to anatomise 'the darkness of man's heart' (LF p. 223):

> What man *is*, whatever man is under the eye of heaven, that I burn to know and that—I do not say this lightly—I would endure knowing. The themes closest to my purpose, to my imagination have stemmed from that preoccupation, have been of such a sort that they might move me a little nearer that knowledge. They have been themes of man at an extremity, man tested like a building material, taken into the laboratory and used to destruction; man isolated, man obsessed, man drowning in a literal sea or in the sea of his own ignorance. (MT p. 199)

In *King Lear* the trial by ordeal of human nature takes place on the inhospitable landscapes of a storm-blasted Dark Age Britain; the laboratory in which Golding's schoolboys are used to destruction is the apparently more idyllic world of a tropical island. As we shall see, there are many islands, both real and metaphorical, in Golding's fiction: in *The Inheritors* the new people (i.e. we humans) are first discovered on an island and it is characteristic of them that they are isolated from each other in a way that the Neanderthal people are not; in *Pincher Martin* the central figure finds himself utterly alone and forgotten on a mere rock in the ocean; to Jocelyn in *The Spire* the great ship of the cathedral seems to offer insulation against the evils of the dangerous sea of the world; Wilfred Barclay in *The Paper Men*, despite his credit-card-given ability to travel anywhere at anytime, is isolated from his fellow man and from his own past by his alcoholism and his spiritual crisis occurs on one of the Lipari islands. Isolation is everywhere.

In confining the boys to a small island in *Lord of the Flies* Golding is using a long-established literary method of examining human nature and human polity in microcosm, as in Shakespeare's *The Tempest* or Thomas More's *Utopia*, in Defoe's *Robinson Crusoe* or Swift's *Gulliver's Travels*. These books provide a literary background to the boys' adventures on their island. In such works we find a tendency to present human nature at an extreme: in More's utopian fantasy and in Aldous Huxley's *Island* we see human nature and society at their best. In his introduction to the former Paul Turner remarks:

> The old-fashioned method of getting to Utopia is to be wrecked on an island, preferably in the South Seas, and Huxley's last essay in the genre [*Island*] is to this extent traditional. So is William Golding's *Lord of the Flies* . . . , which may, I think, be considered a rather individual form of Dystopia.[6]

The South-Sea island setting suggests everyone's fantasy of lotus-eating escape or refuge from troubles and cares. But for Golding this is the sheerest fantasy: there is no escape from the agony of being human, no possibility of erecting utopian political systems where all will go well. Man's inescapable depravity makes sure 'it's no go' on Golding's island just as it does on the various islands visited by Gulliver in Swift's excoriating examination of the realities of the human condition.

Robinson Crusoe belongs in part to the world of sheer escapist boys' adventure stories which also contribute to the literary background of *Lord of the Flies*. The castaway boys themselves are reminded of *Treasure Island*, *Swallows and Amazons* and Ballantyne's *The Coral Island*: prompted by the mention of these works, Ralph assures them: '"It's a good island. Until the grown-ups come to fetch us we'll have fun"' (p. 38). The boys imagine that they can have fun not only in swimming and hunting but in imposing decent, civilised English values upon their island, as Ralph, Jack and Peterkin Gay had done on Ballantyne's island and as Robinson Crusoe had done by converting his island to an English gentleman's country estate. But their efforts in this direction are a dismal failure. Things fall apart, or 'break up' in Ralph's phrase (p. 89), into atavism, savagery and bloodshed.[7] The boys regress to what might be called a state of nature, but the experience of this is not of an earthly paradise but a hell on earth.

Golding is determined to disabuse us not only of naïve optimism about the nature of children but also of the sort of faith in the goodness of all things natural described by Aldous Huxley in his essay 'Wordsworth in the Tropics':

> In the neighbourhood of latitude fifty north, and for the last hundred years or thereabouts, it has been an axiom that Nature is divine and morally uplifting ... To commune with the fields and waters, the woodlands and the hills, is to commune, according to our modern and northern ideas, with the visible manifestations of the 'Wisdom and Spirit of the Universe'.[8]

Such an optimistically Romantic view of the beneficence of the natural world is not confirmed by the visit of Golding's northern boys to the tropics. Golding has remarked of Huxley: 'I owe his writings much myself, I've had much enjoyment and some profit from them—in particular, release from a certain starry-eyed optimism' (MT p. 181). Huxley proposes in 'Wordsworth in the Tropics' that a visit to the tropics would cure any Wordsworthian of his faith in nature. The tropical island of Golding's novel, which seems to the boys paradisial in its unspoilt wildness, proves to be an inferno, a sort of pressure-cooker heated by a vertical sun which aims blows at the boys' heads in its violent intensity, which fires 'down invisible arrows' (p. 67) like an angry or malevolent god. It is just as Huxley describes: 'Nature, under a vertical sun, and nourished by the equatorial rains, is not at all like that chaste, mild deity who presides over ... the prettiness, the cosy sublimities of the Lake District.'[9] Prettiness and cosiness are important elements in Ralph's memories of natural wildness back in England, but Ralph's experience of nature is hopelessly limited and naïvely comfortable: 'But the remembered cottage on the moors (where "wildness" was ponies, or the snowy moor seen through a window past a copper-kettle ...) is utterly out of reach and unreal; a flimsy dream.'[10] The reality of nature in the tropics is profoundly sinister and threatening. From their experience of this natural environment the boys derive a sort of religion, but their theology is a demonology, their lord or god is a devil. In this they merely conform to the ways of indigenous jungle-dwellers as described by Huxley: 'The sparse inhabitants of the equatorial forest are all believers in devils.'[11]

The boys' physical surroundings are terrifying and encourage in them a belief in a malevolent god; the boys' own physical condition also is not improved by their stay on the island. Their return to a state of nature, insofar as it implies a lack of toilet facilities and wholesome food, has a very unpleasant effect on them. The 'littluns' in particular quickly become 'filthily dirty' and are affected by 'a sort of chronic diarrhoea' (p. 64). One of Ralph's problems as chief is that the boys fail to abide by the rule that only one clutch of tide-washed rocks should be used as a lavatory: 'Now people seem to use anywhere. Even near the shelters and the platform' (p. 87). Man seems to be a natural producer of filth as well as evil, and the one is a symbol of the other. Of this aspect of the boys' plight Leighton Hodson writes: 'the odour of decay pervades life from the diarrhoea of the littluns ... to Jack hunting the pigs by following their steaming droppings; the association of the Beast, evil, excrement, and blood is both overpowering and purposeful.'[12] This physical degeneration is matched by an upsurge of cruelty, bloodlust and violent rapacity as the Beast, which they take to be a spirit or monster outside of themselves, rises up within them and takes over their lives. Overwhelmed by the horrors that have entered their lives, littluns will isolate themselves to wail, gibber and howl at the misery of their condition. Were Lemuel Gulliver to land on the island, he would instantly recognise that he had returned to a land inhabited by Yahoos.

In Book Four of *Gulliver's Travels* the hero lands on an island dominated by the Houyhnhnms, a nation of intelligent horses whose name signifies '*the perfection of nature*'[13] and whose generally very admirable way of life is lived in accordance with nature or, more precisely, with reason, which they take to be the supreme gift of nature. The peacefulness, cleanliness and reasonableness of their lives make their society an ideal towards which we humans might well wish to aspire. The humanoids of the island, however, have no such aspirations for they are, as Gulliver is mortified to discover, a disgusting race of passionate, violent, irrational, greedy and lustful creatures: these are the Yahoos. Their appearance and presence are rendered particularly offensive by 'their strange disposition to nastiness and dirt'.[14] They wallow in their filth, symbolising their propensity towards evil and the dark, perverse psychological forces which make them incapable of behaving reasonably or organising and maintaining a rational society. Swift thus gives us a painfully simple sketch of the human condition: we aspire to reasonableness and would like to construct and live in rational societies, but the nature of the beast within us, the innate propensity towards violence, cruelty and selfish and self-destructive wickedness, makes such optimistic schemes incapable of realisation. Swift rubs our noses mercilessly in our own filth. John S. Whitley has suggested that 'the Hebrew word "Beelzebub", though it means literally "Lord of flies", might be rendered in English as "lord of dung", that substance around which flies gather'.[15]

The Yahoo-nature inevitably brings about misery. It is not surprising that even the insensitive, brute Yahoo is driven at times 'to retire into a corner, to lie down and howl, and groan' like the half-demented littluns on Golding's island.[16] The transformation from schoolboys to Yahoos forces upon us the bitter truth of *Gulliver's Travels*, that we are creatures whose nature renders us incapable of maintaining rational, equable and peaceful societies such as that of the Houyhnhnms. Ralph and Piggy attempt to create such a society on the island. Piggy in particular has great faith in Houyhnhnm-like values, believing in government by persuasion, deciding issues by debate, above all in reason itself. For Piggy the world is reasonable: at one point he seems amusingly reminiscent of René Descartes: 'I been in bed so much I done some thinking' (p. 102). But Piggy's rationalism is as inadequate as his grammar. His reason cannot control the boys, his belief that science can explain everything makes him unable to comprehend the reality of the Beast, his democracy crumbles before the onslaught of the atavistic Jack, intuitively adept at using the Beast for his own ends. Piggy may be the brains of the outfit but the Beast in Roger, by smashing his skull, makes those brains useless. Piggy's body is quickly swallowed by the sea, which in the chapter 'Beast from Water' was suggested as a possible dwelling-place of the Beast. When Ralph first inspects the spot where Piggy dies, the sea's motion is described by the narrator as 'like the breathing of some stupendous creature', 'the sleeping leviathan' (p. 115). The sea is an insuperable obstacle to the boys' escape and one is tempted to detect a reference to Thomas Hobbes' *Leviathan*, wherein the life of man in a state of nature is characterised as being just as Yahoo-like as the boys discover it to be. It is, in Hobbes' famous phrase, 'solitary, poor, nasty, brutish, and short'.[17] *Lord of the Flies* insists that this is a truth, a grim reality, from which there is no escaping.[18]

The boys' return to nature, then, is not an idyll but a nightmare. It is tempting to see their misadventures as a regression from the Houyhnhnm-like values of our civilisation into the caveman world of the Yahoos. This is Piggy's view of the matter: if only they would behave like grown-ups all would be well; if only a ship carrying grown-ups would spot them they would be saved. This is a comforting view of the book since it seems to put us grown-ups on the side of the angels and endorse the view that our civilisation is rational, peaceful and even salvific. To take such a view is, however, to fall into what Golding suggests is one of the most dangerous of errors: to attempt to deny that the Beast is in us and to limit its existence or operancy to some other time, place, or group of people. Such a reading of the book is untenable. Piggy's faith in grown-ups is shown to be sadly misplaced. Here, displaying typical common sense and faith in the known laws of science, he tries to reassure Ralph: '"The trouble is: Are there ghosts, Piggy? Or beasts?" "Course there aren't." "Why not?" "'Cos things wouldn't make sense. Houses an' streets, an'—TV—they wouldn't work."' (p. 101). But the horrible truth is that man's organised civilisation and sophisticated systems of communication have failed to work, have been destroyed or have broken down in the nightmare of nuclear war.

Civilised values *are* endorsed by the novel—it is heartbreaking to see how friendship and fair-play are replaced by hostility and tyranny—but our actual civilisations are condemned as barbaric and monstrously destructive. Ralph and Jack, chiefs of rival gangs or tribes on the island, are 'two continents of experience and feeling, unable to communicate' (p. 60). They are thus an image of the tragic state of world politics in the mid-twentieth century and of the seemingly eternal need of civilisations to find rivals with whom to quarrel, the perennial argy-bargy of history which Joyce in *Finnegans Wake* sums up as 'wills gen wonts'.[19] When the Lord of the Flies himself, the focus of evil in the book, condescends to speak, it is with the voice of a schoolmaster, whose duty it is to instil the values of our civilisation into developing children. That these values are, to say the least, defective is made very clear by an outburst from Piggy just before his fatal fall: '"Which is better—to be a pack of painted niggers like you are, or to be sensible like Ralph is?"' (p. 199). Piggy *in extremis* lets slip that being 'sensible' may well involve adhering to tribal values and loyalties, regarding whomever is judged to be alien with contempt or loathing and treating them accordingly. But then Piggy knows what it is to be an alien, because he is made an outsider in part by his being physically unattractive but also as a function of that prominent feature of English civilisation, the class system.

Golding's later novels, especially *The Pyramid* and *Rites of Passage*, make abundantly clear his deep bitterness at and hatred of the evils of class. But even in this first novel, even on a desert island, this Golding obsession is in evidence. The novelist Ian McEwan has written of his adolescent reading of *Lord of the Flies*: 'As far as I was concerned, Golding's island was a thinly disguised boarding school.'[20] At one point the narrator seems to claim that class is of no importance in the alienation and persecution of Piggy: 'There had grown up tacitly among the biguns the opinion that Piggy was an outsider, not only by accent, which did not matter, but by fat, and ass-mar, and specs, and a certain disinclination for manual labour' (p. 70). But the narrator implicitly admits that accent, a mark of class, is an alienating factor ['not only'] and actually mocks, in passing, Piggy's way of speaking. The view that class does not matter in Piggy's misfortunes is scarcely borne out by events. From the very outset Piggy is isolated, stranded on an island within the island, by being lower-class. On the book's first page Ralph's 'automatic gesture' of pulling up his socks makes 'the jungle seem for a moment like the Home Counties' (p. 7) and unfortunately Piggy just does not fit into the middle-class ambience implied thereby. Ralph is a good-natured boy, but in this initial scene he seems very reluctant to accept the friendship of the one companion he has so far found on the desert island: '"What's your name?" "Ralph." The fat boy waited to be asked his name in turn but this proffer of acquaintance was not made' (p. 9). One has the uncomfortable feeling throughout this scene that Ralph has been conditioned to be unfriendly towards boys who talk like Piggy. Ralph is not slow to inform Piggy that his father is officer-class, but in response to the crucial question '"What's your father?"' Piggy can produce only the poignant reply: '"My dad's dead," he said quickly, "and my mum—"' (p. 14). The unseemly haste with which Piggy announces that his father is dead suggests a reluctance to reveal his place in life and the blank after the mention of his mum speaks unhappy volumes. Piggy has failed to produce satisfactory credentials. It is at least partly for this reason that Piggy is doomed to become 'the centre of social derision so that everyone felt cheerful and normal' (p. 164). Life seems cheery and normal provided there are the likes of Piggy around to be looked down on and derided.

Piggy's main persecutor is Jack, who from the first evinces contempt and hatred for Piggy, whom he seems to regard as an upstart. Jack's education appears to have instilled in him the belief that it is his right to give commands, to rule: '"I ought to be chief," said Jack with simple arrogance, "because I'm chapter chorister and head boy"' (p. 23). His privileged choir-school background has no doubt taught him much about the necessity of hierarchies, including the notion that head boy from such a school ought to be top man anywhere. Whitley comments: 'This assumption of leadership, bred by being part of a civilised elite, is maintained when he becomes a member of a primitive elite. The perfect prefect becomes the perfect savage.'[21] It would be difficult to imagine anything more suggestive of innocence than a group of cathedral choristers, but we first see the choir as 'something dark' in the haze, as 'the darkness' (p. 20): the choir is from the outset associated with evil. A cathedral choir connotes also a certain English middle-class cosiness, a social world 'assured of certain certainties'. Here is Jack at his most 'sensible', declaring some important certainties: '". . . We've got to have rules and obey them. After all, we're not savages. We're English; and the English are best at everything"' (p. 47). Golding has written that such cosy English chauvinism was something he particularly wished to attack in *Lord of the Flies*:

> One of our faults is to believe that evil is somewhere else and inherent in another nation. My book was to say: you think that now the war is over and an evil thing destroyed, you are safe because you are naturally kind and decent. (HG p. 89).

The English error is to objectify and externalise the Devil, as the boys do, and this self-congratulatory attitude is dangerous because it allows the Devil to go to work, evils to be perpetrated, under cover of the belief that English people are good, decent and fair-minded. The classic jingoistic expression of such an attitude might be: 'Come off it! This is *England*! Something like that couldn't happen in England!' Whoever adopts such an attitude blinds himself to the evils which do exist in English life, prominent among which is the class system. Golding tries to expose the truth about this evil by translating it from England to a desert island: Jack's hatred of and violence towards Piggy is the raw naked truth about English social organisation. Classist attitudes not only ensure that under the motto of fair play a very unfair deal is given to most members of a society, they also bring about the reification of people. Thus a person may be treated not on the merits of his complex make-up as an individual but merely in accordance with his being recognised as a component of a mass class-group. The final blow dealt to Piggy transforms the extraordinary and miraculous complexity and beauty of his brain, the seat of consciousness and what makes him the particular and unique person he is, into mere 'stuff'.

The treatment meted out to Piggy makes the view that the boys' story is one of simple regression and degeneration a very difficult one to hold. But such a view is completely undermined by the adventitious arrival of the naval officer at the close. Every reader of the novel must have felt profoundly relieved when Ralph stumbles upon this white-clad saviour. All will be well now that the authority and values of civilisation have returned in the figure of this man, who might indeed almost be Ralph's father come to rescue them all. Critics have long recognised, however, that this warrior who stops the boys' war is anything but snowy-white morally. Virginia Tiger sums the matter up thus:

> There is no essential difference between the island world and the adult one and it is the burden of the fable's structure . . . to make it clear that the children's experiment on the island has its constant counterpart in the world outside.[22]

The officer is a warrior, a killer, and he is right to regard the boys' war as mere 'Fun and games', because compared to the massive death-dealing of the nuclear war in which he is involved it is very small-scale indeed. But the officer is nonetheless dismayed that a group of British boys should have degenerated into savages, should have failed 'to put up a better show than that'. Show, the keeping-up of a good appearance, is what this ultra-English officer is all about. The white uniform, the gold buttons, the 'trim cruiser' of the closing sentence are all signs of the officer's belief in orderliness, cleanliness, and of his and his nation's belief in their moral rectitude. The officer's first, and apparently kindly, thought about Ralph is that he 'needed a bath, a hair-cut, a nose-wipe and a good deal of ointment' (pp. 221–3). An advocate, no doubt, of the stiff upper lip, he is embarrassed by Ralph's heartbroken tears. The officer is no saviour at all. He is doubly guilty: of being a warrior on behalf of one of the world's two tribes and of sanitising the killing, the vast butchery, involved in such conflicts, of cleaning and dressing it up so that it seems sane and sensible. He is able to masquerade as a peacemaker, a bringer of light to the savages. He dislikes the blood and filth of the boys, he is embarrassed by Ralph's open display of emotion, but the blood and filth are the true symbols of war or warriors and Ralph's grief is an absolutely human and appropriate reaction to the revelations of the island.

The officer comes ashore like Lemuel Gulliver to discover a pack of Yahoos. Like Gulliver, he finds them distasteful. But Gulliver gradually comes to see that supposedly civilised humans are worse than Yahoos because they have all the filth and vices of the Yahoos, though they hide these under clothes and a clothing of pride in their own supposed moral rectitude, and have abused what reason they have by employing it in the invention of new ways in which to express their viciousness. It is a uniform-wearing Yahoo that has come to rescue the boys: there is even more reason than Ralph thinks to weep for 'the darkness of man's heart'. The phrase describes succinctly enough the central concern of Swift's writing but asks us specifically to think of Conrad. The overall picture of man's nature which emerges from *Lord of the Flies* is indeed similar to the one we find in *Heart of Darkness*. A return to the state of nature, an escape into primitivism such as that attempted by Conrad's Kurtz, leads only to the unleashing of brutality, greed for power, and sadism in the most naked and brutal forms, to the horror of orgiastic and murderous midnight dances and human heads stuck on poles. But the forces of civilisation, clad in shiny white to proclaim their moral excellence, are mere whited sepulchres, every bit as guilty as Kurtz and lacking even the honesty of open savagery. Both books offer this grim view of the human condition: there is no rescue, no way out, and the ending of *Lord of the Flies* is anything but happy. To regard it as such would be to ignore the prophetic voice of Simon.

In *The Coral Island* Ballantyne's three young adventurers had the names Ralph, Jack and Peterkin Gay. In Golding's novel we find a Ralph and a Jack but two boys seem to share the derivation of their names from the third member of Ballantyne's jolly-sounding trio: Piggy's name is an approximate and unpleasant contraction of Peterkin Gay, but the name Simon, we know from the Bible, was the original name of St Peter, so Simon has a claim too. Simon and Piggy are, indeed, alike in sharing a role in *Lord of the Flies*, the role of outsider, scapegoat and victim of murder. Though the two are alike in this way, however, they are otherwise very different from one another and represent, indeed, two mighty opposites, two warring ways of looking at the world, which occur again and again in Golding's fiction. Faith in science and rationality, with a marked disbelief in anything supernatural, is characteristic of Piggy. Simon, by contrast, is intuitive, introspective, other-worldly; his central insight is gained in a vision or trance; Simon represents and has access to a dimension of experience it is proper to call religious. Piggy cannot understand Simon and thinks him mad.

This conflict between the contrasting world-views of science or ratiocination and religious or visionary experience, between worldly commonsense and other-worldly mysticism, is dramatised time and again by Golding: in the figures of Nick Shales and Rowena Pringle in *Free Fall*, in Roger Mason and Jocelin in *The Spire* and in Edmund Talbot and Robert James Colley in *Rites of Passage*. This conflict is clearly of great importance to Golding and it would be true to say that, though he is at pains to be fair to and make a strong case for the scientific or worldly side, his sympathies ultimately lie with the Simons, Jocelins and Colleys. In an essay on education he writes: 'it cannot be said often enough or loudly enough that "Science" is not the most important thing' (HG p. 129). This too has a Swiftian air to it. In Book Three of *Gulliver's Travels* Swift demonstrates powerfully that the analytical intellect, alone and unaided by any higher insight, cannot even begin to offer solutions to the problems of being human. Golding has expressed admiration for Copernicus, whom he characterises as a man devoted to the quest for scientific truth but who nonetheless bears the signs of an inclination towards mysticism.[23] In *Lord of the Flies* Golding's bias in this matter is perhaps most clearly seen in the differing degrees of respect accorded to Piggy and Simon by the narrative in their deaths. Leighton Hodson describes this succinctly:

> Golding manages to deepen his meaning of what the boys' attitudes represent by providing them, in their common ends, with descriptions that correspond to the limited practical intelligence in the case of Piggy—dry in tone—and the intuitive depth of understanding in the case of Simon—eloquent and transfiguring.[24]

The limitations of Piggy's practical intelligence are, indeed, particularly highlighted by comparison with Simon. Piggy's clever and sensible schemes fail to bring about the rescue the boys desperately need; his rational approach is unable to sway the mass of boys in debate or preserve order among them; above all, he rejects Simon's suggestion that the Beast is a reality within the boys themselves. Piggy rightly condemns the notion that there is an external Beast that lives in the forest or the sea, but under great pressure comes to believe that Jack is the Beast or Devil, failing to see that this too is an externalisation, an avoidance of his own guilt. Piggy's scientific views dictate that there is no Devil in the world, but if he must allow that there is evil he is determined to 'believe that evil is somewhere else' and in someone else. He is himself, however, involved in the murder of Simon, for all his predictable attempts to exculpate himself and explain the killing away as an accident.

Simon is murdered by the boys when he emerges from the forest into the frenzy of their dance, supposedly a charm against the Beast. Their defence against an imagined external Beast allows the beast within them to gain absolute control and transform them into murderers. Simon had come to tell them that the creature on the mountain they thought to be the Beast was merely the horribly damaged body of a pilot, evidence of the effects of the beast within us in the world of warring adults. Simon had come to bring them confirmation of the truth that he had proposed earlier and for which he had been shouted down and derided, the dark truth that the Beast is within them, each and every one of them. The reception he is given proves his point once and for all. The truth which Simon offers is a grim one, but Simon himself is not at all a grim or dark figure. He is affectionate, gentle and kind, helping the littluns to find good fruit, for example, but also a loner, a 'queer' boy who isolates himself in a forest glade reminiscent of a church and goes into reveries. It is small wonder that the other boys regard this youthful mystic as mad or 'batty', a fool. We must take Simon a great deal more seriously. The traditional role of the prophet is to awaken men to the truth of their own sinfulness: this Simon does, and he also succeeds in fulfilling the popular view of the prophet's task by foretelling the future. He tells Ralph that he will get home safely and his voice comes back to Ralph just before he is in fact rescued. The boys are living in the dangerous error of believing that the Beast is an evil creature at the mountaintop, so Simon the prophet goes to the mountain to discover the truth. On his way he finds a forest glade desecrated by a sow's head on a stick, a gift for the Beast. Simon falls into a fit, or hallucination, or vision, in which the Lord of the Flies, the Devil, speaks to him through the foul mouthpiece of the head and tells him that he is '"part of you"'. He warns Simon to go back and fall into line or the boys will 'do' him (pp. 157–9). Simon defies the threat, climbs the mountain, finds the parachutist and descends to the beach to be slaughtered.

Amidst the bloody chaos of the storm and the demonic dance we are told that 'Simon was crying out something about a dead man on a hill' (p. 168) as he is being assaulted. He refers of course to the parachutist, but we must hear also a suggestion of the death of Christ on Calvary and realise that, in killing the true prophet who had come down to reveal to them their real nature, their sinfulness, and thus set them on the road towards saving themselves, the boys are re-enacting the crucifixion of Jesus Christ. Simon's life and death are an imitation of Christ. In ascending the mountain and returning to the boys, despite the warnings of the Lord of the Flies about what will happen to him, he takes up and shares the Cross like his namesake from Cyrene: '"Simon. He helps"', as Ralph earlier remarks (p. 59). His self-sacrifice does not, however, achieve an instant conversion of the boys to goodness. Nor did Christ's with regard to mankind as a whole. Piggy blames him for bringing his death on himself: '"Coming in the dark—he had no business crawling like that out of the dark. He was batty. He asked for it"' (p. 173). He walked right into his own death, so he must have been mad, a fool, a Simple Simon.

To suggest that a person or character is a fool would normally undermine any confidence we might have that the person or character concerned had wisdom to offer us. Here this is not the case. Simon imitates the folly of that supreme fool Christ, who allowed himself to be crucified and whose teachings must seem foolish to the worldly-wise. Christ the holy fool is admirably described by Erasmus in the *Praise of Folly*:

> Christ too, though he is the wisdom of the Father, was made something of a fool himself in order to help the folly of mankind, when he assumed the nature of man and was seen in man's form ... Nor did he wish them to be redeemed in any other way save by the folly of the cross and through his simple, ignorant apostles, to whom he unfailingly preached folly.[25]

To those in darkness, to those under the sway of the Lord of This World who is the Lord of the Flies, the wisdom of Christ must indeed appear utter folly. Simon is the first of Golding's holy fools, characters who in many respects are holy or Christ-like and yet, almost by that very token, are ill-fitted for survival in the world of fallen man: two clear examples, whom we shall examine later, are Nathaniel in *Pincher Martin* and Matty in *Darkness Visible*. The holy or prophetic fool dares to challenge the cosy but delusive beliefs of the majority and so must be laughed at, dismissed, driven out or slaughtered by that majority.

The message or wisdom which Simon offers—that the Beast is in us, that we must acknowledge the 'thing of darkness' as our own—is disturbing and negative. He does not appear to bring the good news of redemption or salvation. But his life and death offer some hope in the book's pervasive gloom inasmuch that among all the boys, so to say, at least one good man has been found, one person who is capable of imitating Christ's redemptive example. At the mountaintop he is able to free the dead pilot, according to Golding a symbol of the nightmare of human history (HG p. 90), and allow him to fly off, just as Christ, from an orthodox point of view, changed the nature of history by freeing man from the bondage of sin, offering the *possibility* of escape from the endless backsliding and tribulations of human and personal history. There is, furthermore, the 'eloquent and transfiguring' description of the sea's disposal of Simon's body. Simon is carried 'towards the open sea' by the tide, attended by 'strange, moonbeam-bodied creatures with fiery eyes' who weave a halo of brightness around his head (pp. 169–70). These beautiful and seemingly magical little entities we have seen before in broad daylight:

> There were creatures that lived in this last fling of the sea, tiny transparencies that came questing in with the water over the hot, dry sand ... Perhaps food had appeared where the last incursion there had been none; bird droppings, insects perhaps, any of the strewn detritus of landward life. Like a myriad of tiny teeth in a saw, the transparencies came scavenging on the beach. (p. 66)

But there is no beauty or magic or mystery. The creatures are simply the lowest point in the ugly world of living nature, vile scavengers as coldly destructive as sawteeth. It is Simon's self-sacrifice that transforms them to beauty, goes some way towards redeeming the world of nature and reestablishing its beauty and harmony.

What light there is in the book does, indeed, seem to be concentrated around Simon. There are, however, certain other aspects of the novel which may be seen as mitigating the generally excoriating treatment of human nature. 'I am by nature an optimist' Golding has remarked 'but a defective logic—or a logic which I sometimes hope desperately is defective—makes a pessimist of me' (HG p. 126). Though this is rather a dark utterance, it does make explicit that tension between optimism and pessimism, between hope and despair, which is characteristic of Golding's fiction. Indeed, from *The Spire* onwards it seems appropriate to characterise his fiction as broadly tragi-comic. Though comedy is a grotesquely inappropriate term to apply to *Lord of the Flies*, the outlook of the novel is not entirely pessimistic.

There is first the essential decency of Ralph, 'the fair boy' whose eyes proclaim 'no devil' and who tries to keep the other boys' eyes on the values of civilisation, tries 'to keep a clean flag of flame flying' (pp. 8, 11, 45). Though the book suggests that we should be sceptical about such an ocular proclamation and about 'Rally round the flag, boys!' sentiments, there is no doubt that Ralph does strive earnestly and sincerely to be fair and decent. There is also the goodness, the sheer vitality, of the twins Samneric, Ralph's most loyal supporters. Not only are they kind, loyal and generous, but their apparent blending into one another makes them seem representative of average everyday man, the 'man on the Clapham omnibus'. Moreover, we sympathise strongly with this group and abominate Jack and Roger. It seems that we can at least say of ourselves that we would *like to be* decent, fair and good. Our sympathy or even identification with Ralph is also very effective in intensifying the 'thriller' aspect of the novel: in the final chapter we have the very unpleasant feeling that *we* are being hunted by Jack and Roger.

How we fear and loathe their extravagant and insatiable evil! There is some comfort to be taken in this, but we must remember that Ralph and Samneric, those models of decency, were involved in the murder of Simon and, like another decent man caught up in evil, they try to wash the innocent martyr's blood from their hands by their denial that they were present at the killing. Further, Samneric are coerced into joining Jack's tribe and in Ralph's final interview with them they have become, for all the kindness towards Ralph which they cannot quite fight down, guardians of a regime where all rules have disappeared except the rule of sadism. Samneric, like other ordinary men before them, have been transformed into concentration camp guards, porters at the Gate of Hell. Ralph's conversation with them at the Castle Rock is perhaps the most heartrending section of the entire book and there is every reason why that should be so.[26]

Just as we sympathise with the nature of Ralph, Samneric and, indeed, even Piggy, so too we are attracted to the democratic system they create. The gentle, exhortatory paternalism of Ralph and Piggy seems both fair and sensible as a way of organising government. It is manifestly preferable to Jack's absolutist tyranny. Again our hearts seem to be in roughly the right place. And yet Jack's system has greater attraction for the boys, who desert Ralph's tribe in droves. In fairness to Jack it must be said that in certain important respects his reign of terror is a more effective form of government than Ralph's. He gives the boys meat and he is able to keep them in order, to put a stop to quarrels, fragmentation and even sheer laziness in a way which Ralph was not: '"See? They do what I want"' (p. 198), he pointedly remarks to Ralph, who has just become a one-man tribe. Once again the Leviathan raises its head: Hobbes' pessimistic view is that human fractiousness requires to be quelled and governed by an absolute monarch. *Lord of the Flies* could never be said to advocate Jack's monarchy however, since though in some ways it clearly 'works' it also panders to and is an expression of the worst aspects of human nature; greed, cruelty and lust. Like a vicious Roman emperor he provides food and entertainment for his mob, entertainment taking the form of beating littluns, murderous ritual dances, and the obscene and rapacious violence of the hunt: 'The sow collapsed under them and they were heavy and fulfilled upon her' (p. 149). Jack intuitively knows all about the lowest and vilest elements in our nature and how to exploit them:

> Simon became inarticulate in his effort to express mankind's essential illness. Inspiration came to him.
>
> "What's the dirtiest thing there is?"
>
> As an answer Jack dropped into the uncomprehending silence that followed it the crude expressive syllable. Release was like an orgasm ... The hunters were screaming with delight. (p. 97)

Obscenity can be delightful: that is a symptom of our essential illness.

Jack may be successful in satisfying in the short-term certain basic and base human cravings, but his system offers no hope of rescue. Behaviour such as Jack indulges in and encourages seems to preclude redemption or salvation, even if salvation is no more than the imitation of Christ in *this* world which we see in Simon, whom Jack and his minions kill. The symbol of his terrible régime is the stick sharpened at both ends, the support of the totem Lord of the Flies, a weapon which seems to suggest that its killing-power may rebound against the user. It is a symbol which reminds us of the self-defeating nature of the weaponry deployed for nuclear war by those who build fortresses and bunkers against imagined external threats and evils in the world outside the island. The spear is sharpened by Roger and, for all that has been said about Jack's ability to command obedience, it is not difficult to imagine this sinister figure returning Jack's violent means to power upon him and completing his bloody and Macbeth-like career by sticking *his* head on a pole.

At the close the naval officer arrives to find the island paradise lost and burning, the scene 'with dreadful faces thronged and fiery arms'.[27] Coming from his warship, he is a veritable *deus ex machina* descending from the 'above' of the adult world to set things right and rescue the erring children. Despite the sinister associations of the naval officer, might he not still be seen as the caring and omnipotent God who finally intervenes in man's world to stop the course of the bloody history of fallen man and restore peace forever? Such a view would offer a glimmer of religious light at the end of the tunnel. Such a reading is perhaps allowable, but there is evidence in the novel which counts against it and which ought not to be ignored. There seems to be no haven for the boys to be rescued *to*. We are told much earlier that 'Roger's arm was conditioned by a civilisation that knew nothing of him and was in ruins' (p. 67). When the boys first spot a passing ship on the horizon the narrative speaks of 'the smoke of home' beckoning to them (p. 73), a touching phrase since it suggests both the homeliness the boys long for and the smoking ruins that are all that remain of home. Having been terrified by the dead parachutist that seems to be the Beast, Ralph complains that the 'thing squats by the fire as though it didn't want us to be rescued' (p. 138), and the corpse is, indeed, a sign that the civilisation which might rescue them has been destroyed by war. The naval officer has played a part in that war. Perhaps there is no comfort in seeing him as an image of God, because the image is of a flawed and irresponsible god, perhaps like the forgetful or lazy creator of the island's reef: 'The coral was scribbled in the sea as though a giant had bent down to reproduce the shape of the island in a flowing, chalk line but tired before he had finished' (p. 31). The creator's signature does not inspire confidence in his character and evidences from nature generally, as we have seen, from the 'enmity' of the sun, that traditional symbol of the Godhead, downwards, are not such as to encourage faith in absolute beneficence (pp. 13–15). The weight of evidence would seem to indicate that any creator must be a cruel selfish wielder of power, that the gods are indeed as Gloucester described them, swatting men like flies with an ease the naval officer might well envy or might even match, a source of no comfort or hope. What desperate hope the book offers is simply the example of Simon, the acknowledgement of our guilt, of the 'thing of darkness' within us, and the overcoming of this guilt and darkness in generous, if unsuccessful, self-sacrifice for the sake of others. Simon, like Cordelia, allows a little room for hope, but the book's abiding impression remains like that of *King Lear*: 'grief, sheer grief, grief, grief, grief'.

Notes

1. *King Lear*, III. 7. 81.

2. Ibid., V. 3. 197.

3. Compare *King Lear*, IV. 6. 4.

4. *King Lear*, III. 7. 81.

5. Ibid., III. 6. 74.

6. More, p. 20.

7. Alastair Niven suggests that 'Ralph's words are an uncomprehending child's expression of what W.B. Yeats wrote in his poem "The Second Coming"'. Niven, *William Golding*, p. 21.

8. Huxley, *Do What You Will*, p. 113.

9. Ibid.

10. Kinkead-Weekes and Gregor, *William Golding*, p. 40.

11. Huxley op. cit., p. 114.

12. Hodson, *William Golding*, p. 38.

13. Swift, *Gulliver's Travels*, p. 190 (Book IV, Chapter 3).

14. Swift op. cit., p. 212 (Book IV, Chapter 6).

15. Whitley, Golding p. 43:

16. Swift op. cit., p. 213 (Book IV, Chapter 6).

17. Hobbes, *The Leviathan*, p. 186 (Book II, Chapter 13).

18. The importance of Hobbes as background-reading for *Lord of the Flies* is stressed by Alastair Niven. See Niven op. cit., p. 38.

19. Joyce, *Finnegans Wake*, p. 4.

20. Ian McEwan, 'Schoolboys', in Carey, *William Golding*, p. 158.

21. Whitey op. cit., p. 28.

22. Tiger, *William Golding*, p. 51.

23. See 'Copernicus' in *The Hot Gates*.

24. Hodson op. cit., p. 29.

25. Erasmus, *Praise of Folly*, pp. 198–9.

26. *The Tempest*, V.1. 275.

27. Milton, *Paradise Lost*, XII. 644.

L.L. DICKSON

Lord of the Flies

Of Golding's nine novels, *Lord of the Flies* is most clearly an allegory. It has been criticized as both too explicit[1] and too ambiguous.[2] Walter Allen's skepticism is typical: "The difficulty begins when one smells allegory."[3] More accurately, Golding's *Lord of the Flies* combines the best features of realistic and allegorical fiction; the novel allows for "the simultaneous operation of the factual and the fabular."[4]

The tension between realistic novel and allegorical fable is established in the setting for the action in *Lord of the Flies*: the isolated island provides an appropriate stage for the survival story of the deserted boys, but also suggests a universal, timeless backdrop for symbolic action. Golding creates a microcosm, a procedure common "to the great allegorists and satirists," and then "examines the problem of how to maintain moderate liberal values and to pursue distant ends against pressure from extremists and against the lower instincts."[5] The protagonist's ironic "rescue" by a naval officer, who is himself engrossed in the savage business of international warfare, reveals that the chaotic island-world is but a small version of a war-torn adult world. The novel does not imply that children, without the disciplined control of adults, will turn into savages; on the contrary, it dramatizes the real nature of all humans. The nightmare world, which quickly develops on the island, parallels the destruction of the outside world through atomic warfare. The dead parachutist, whom the boys mistake

From *The Modern Allegories of William Golding*, pp. 12–26, 141–142. © 1990 by the Board of Regents of the State of Florida.

for the Beast, is a symbolic reminder of the human history of self-destruction; the parachutist is literally and figuratively a "fallen man."

At first, the island world is compared to Eden: the boys "accepted the pleasure of morning, the bright sun, the whelming sea and sweet air, as a time when play was good and life so full that hope was not necessary and therefore forgotten."[6] But this setting is simultaneously sinister and hostile. The boys are scratched by thorns and entrapped by creepers. "The ground beneath them was a bank covered with coarse grass, torn everywhere by the upheavals of fallen trees, scattered with decaying coconuts and palm saplings. Behind this was the darkness of the forest proper and the open scar" (p. 6). Eventually the island becomes a burning hell: "Smoke was seeping through the branches in white and yellow wisps, the patch of blue sky overhead turned to the color of a storm cloud, and then the smoke bellowed around him" [Ralph, the protagonist] (p. 233). The island is a microcosm from the adult world; indeed, "you realize after a time that the book is nothing less than a history of mankind itself."[7]

The personified agents in *Lord of the Flies* are developed in all the four ways discussed in the first chapter. First, the analogy through nomenclature is the most obvious method by which the characters take on additional dimensions. Golding's novel represents an ironic treatment of R. M. Ballantyne's *The Coral Island*, a children's classic that presents the romantic adventures of a group of English schoolboys marooned on an Eden-like South Sea island. By mustering their wits and their British courage, the boys defeat the evil forces on the island: pirates and native savages. Not only is Golding's island literally a coral island (p. 12) where the boys "dream pleasantly" and romantically, but there are specific references to Ballantyne: "'It's like in a book.' At once there was a clamor. 'Treasure Island—' 'Swallows and Amazons—' 'Coral Island—'" (p. 37). At the conclusion of the novel, the dull-witted naval officer who comes to Ralph's rescue makes an explicit comparison: "Jolly good show. Like the Coral Island" (p. 242). Golding uses the same names for his main characters as Ballantyne did. Ralph, Jack, and Peterkin Gay of *The Coral Island* become Golding's Ralph, Jack, and Simon ("Simon called Peter, you see. It was worked out very carefully in every possible way, this novel"[8]). Golding's characters, however, represent ironic versions of the earlier literary work, and their very names, inviting comparison to Ballantyne, add ironic impact to the characterization.

The change of Peterkin's name to Simon better supports that character's function as a "saint" figure in Golding's novel. Obviously Piggy's name contributes to the symbolism: Piggy will become identified with a hunted pig, and eventually will be killed too, as the boys' savage hunt turns to human rather than animal victims. When Piggy falls to his death, his arms and legs twitch "like a pig's after it has been killed" (p. 217). Jack's name is a variant of John, the disciple of Christ, and indeed Jack is an ironic distortion of the religious connotations of his name, in the same manner as is Christopher Martin, the egocentric protagonist of Golding's third novel.

Second, the characters in *Lord of the Flies* become allegorical agents through the correspondence of a state of nature with a state of mind. The more the boys stay on the island, the more they become aware of its sinister and actively hostile elements. The description of the pleasant Coral island fantasy world quickly dissolves into images of darkness, hostility, danger. The boys accept "the pleasures of morning, the bright sun" and the unrestricted play, but by afternoon the overpowering sunlight becomes "a blow that they ducked" (p. 65). Though dusk partly relieves the situation, the boys are then menaced by the dark: "When the sun sank, darkness dropped on the island like an extinguisher and soon the shelters were full of restlessness, under the remote stars" (p. 66).

The boys' attitude of childish abandon and romantic adventure changes to a much more sober one when the possibility of a beast is introduced. At that point the island is transformed into a dark haven for unspeakable terrors. The boys' increasing apprehension about their immediate physical safety parallels the gradual awareness that is taking shape in the minds of Simon, Piggy, and particularly Ralph, concerning the *real* evil of the island. The boys mistakenly project their own bestiality on an imaginary animal roaming the island, but Simon hesitantly speculates, "maybe it's only us" (p. 103). The others do not understand. They look into the blackened jungle for signs of the beast's movement. The darkness is "full of claws, full of the awful unknown and menace" (p. 116). Simon's inner vision, however, tells him that it is the human being who is "at once heroic and sick" (p. 121). When Simon confronts the Lord of the Flies, the pig's head on a stick, it tells him (but really he tells himself), "Fancy thinking the Beast was something you could hunt and kill! . . . You knew, didn't you? I'm part of you?" (p. 172). The hostile island and its dark mysteries are only a symbolic backdrop reinforcing the images of savagery, bestiality, and destruction that describe, and reveal, the boys themselves.

A third method by which the characters assume allegorical significance is through the implicit comparison of an action with an extrafictional event. James Baker was the first to point out similarities between Euripides' *The Bacchae* and Golding's novel. The mistaken slaying of Simon recalls Pentheus's murder at the hands of the crazed bacchantes of Dionysus. Pentheus's pride and his inability to recognize Dionysus's powers lead to his downfall: "This same lesson in humility is meted out to the schoolboys of *Lord of the Flies*. In their innocent pride they attempt to impose a rational order or pattern upon the vital chaos of their own nature. . . . The penalties (as in the play) are bloodshed, guilt, utter defeat of reason."[9]

Both the novel and the play contain a beast-god cult, a hunt sequence, and the dismemberment of the scapegoat figure.[10] Though Simon is the clearest equivalent for Pentheus, Piggy and finally Ralph are cast in similar roles. Piggy is destroyed, though not dismembered, by Jack's forces. Ralph is chased by frenzied hunters but is "saved" (by a deus ex machina process similar to that of the end of Euripides' play) from the prospect of beheading. Ralph fittingly becomes Golding's version of Agave. The boy, like Pentheus's mother, mistakenly takes part in a killing and then must live sorrowfully with the knowledge of his, and all humanity's, capacity for blind destruction.

The actions that help establish parallels to religious events emphasize biblical analogues. Ralph's first blowing of the conch, proclaiming survival after the crash on the island, recalls the angel Gabriel's announcing good news. Inasmuch as the boys' "survival" is quite tentative, however, the implied comparison to Gabriel is ironic. Simon's fasting, helping the little boys, meditating in the wilderness, going up on the mountain—all these actions solidify the Christ parallel. The recurring pattern of falls—the falling parachutist, Piggy's fall to his death, the destruction of the conch in the same fall, Ralph's tumbling panic at the end of the novel—emphasizes the fall of humankind motif.

The extrafictional events pertaining to classical mythology or to Christ's passion enlarge the surface action with additional symbolic meanings.

The fourth and final technique for intensifying allegorical agents concerns the manifestation in an action of a state of mind. In *Lord of the Flies* a series of hunts, for either pigs or humans, symbolically demonstrates the boys' gradual deterioration into savages. Moral order is corrupted and the end result is chaos. William Mueller has established convincingly that "the book is a carefully structured work of art whose organization—in terms of a series of hunts—serves to reveal with progressive clarity man's essential core."[11] Mueller identifies six "hunts," but there are at least nine separate instances where this symbolic act occurs: (1) the first piglet, "caught in a curtain of creepers," escapes when Jack is mentally unable to kill the helpless creature (p. 32); (2) a second pig eludes the hunters, much to Jack's disgust (p. 55); (3) Jack is successful the next time, and the hunters conceive the ritual chant of "Kill the Pig. Cut her throat. Spill her blood" (p. 78); later Maurice briefly pretends to be the pig (p. 86); (4) during a mock ceremony that gets out of hand, Robert plays the role of the pig, in a scene that sinisterly foreshadows the transition from nonhuman to human prey (pp. 135–36); (5) after another successful hunt, the boys smear themselves with animal blood, and Maurice plays the pig while Robert ritually pokes him with a spear, to the delight of Jacks's hunters (pp. 161–63); (6) Jack and Roger play hunter and pig respectively, as Piggy and Ralph "find themselves eager to take a place in this demented but partly secure society" (p. 181); (7) Simon is mistaken for the beast and is torn to pieces; (8) Piggy is killed by Roger, who acts "with a sense of delirious abandonment" (p. 216); (9) and finally Ralph is the object of the last murderous hunt.

The two fundamental patterns by which allegorical action is resolved are those of "progress" and "battle." The journey motif is first established by the plot circumstances of the opening chapter. A group of boys has been taken by airplane from a war-threatened England to a safer territory, but in the process their plane is attacked and they have been dropped to safety on a deserted island. Their thwarted flight is mentioned in the opening exposition. Though their physical, outer journey has ended, they soon begin a more recondite "journey." Through their quest for the beast, they (or at least Simon and Ralph) discover the real beast, humanity's own predilection for evil.

The structure of *Lord of the Flies* provides for a gradual revelation of insight, as Ralph sees his friends slowly turn into beasts themselves. The significance of the final scene, in which the naval officer reestablishes an adult perspective, is not what James Gindin once contended: "a means of cutting down or softening the implications built up within the structure of the boys' society on the island."[12] The officer's presence does not reaffirm that "adult sanity really exists," nor is it merely a gimmick that "palliates the force and the unity of the original metaphor"[13] on the contrary, it provides the final ironic comment: Ralph is "saved" by a soldier of war, a soldier who cannot see that the boys have symbolically reenacted the plight of all persons who call themselves civilized and yet continue to destroy their fellow humans in the same breath.

The irony of this last scene is consistent with Golding's sarcastic treatment of Ballantyne, and it also emphasizes the universality of Ralph's experience. There is no distinction between child and adult here. The boys' ordeal is a metaphor for the human predicament. Ralph's progress toward self-knowledge culminates in his tears: "Ralph wept for the end of innocence, the darkness of man's heart, and the fall through the air of the true, wise friend called Piggy" (p. 242). Because Piggy represents the failure of reason, the use of "wise" offers a further irony.

The battle motif is developed in both physical confrontations and rhetorical "combat." Initially, the pig hunts are ritualized tests of strength and manhood, but when the hunters eventually seek human prey (Simon, Piggy, and finally Ralph) the conflict is between the savage and the civilized; blind emotion and prudent rationality; inhumanity and humanity; evil and good. This conflict is further established in the chapter entitled "The Shell and the Glasses," when Jack's hunters attack Ralph's boys and steal Piggy's glasses. Jack carries the broken spectacles—which have become symbolic of intellect, rationality, and civilization—as ritual proof of his manhood and his power over his enemies: "He was a chief now in truth; and he made stabbing motions with his spear" (p. 201). In the "Castle Rock" chapter, Ralph opposes Jack in what is called a "crisis" situation: "They met with a jolt and bounced apart. Jack swung with his fist at Ralph and caught him on the ear. Ralph hit Jack in the stomach and made him grunt. Then they were facing each other again, panting and furious, but unnerved by each other's ferocity. They became aware of the noise that was the background to this fight, the steady shrill cheering of the tribe behind them" (p. 215).

More subtle forms of "battle"—debate and dialogue—are dramatized in the verbal exchanges between Jack and Ralph. Golding emphasizes their polarity: "They walked along, two continents of experience and feeling, unable to communicate" (p. 62). Later when Jack paints his face and flaunts his bloodied knife, the conflict is heightened: "The two boys faced each other. There was the brilliant world of hunting, tactics, fierce exhilaration, skill; and there was the world of longing and baffled common-sense" (p. 81). When Ralph does not move, Jack and the others have to build their fire in a less ideal place: "By the time the pile [of firewood] was built, they were on different sides of a high barrier" (p. 83). Different sides of the wood, different continents, different worlds—all these scenes intensify the symbolic as well as physical conflict. Here we encounter "a structural principle that becomes Golding's hallmark: a polarity expressed in terms of a moral tension. Thus, there is the rational (the firewatchers) pitted against the irrational (the hunters)."[14]

In both chapter 2, "Beast from Water," and chapter 8, "Gift for the Darkness," the exchange of views about whether there is a beast or not "becomes a blatant allegory in which each spokesman caricatures the position he defends."[15] Ralph and Piggy think that rules and organization can cure social ills, and that if things "break up," it is because individuals are not remembering that life "is scientific," rational, logical (p. 97). Jack hates rules, only wishes to hunt, and believes that evil is a mystical, living power that can be appeased by ritual sacrifice (p. 159). Simon feels that evil is not outside but rather within all human beings, though he is "inarticulate in his effort to express mankind's essential illness" (p. 103). He uses comparisons with excrement and filth to describe his notion of human inner evil.

Simon's confrontation with the pig's head on a stick, the Lord of the Flies, is another instance of allegorical dialogue. At first, Beelzebub seems to triumph: Simon is mesmerized by the grinning face (p. 165); he is warned that he is "not wanted," for Simon is the only boy who possesses a true vision of the nature of evil; and finally he faints (p. 172). However, Simon recovers, asks himself, "What else is there to do?" (p. 174), discovers the dead parachutist, and then takes the news about the "beast" to the rest of the boys. The entire scene with the pig's head represents the conflict that is occurring within Simon's own consciousness. The Lord of the Flies is only an externalization of the inner evil in all humans. Later when Ralph comes upon the pig's head, "the skull [stares at] Ralph like one who knows all the answers and won't tell" (p. 22). Though Ralph does not understand the significance of the pig, he does feel a "sick fear." In desperation he hits the head, as if breaking it would destroy the evil on the island. However, the broken pig's head lies in two pieces, "its grin now six feet across" (p. 222). Rather than being destroyed, it ironically has grown. In the final pages of the novel, when Ralph is desperately fleeing from the hunters, he runs in circles and retraces his steps back to the broken pig's head, and this time its "fathom-wide grin" entirely dominates the burning island.

Four patterns of imagery reinforce the symbolism in *Lord of the Flies*. Images pertaining to excrement, darkness, falling, and animalism help define the human capacity for evil and savagery.

The many references to excrement, and also to dirt, underline thematically the vileness of human nature itself. As the boys' attempts at a sanitation program gradually break down, the inherent evil in human nature is symbolically manifested in the increasing images that refer to dung: "the two concepts merge in Golding's imagination—covertly in *Lord of the Flies* and manifestly in *Free Fall*, which is a literary cloaca, full of that revulsion psychologists try to explain in terms of the proximity and ambiguity of the apertures utilized for birth and excreta."[16]

Images associated with excrement (and more generally, dirt) are used in a negative sense, depicting human corruption. The conch makes "a low, farting noise" (p. 15). Johnny, the first "littlun" Ralph and Piggy meet, is in the act of defecating (p. 16). Pig droppings are closely examined by Jack's hunters to determine how recently the pig has left a particular place; the temperature of feces has become the central subject of interest (pp. 54 and 132). Ralph slowly loses his battle against filth: "With a convulsion of the mind, Ralph discovered dirt and decay, understood how much he disliked [his own long, dirty hair]" (p. 88). Even when Piggy tries to clean his glasses, the attempt is in vain (p. 11). He is appalled at the increasing filth on the island: "'We chose those rocks right along beyond the bathing pool as a lavatory. . . . Now people seem to use anywhere. Even near the shelters and the platform. You littluns, when you're getting fruit; if you're taken short—'. The assembly roared. 'I said if you're taken short you keep away from the fruit. That's dirty'" (p. 92).

Weekes and Gregor recognize the realistic level of description here— eating nothing but fruit does indeed bring on diarrhea—but they add, "The diarrhea might seem to invite allegorical translation—the body of man is no longer fit for Eden."[17] At one significant point, the inarticulate Simon tries to think of "the dirtiest thing there is" (p. 103) in order to describe the fallen human condition, and Jack's answer, "one crude expressive syllable," reaffirms the metaphor of excrement, which prevails throughout the novel. The area near the decaying, fallen parachutist is "a rotten place" (p. 125). When the pig's head is mounted on the stick, it soon draws a "black blob of flies"; it is literally a lord of the flies, as well as figuratively Beelzebub, from the Hebrew *baalzebub*, "lord of flies." Sometimes this name is translated "lord of dung." By the end of the novel, Ralph himself has been reduced to a dirty, piglike animal.

Golding uses light–dark contrasts in a traditional way: the numerous images of darkness underline the moral blackness of the boys' crumbling society. The normal associations with the sinister, with death, with chaos, with evil are suggested by this imagery. Decaying coconuts lie "skull-like" amid green shadows (p. 7); Jack's choirboys are clothed in black; the beast is naturally associated with the coming of night (p. 39); the "unfriendly side of the mountain" is shrouded in hushed darkness (p. 48). Roger is described as a dark figure: "the shock of black hair, down his nape and low on his forehead, seemed to suit his gloomy face and make what had seemed at first an unsociable remoteness into something forbidding" (p. 68).

With a Hawthornesque touch, Golding describes the subtle change that has come over all the boys' faces, after the group has become largely a hunting society: "faces cleaned fairly well by the process of eating and sweating but marked in the less accessible angles with a kind of shadow" (p. 130). Jack is described as "a stain in the darkness" (p. 142). Generally, the coming of night turns common surroundings into a nightmare landscape of imaginary horrors: "The skirts of the forest and the scar were familiar, near the conch and the shelters and sufficiently friendly in daylight. What they might become in darkness nobody cared to think" (p. 155).

Images of light and brightness are identified with spirit, regeneration, life, goodness. The description of Simon's dead body as it is carried out to sea suggests transcendence: "Softly, surrounded by a fringe of inquisitive bright creatures, itself a silver shape beneath the steadfast constellations, Simon's dead body moved out toward the open sea" (p. 184). The contrast between the bright, gaudy butterflies and the black flies on the pig's head emphasizes the symbolic conflict between good and evil used throughout the novel. The bright butterflies are drawn to the sunlight and to open places (p. 64); they surround the saintly Simon (p. 158); they are oblivious to the brutal killing of the sow: "the butterflies still danced, preoccupied in the centre of the clearing" (p. 162). in this particular instance, they remind the reader of those indifferent seagulls in Stephen Crane's "The Open Boat"—simply a part of nature, not threatened by the environment, and a mocking contrast to the violent predicaments that human beings either perpetuate or suffer. But the butterflies represent a more positive force, and significantly they desert the open space dominated by the grinning pig's head.[18]

Golding's obsession with the fallen human state permeates the imagery of *Lord of the Flies*. The opening chapter is typical. Ralph appears amid a background of fallen trees. He trips over a branch and comes "down with a crash" (p. 5). He talks with Piggy about coming down in the capsule that was dropped from the plane. He falls down again when attempting to stand on his head (p. 25). He pretends to knock Simon down (p. 28). In addition to the descriptions of the fallen parachutist, Simon's fainting spells, Ralph's "nightmares of falling and death" (p. 229), and his final collapse at the feet of the naval officer, the act of falling is closely associated with the idea of lost innocence. Ralph weeps for "the end of innocence . . . and the fall through the air" of Piggy.

Animal imagery reinforces the boys' transformation into savages and subhumans. Predictably, evil is associated with the beast, the pig's head, or a snake, but as the story progresses, the boys themselves are described with an increasing number of animal images.

The boys' disrobing early in the novel at first suggests a return to innocence, but as the hunters become more and more savage, their nakedness merely underscores their animalism. Sam and Eric grin and pant at Ralph "like dogs" (pp. 17 and 46). Jack moves on all fours, "dog-like," when tracking the pig (p. 53); during the hunt he hisses like a snake, and is "less a hunter than a furtive thing, ape-like among the tangle of trees" (p. 54). Ralph calls him a "beast" (p. 214). Piggy, whose very name suggests an obvious comparison, sees that the boys are becoming animals; he says that if Ralph does not blow the conch for an assembly, "we'll soon be animals anyway" (p. 107). Without his glasses, Piggy laments that he will "have to be led like a dog" (p. 204). When he dies, his body twitches "like a pig's after it has been killed" (p. 217). Simon, hidden in the shadows of the forest, is transformed into a "thing," a "beast," when the narration shifts to the other boys' view (pp. 182–83).

Ralph's transformation is slower than the others, but it is clearly discernible. Early in the novel, he viciously accepts the hunters' raw pig meat and gnaws on it "like a wolf" (p. 84). He is caught up in the savage ritual when Roger plays the pig (p. 181); he is part of the unthinking gang that murders Simon. When Piggy is killed, Ralph runs for his life and obeys "an instinct that he did not know he possessed" (p. 217). In the last chapter, Ralph is little more than a cornered animal. Ironically he sharpens a stick in self-defense and becomes a murderous hunter himself. "Whoever tried [to harm him] would be stuck, squealing like a pig" (p. 231). We are told that he "raised his spear, snarled a little, and waited" (p. 233). Ralph's transformation is both shocking and saddening. Alone in the forest, he brutally attacks the first adversary he meets: "Ralph launched himself like a cat; stabbed, snarling, with the spear, and the savage doubled up" (p. 234). When Ralph is trapped in the underbrush, he wonders what a pig would do, for he is in the same position (p. 236).

Related to these animal images is the continual reference to the word savage. In *Lord of the Flies* the distinction between civilized human being and savage becomes increasingly cloudy and a source of further irony. Early in the novel Jack himself proclaims, "I agree with Ralph. We've got to have rules and obey them. After all, we're not savages" (p. 47). Piggy asks more than once, "What are we? Humans? Or animals? Or savages?" followed by the double irony, "What's grownups going to think?" (p. 105). The painted faces of the hunters provide "the liberation into savagery" (p. 206), an ironic freedom to destroy society; and the animal imagery contributes to this idea.

Several "levels" of meaning operate in *Lord of the Flies*, apart from the surface narrative. First, from a particular psychological viewpoint, the tripartite organization of the human psyche—ego, id, superego—is dramatized symbolically in the characters of Ralph, Jack, and Piggy, respectively. The conflict between Ralph, the level-headed elected leader of the boys' council, and Jack, the self-appointed head of the hunters, corresponds to an ego–id polarity. Ralph realistically confronts the problem of survival and works out a practical plan for rescue. Jack is quick to revert to savagery, dishonesty, violence. Piggy, the fat, bespectacled rationalist, reminds Ralph of his responsibilities, makes judgments about Jack's guilt, and generally represents the ethical voice on the island. Since Piggy does not acknowledge his own share of guilt for Simon's death, Oldsey and Weintraub conclude that this inconsistency "spoils the picture often given of Piggy as superego or conscience."[19] However, the many times Piggy reminds the weakening Ralph of what must be done far outweigh this one reversal.

A second level of symbolism emerges from the archetypal patterns in the novel. The quest motif is represented by Ralph's stumbling attempts at self-knowledge. His is literally an initiation by fire. Ironically the knowledge he acquires does not allow him to become an integrated member of adult society, but rather it causes him to recoil from the nightmare world he discovers. He is a scapegoat figure who must be sacrificed as atonement for the boys' evils. Simon and Piggy are also variants of the scapegoat symbol. Simon is most clearly the saint or Christ figure. The Dionysian myth is also reworked, as the boys' blindness to their own irrational natures leads to their destruction. As James Baker has observed, Euripides' *Bacchae* "is a bitter allegory" of not only the degeneration of society but also of essential human blindness: "the failure of rational man who invariably undertakes the blind ritual-hunt in which he seeks to kill the threatening 'beast' within his own being."[20]

On still another level, *Lord of the Flies* accommodates a political allegory in which Ralph represents democracy and Jack totalitarianism. Golding has often stressed the impact of World War II on his own life and his change from an idealist who believed in human perfectibility, to a more skeptical observer who had discovered a dark truth "about the given nature of man."[21] In his most explicit statement about the effect of the war on his estimation of humanity and its political systems, Golding says:

> It is bad enough to say that so many Jews were exterminated in this way and that, so many people liquidated—lovely, elegant word—but there were things done during that period from which I still have to avert my mind lest I should be physically sick. They were not done by the headhunters of New Guinea, or by some primitive tribe in the Amazon. They were done, skillfully, coldly, by educated men, doctors, lawyers, by men with a tradition of civilization behind them, to beings of their own kind. . . . When these destructive capacities emerged into action they were thought aberrant. Social systems, political systems were composed, detached from the real nature of man. They were what one might call political symphonies. They would perfect most men, and at the least, reduce aberrance.
>
> Why, then, have they never worked?[22]

Such statements not only define Golding's own social background but also illuminate his use of the microcosmic island society in *Lord of the Flies*.

Golding's own comments about *Lord of the Flies* continually focus on the potentials and the limitations of the democratic ideal. Though he supports a democratic doctrine, he recognizes its weaknesses: "You can't give people freedom without weakening society as an implement of war, if you like, and so this is very much like sheep among wolves. It's not a question with me as to whether democracy is the right way so much, as to whether democracy can survive and remain what it is."[23] By giving up all its principles, the island society of *Lord of the Flies* demonstrates the inefficacy of political organizations that attempt to check human beings' worst destructive instincts. It is only by first recognizing these dark powers that democracy can hope to control them.

The fourth level of meaning is the moral allegory, which focuses on the conflicts between good and evil, and encourages philosophical or theological interpretations. Golding is defining the nature of evil. Whether it is embodied in a destructive, unconscious force, a mistaken sacrifice that unsuccessfully atones for the boys' collective guilt, or a dictatorial power opposing the democratic order (corresponding to the psychological, archetypal, and politico-sociological levels, respectively), the problems of moral choice, the inevitability of original sin and human fallibility, the blindness of self-deception create a fourth level of meaning in the novel.

The island is not only a stage on which characters must make crucial moral decisions but also a microcosm for the human mind, in which ethical conflicts similarly occur. Because Golding believes that "a fabulist is always a moralist," he assigns a significant pattern of imagery to Ralph, "the fair boy" (p. 5), who unties the "snake-clasp of his belt" (p. 7). Ralph possesses a "mildness about his mouth and eyes that proclaims no devil" (p. 7); he rallies the boys to the open, sunlit part of the island; his conch sounds a Gabriel-like note unifying (if only temporarily) his followers. Jack, on the other hand, is identified with darkness and violence: when his band of choirboys first appears, it is described as "something dark," like a "creature" (p. 19); the black caps and cloaks hide their faces; Jack's red hair suggests a devilish element; his impulsive decision to be a hunter and kill pigs foreshadows his demonic monomania for destruction; when he first meets Ralph, Jack is sun-blinded after coming out of the dark jungle.

However, because Golding complicates the characterization and shows Ralph to be susceptible to evil forces and at times paradoxically sympathetic to Jack, the reader recognizes ambiguities not easily compatible with a neat but rigid system of symbols. If *Lord of the Flies* "teaches" through its moral allegory, it is the lesson of self-awareness: "The novel is the parable of fallen man. But it does not close the door on that man; it entreats him to know himself and his Adversary, for he cannot do combat against an unrecognized force, especially when it lies within him."[24]

Notes

1. See Douglas Hewitt, "New Novels"; Francis E. Kearns, "Salinger and Golding: Conflict on the Campus," p. 139; Howard S. Babb, *The Novels of William Golding*, p. 19.

2. Margaret Walters, "Two Fabulists: Golding and Camus," p. 23. Walters criticizes *Lord of the Flies* for its "deliberate mystifications" paradoxically combined with "crude explicitness."

3. Walter Allen, "New Novels."

4. Clive Pemberton, *William Golding*, p. 9. For a detailed study of the close relationship between fantasy and realism in the modern novel, see Patrick Merla, "'What Is Real?' Asked the Rabbit One Day." A similar view is expressed by James Stern, "English Schoolboys in the jungle": "Fully to succeed, a fantasy must approach very close to reality."

5. Phillip Drew, "Second Reading," 79.

6. William Golding, *Lord of the Flies*, p. 65. Subsequent references are to this edition, and hereafter page numbers will be indicated in the text.

7. Wayland Young, "Letter from London," pp. 478–79.

8. Golding and Kermode, "Meaning," p. 10.

9. Baker, *Golding*, p. 9.

10. Bernard F. Dick, *William Golding*, p. 31.

11. William Mueller, "An Old Story Well Told: Commentary on William Golding's *Lord of the Flies*," p. 1203.

12. James Gindin, *Postwar British Fiction*, p. 198.

13. Ibid., p. 204. For other adverse criticism of Golding's "gimmick endings," see Young, "Letter," p. 481, and Kenneth Rexroth, "William Golding."

14. Dick, *Golding*, p. 21.

15. Baker, *Golding*, p. 10.

16. Bernard S. Oldsey and Stanley Weintraub, *The Art of William Golding*, p. 30.

17. Mark Kinkead-Weekes and Ian Gregor, *William Golding: A Critical Study*, p. 25.

18. Also see Robert J. White, "Butterfly and Beast in *Lord of the Flies*," in which he identifies the butterflies with the Greek word for butterfly, *psyche*, meaning "soul."

19. Oldsey and Weintraub, *Art*, p. 22.

20. Baker, *Golding*, p. 7. Also see Dick, *Golding*, pp. 29–33: "*Lord of the Flies* can also be read in the light of the Dionysian-Apollonian dichotomy" (i.e., the conflict between the irrational and rational worlds).

21. Granville Hicks, "The Evil that Lurks in the Heart," p. 36.

22. Golding, *Hot Gates*, pp. 86–87.

23. Keating and Golding, "Purdue Interview," pp. 189–90. Also see Douglas M. Davis, "A Conversation with Golding," p. 28; Maurice Dolbier, "Running J. D. Salinger a Close Second," p. 6.

24. Mueller, "Old Story," p. 1206.

LAWRENCE S. FRIEDMAN

Grief, Grief, Grief:
Lord of the Flies

*L*ord *of the Flies* opens in Eden. Ralph, fair-haired protagonist, and Piggy, faithful companion and resident intellectual, look about them and pronounce their island good. And so it is, for William Golding has set his young castaways down upon an uninhabited Pacific island as lush as it is remote. Fruit hangs ripe for the picking; fresh water flows abundantly from a convenient mountain; and the tropical climate soon prompts the boys to throw off their clothes. Ralph joyfully stands on his head, an action he will repeat at moments of high emotion. It is easy to forget that the world is at war, and that the plane that carried Ralph, Piggy, and the many other English boys stranded on the island, was shot down by the enemy.

As war and plane crash recede from memory, the visible world shrinks to the desert island and its populace of six- to twelve-year-old-boys. Because of the island's fecundity and mild climate the boys are largely exempt from the struggle for food and shelter; because of their youth they are exempt from sexual longing and deprivation; because of their isolation they are exempt from adult constraints. Free to live as they choose, they can act out every boy's dream of romantic adventure until their eventual rescue. *Lord of the Flies* begins, therefore, as a modern retelling of R. M. Ballantyne's Victorian children's classic, *Coral Island*. Indeed Golding traces his book's genesis to a night when he had finished reading just such an island adventure story

From *William Golding*, pp. 19–32, 172. © 1993 by Lawrence S. Friedman.

to his eldest child.[1] Exasperated by the familiar cutout characters and smug optimism of the original, he conceived of breathing life into a moribund genre by isolating boys on a desert island and showing how they would *really* behave. Ballantyne's shipwrecked boys, somewhat older than Golding's, lead an idyllic life on their remote South Seas island. Tropical nature is benign, the boys' characters conventionally innocent. What evil exists on Coral Island enters in the form of such adult intruders as savage cannibals or pirates. Ballantyne's vision is doubly optimistic: man is inherently good; and good will win out in the end. Like most fairy tales, *Coral Island* is an amalgam of faith and hope.

On Golding's coral island, Piggy's allusions to atomic war, dead adults, and uncertainty of rescue barely ripple the surface of Ralph's pleasant daydreams. Soon the boys recover a conch from the lagoon. More than a plaything, the conch will become a means of communication, and ultimately a symbol of law and order. Instructed by the wise but ineffectual Piggy, Ralph blows on the conch, thereby summoning the scattered boys. Possession of the conch ensures Ralph's election as chief. Later the assembled boys agree that whoever wishes to speak must raise his hand and request the conch. Cradling the conch in one's hands not only confers instant personal authority but affirms the common desire for an orderly society.

Read as a social treatise, Golding's first chapter seems to posit notions of fair play and group solidarity familiar to readers of *Coral Island*. But the same chapter introduces us to Jack Merridew marching at the head of his uniformed column of choirboys. Clad in black and silver and led by an obviously authoritarian figure, the choirboys seem boy Nazis. Frustrated by Ralph's election as chief, Jack barely conceals his anger. The chapter ends with Jack, knife in hand, reflexively hesitating long enough on the downward stroke to allow a trapped piglet to escape. The civilized taboo against bloodletting remains shakily in place as the angry boy settles for slamming his knife into a tree trunk. "Next time," he cries.

It is the exploration of Jack's "next time" that will occupy much of the remainder of *Lord of the Flies*. By fixing incipient evil within Jack, Golding reverses the sanguine premise of nineteenth-century adventure stories that locate evil in the alien or mysterious forces of the outside world. According to Golding his generation's "liberal and naïve belief in the perfectibility of man" was exploded by World War II. Hitler's gas chambers revealed man's inherent evil. His followers were not Ballantyne's savage cannibals or desperate pirates whose evil magically dissipated upon their conversion to Christianity. Rather they were products of that very Christian civilization that presumably guarantees their impossibility. Nor does it suffice to accept Ballantyne's implication that his boys' Englishness, like their Christianity, marks them as inevitably good. "We've got to have rules and obey them. After all, we're not savages. We're English, and the English are best at everything.

So we've got to do the right things." Coming from Golding's Jack, these words effectively shatter Ballantyne's easy optimism. Conditioned no less by the theology of man's fall than by Nazi atrocities, *Lord of the Flies* traces the spreading stain of man's depravity from its first intimations in Jack to its near-total corruption of the boys and their social order. "I decided," explained Golding, "to take the literary convention of boys on an island, only make them real boys instead of paper cutouts with no life in them; and try to show how the shape of the society they evolved would be conditioned by their diseased, their fallen nature."[2]

Too immature to account for the enemy within, the boys project their irrational fears onto the outside world. The first of these projections takes the shape of a snakelike "beastie," the product of a small boy's nightmare. One side of the boy's face "was blotted out by a mulberry-colored birthmark," the visible sign of the dual nature of fallen man. More by force of personality than by reason, Ralph succeeds in exorcising the monster from the group consciousness. Now the boys struggle to drag logs up the mountain for a signal fire, Ralph and Jack bearing the heaviest log between them. Jack's momentary selflessness combined with the manipulation of the lenses of Piggy's spectacles to start their fire—as well as the very act of fire building itself—signal a resurgence of civilized values. But the fire soon rages out of control; exploding trees and rising creepers reinvoke cries of "Snakes!, Snakes"; and the small boy with the birthmark has mysteriously disappeared. The seed of fear has been planted. Reason has failed to explain the darkness within and the island paradise begins its fatal transformation into hell.

Soon Ralph and Jack find communication impossible, the former talking of building shelters, the latter of killing pigs. Increasingly obsessed with his role as hunter, Jack neglects his more important role as keeper of the signal fire. Painting a fierce mask on his face he is "liberated from shame and self-consciousness." Shortly thereafter he and his frenzied followers march along swinging the gutted carcass of a pig from a stake to the incantory chant, "Kill the pig. Cut her throat. Spill her blood." Abandonment to blind ritual has displaced the reasoned discourse governed by the conch. Meanwhile the untended fire has gone out, and a ship has sailed past the island. Lost in blood lust, Jack's thoughts are far from rescue, and he at first barely comprehends Ralph's anger. When he does, he strikes out at the helpless Piggy, shattering one of his lenses. Reason henceforth is half-blind; the fragile link between Ralph and Jack snaps; and ritual singing and dancing resume as the boys gorge themselves on the slaughtered pig. That Ralph and Piggy join in the feast indicates the all-too-human failure to resist the blandishments of mass hysteria.

Killing marks the end of innocence. It is a wiser Ralph who "found himself understanding the wearisomeness of this life where every path was an improvisation and a considerable part of one's waking life was spent watching one's feet ... and remembering that first enthusiastic exploration as though it were part of a brighter childhood, he smiled jeeringly." Here at the beginning of the important fifth chapter, "Beast from Water," the regression and initiation themes converge. On the basis of his newfound knowledge, Ralph assembles the boys to discuss such practical matters as sanitation, shelter, and, most crucially, the keeping of the fire. But the tension among the boys is palpable, and Ralph soon confesses, "Things are breaking up. I don't understand why. We began well, we were happy." And he concludes, "Then people started getting frightened." Piggy's theory that life is scientific is countered by new reports of a beast from the sea. Neither Piggy's logic nor Ralph's rules can hold the boys together, and the meeting scatters in confusion.

E. M. Forster pleads in his introduction to the 1962 American edition of *Lord of the Flies* for more respect for Piggy.[3] Of course he is correct. Faced with specters of water beasts and Jack's authoritarian violence, who could fail to opt for Piggy's rationalism? Yet unaided reason cannot tell Ralph why things go wrong; it can only deny the physical reality of the beast. It is left to Simon, the skinny, inarticulate seer to "express mankind's essential illness" by fixing the beast's location: "What I mean is ... maybe it's only us." Golding's moral—that defects in human society can be traced back to defects in human nature—can be illustrated by the fable of the scorpion and the frog:

> "Let me ride across the pond on your back," pleads the scorpion.
>
> "No," replies the frog, "for if I let you on my back your sting will prove fatal."
>
> "Listen to reason," cries the scorpion. "If I sting you, you'll sink to the bottom of the pond, and I'll drown."
>
> So the frog takes the scorpion on his back and begins swimming. Midway across the pond, he feels the scorpion's fatal sting. "How could you," gasps the frog with his dying breath. "Now you'll drown."
>
> "I couldn't help it," sighs the scorpion. "It's my nature."[4]

Though his irrationality, like the scorpion's, may cost him his life, man is his own worst enemy. Undone by the beast within, man self-destructs no matter what form of social organization he adopts.

"Beast from the Air" opens with the sign from the world of grown-ups that answers Ralph's desperate cry for help after the breakup of the assembly. Dropping from the air battle high above the island, a dead parachutist settles on the mountaintop where fitful breezes cause him spasmodically to rise and fall. This grotesque "message" recalls the adult savagery that marooned the boys on the island. Moreover, the boys now take the faraway figure for the beast that haunts their dreams. Confronted by its apparent physical reality even Ralph succumbs to fear. The ironic appropriateness of the man-beast foreshadows Jack's growing power and the final unraveling of the social order. Now that the primary task is to kill the beast, Jack assumes command. Promising hunting and feasting he lures more and more boys into his camp. Man regresses from settler to roving hunter, society from democracy to dictatorship.

It is at this point, shortly after the collapse of social order under the pressures of inherent evil associated with Jack and irrational fear embodied in the beast from the air, that Golding paints his most startling and powerful scene. Simon, the only boy who feels the need for solitude, returns to his place of contemplation, a leafy shelter concealed by the dense growth of the forest. There he witnesses the butchering of a frantically screaming sow, its gutting and dismemberment, and the erection of its bleeding head on a pole. This head, abandoned by the hunters as a "gift" to the beast, presides over a pile of guts that attracts great swarms of buzzing flies. And the Lord of the Flies speaks: "Fancy thinking the Beast was something you could hunt and kill. You knew didn't you? I'm part of you? Close, close, close! I'm the reason why it's no go? Why things are what they are?" Looking into the vast mouth, Simon sees only a spreading blackness into which he falls in a faint.

As previously noted, Golding has called himself a fabulist and his novel a fable. All fables contain morals; and the moral of *Lord of the Flies* is stated most explicitly in the confrontation between Simon and the pig's head. "I included a Christ-figure in my fable. This is the little boy Simon, solitary, stammering, a lover of mankind, a visionary."[5] Since the Lord of the Flies is Beelzebub, the Judeo-Christian prince of devils, the scene dramatizes the clash between principles of good and evil. To accept the consequences of Golding's symbolism is to recognize the inequality of the struggle between Simon and the head. The Lord of the Flies has invaded Simon's forest sanctuary to preach an age-old sermon: evil lies within man whose nature is inherently depraved. Simon cannot counter this lesson. Engulfed by the spreading blackness of the vast mouth, he is overwhelmed by Beelzebub's power and loses consciousness. While it does not necessarily follow that Christ's message is similarly overpowered by Satan's, the forest scene strongly implies that innocence and good intentions are lost amidst the general ubiquity of evil. That evil cannot be isolated in Jack or in the beast; it is "close, close, close," a part of all of us.

The Simon who awakens from his faint trudges out of the forest "like an old man," stooping under the heavy burden of revelation. Immediately he comes face-to-face with a second awful symbol of human corruption—the rotting body of the downed parachutist. It, too, has been found by the flies; like the pig's head it too has been reduced to a corrupt and hideous parody of life. Releasing the broken figure from the tangled parachute lines that bind it to the rocks, Simon staggers back down the mountain with his news that the beast is harmless. But he stumbles into the frenzied mob of dancing and chanting boys who take him for the beast, fall upon him, and tear him apart.

The ritual murder of Simon is as ironic as it is inevitable. Ironically, he is killed as the beast before he can explain that the beast does not exist. His horrid death refutes his aborted revelation: the beast exists, all right, not where we thought to find it, but within ourselves. Inevitably, we kill our savior who "would set us free from the repetitious nightmare of history."[6] Unable to perceive his truth, we huddle together in the circle of our fear and reenact his ritual murder, as ancient as human history itself. Golding's murderous boys, the products of centuries of Christianity and Western civilization, explode the hope of Christ's sacrifice by repeating the pattern of his crucifixion. Simon's fate underlines the most awful truths about human nature: its blindness, its irrationality, its blood lust.

That the human condition is hopeless is revealed in the fact that even Ralph and Piggy felt the need to join in the "demented but partly secure society" of the hunters just prior to Simon's murder. Later, they console themselves with the excuse that they remained outside the dancing circle. When Ralph recalls the horror of the murder, Piggy first tries to deny its reality. And when Ralph refuses to drop the subject, Piggy shrills again and again that Simon's death was an accident. His desperate rationalizations point to the inability of human reason to cope with the dark reality of human nature. Piggy's excuses are mere frantic attempts to explain away our basest instincts and actions. Their transparent failure to do so marks the limits of the human intellect. Symbolic of the fall of reason is the loss of Piggy's sight. His broken glasses, the means of fire making, are stolen in a raid by Jack and his hunters. As Jack stalks triumphantly off with the glasses dangling from his hand, the reign of savagery is all but sealed.

Jack's victory comes swiftly in the following chapter, "Castle Rock." Again Golding sets up a contest between principles of good and evil. But this time the outcome is a foregone conclusion. The pack of painted savages who blindly murdered Simon has by now abandoned all restraints. Personified by Roger, Jack's fanatical self-appointed "executioner," the hunters turn viciously against Ralph and Piggy and the twins Sam and Eric, the last four remnants of an orderly society. From high atop a cliff Roger pushes a great rock that, gathering momentum, strikes Piggy, killing the fat boy and shattering the conch. Although the conch has long since lost the power to invoke order, its explosion signals the final triumph of lawlessness. Screaming wildly, "I'm chief," Jack hurls his spear at Ralph, inflicting a flesh wound, and forcing the former chief to run frantically for his life.

"Cry of the Hunters," the novel's concluding chapter, marks the final degenerative stage in Golding's fable of man's fall. Ralph's pursuers, freed by Piggy's murder from the faint restraint of reason, have reduced Ralph to their quarry. As the savage pack closes in, the sad lesson of the hunt is inescapable: not that the boys are dehumanized, but that they are all too human. Man's basic instinct is to kill; and the depth of his depravity is measured by the urge to kill his own species. Not only does the metaphor of the hunt complete Golding's definition of the human animal, but it forges a link to analogous hunts in Greek drama that loom in the background of *Lord of the Flies*.

Golding has often acknowledged the formative influence of the ancients. Together with the biblical version of man's fate expressed in the doctrine of original sin, Greek drama fleshes out the myth of the fall. If it is true that a writer's forebears surface most apparently in his early work, then the final hunt of *Lord of the Flies* is second only to Simon's "passion" in fixing the origins of Golding's most cherished ideas. While it is true that Simon's confrontation with the pig's head and his subsequent martyrdom are couched primarily in Christian terms, the Greek influence is also apparent. The pig's head is at once the Judeo-Christian Beelzebub and the king of the Olympian gods. Thus Jean-Paul Sartre's modern reworking of Greek motifs in *The Flies* opens on a public square in Argos, "dominated by a statue of Zeus, god of flies and death. The image has white eyes and blood-smeared cheeks."[7] Zeus himself appears in the play to explain the great swarms of buzzing flies that plague the city. "They are," he says, "a symbol," sent by the gods to "a dead-and-alive city, a carrion city" still festering fifteen years after the original sin of Agamemnon's murder. The citizens of Argos are "working out their atonement." Their "fear and guilty consciences have a good savor in the nostrils of the gods." Zeus implies that man's blood lust is balanced by his reverence for the gods, a view shared by Golding: "As far back as we can go in history we find that the two signs of man are a capacity to kill and a belief in God."[8] Human fear and guilt are perverse affirmations of the gods' existence and therefore find favor with the gods. For Sartre, the existential philosopher, man's awful freedom, won at the expense of breaking his shackles to the gods, is all-important. But for Golding, the Christian believer, man is lost without God. The absence of prayer, even among fearful young choirboys, is one of the darkest aspects of *Lord of the Flies*.

Although *The Flies* may have no direct bearing upon Golding's novel, its title as well as its identification of Zeus as god of flies and death reveal the same backdrop of Greek tradition. At the end of Sartre's play, the hero Orestes, drawn directly from Greek drama, is pursued by the shrieking Furies. No such deities hunt Ralph, only his fellow boys. Yet chase scenes of all kinds fill Greek drama, and Golding the classicist seems indebted not merely to the general metaphor of the hunt but specifically to its powerful treatment in two plays of Euripides: *The Bacchae* and *Iphigenia in Tauris*.

Euripides wrote *The Bacchae*, his greatest and most difficult play, in the wake of a disillusionment with the Peloponnesian War as profound as

Golding's with World War II. As skeptical about human nature as Golding, Euripides had already written the most devastating antiwar play that survives from antiquity, *The Trojan Women*. Both *Lord of the Flies* and *The Bacchae* are anthropological passion plays in which individuals—children in Golding, adults in Euripides—revert to savagery and murder during a frenzied ritual.[9] At Thebes, where Dionysus (Bacchus) comes to introduce his worship to Greece, King Pentheus adamantly denies the new religion. To Dionysus's orgiastic revels Pentheus opposes the rule of reason. Yet he is tempted to disguise himself in the fawn skin of a Dionysian follower in order to watch the rites of the female devotees. Spied by the Bacchants, he is hunted down and torn to pieces by the frenzied women, led by his own mother, Agave. Maddened by the god, the hapless Agave bears Pentheus's head, which she imagines is a lion's, triumphantly back to Thebes. There she comes to her senses and awakens to the horrid proof of Dionysus's power. To deny Dionysus is to deny a fundamental force in human nature. That the destruction of Pentheus is so disproportionate to his offense constitutes poetic justice in *The Bacchae*: Pentheus denies the primitive power of unreason only to become its victim. Yet the orgiastic worship that transforms Agave into the unwitting murderess of her son is hardly preferable to Pentheus's denial. Euripides, in dramatizing the clash between emotionalism and rationalism, may be arguing the primacy of neither. However one interprets *The Bacchae*, its affinities with *Lord of the Flies* are striking:

> Specifically, both drama and novel contain three interrelated ritual themes: the cult of a beast-god, a hunt as prefiguration of the death of the scapegoat-figure, and the dismemberment of the scapegoat. Golding deviates in only one respect from Euripides: logically Ralph, the Pentheus in embryo, should be the scapegoat; but the author assigns this role to Simon, allowing Ralph to live instead with his new-found knowledge of "the darkness of man's heart."[10]

Dionysus is the true hero of *The Bacchae*; his merciless destruction of Pentheus is but the opening salvo in his campaign to establish his worship in Hellas. Golding is no less concerned with the primitive force that Dionysus represents; but his primary concern is the impact of that force upon his hero. Ralph, the latter-day Pentheus, must therefore survive the ordeal of the hunt and live with his hard-won knowledge. Against the backdrop of the flaming island, a hell that once was Eden, the savage tribe pursues Ralph until, stumbling over a root, the frantic boy sprawls helplessly in the sand. Staggering to his feet, flinching at the anticipated last onslaught, Ralph looks up into the astonished face of a British naval officer. Ralph's miraculous salvation completes the drama of his initiation as, in a shattering epiphany, he weeps "for the end of innocence, the darkness of man's heart, and the fall through the air of the true wise friend called Piggy."

Although Golding shifts the focus from God's power to man's knowledge he relies on a familiar Euripidian device for ending his novel. Golding calls the timely arrival of the naval officer a "gimmick," a term subsequently used by critics to plague him. Yet the officer is neither more nor less than the Greek deus ex machina in modern uniform. Employed most strikingly by Euripides, the "god" in the machine is hoisted high above the other actors to solve the problems of the preceding action and to supply a happy ending. Most often, when the deity imposes a happy ending, the normal consequences of the action would be disastrous. Neither *The Bacchae* nor Sartre's *The Flies* employs the device in its purest form. In the former, Dionysus resolves the action by heaping even more woe upon the Thebans who denied his godhead. In the latter, Sartre's Zeus absents himself from the ending, having already explained its significance. Moreover, both gods take major roles from the outset of their respective plays. Neither makes the single in-the-nick-of-time appearance to reverse the action that generally characterizes the deus ex machina.

In *Iphigenia in Tauris*, however, Euripides relies upon the deus ex machina for a resolution markedly similar to that of *Lord of the Flies*. Iphigenia, her brother Orestes, and his friend Pylades, pursued by the minions of the barbarian king Thoas, reach the seacoast where a Greek ship waits to carry them home. But Thoas's troops control the strait through which the ship must pass; and a strong gale drives the ship back toward the shore. Enter the goddess Athena, who warns Thoas to cease his pursuit. It seems that the fates of Iphigenia and her companions have been foreordained, and against this "necessity" even gods are powerless. Thoas wisely relents, the winds grow favorable, and the ship sails off under Athena's divine protection.

Barbarian pursuit, friendly ship, and miraculous rescue are no less present in Golding's conclusion. And when to these elements are added the hunt for sacrificial victims and the bloody rites of the Taurian religion, the resemblances between *Iphigenia in Tauris* and *Lord of the Flies* seem more than skin deep. Yet the lessons of the two works radically differ. Greek drama is ultimately conditioned by the proximity of the gods: omnipresent yet inscrutable they influence human action and determine human destiny. Since, as Sartre's Zeus admits, the gods need mortals for their worship as much as mortals need objects for their devotion, it follows that Greek drama chronicles this interdependence. In *The Flies*, Sartre's Zeus, the fading though still powerful king of the gods, owes his rule to human fear and superstition and relies upon man's willing servitude. When Orestes finally strides boldly into the sunlight, the spell of the gods is broken; henceforth he will blaze his own trail, acknowledging no law but his own. For Sartre, man's freedom begins with his denial of the gods and his full acceptance of responsibility for his actions and their consequences. And while existential freedom is as fearful as it is lonely, it is infinitely preferable to god-ridden bondage. Whether Dionysus stalking through *The Bacchae*, Athena watching over *Iphigenia in Tauris*, or Zeus brooding in *The Flies*, the gods play a role in the human drama. Note that all three deities carefully define their roles: Dionysus to punish the errant Thebans whose king denied him; Athena to ensure the proper worship of her sister, Artemis; and Zeus to warn the recalcitrant Orestes of the consequences of rebellion. So closely are the gods involved with mortals that their interventions, no matter how arbitrary, take on a certain inevitable logic.

What Golding calls the "gimmicked" ending of *Lord of the Flies* and the Greek deus ex machina used most conventionally in *Iphigenia in Tauris* are alike in their technical function: to reverse the course of impending disaster. Yet their effects are quite different. Athena's wisdom is incontrovertible, her morality unassailable. High above the awed mortals she dispels chaos and imposes ideal order. The very fact of her appearance underlines the role of the gods in shaping human destiny. Golding's spiffy naval officer is, however, no god. Nor does he represent a higher morality. Confronted by the ragtag melee, he can only wonder that English boys hadn't put up a better show, and mistakes their savage hunt for fun and games à la *Coral Island*. While he cannot know the events preceding his arrival, his comments betray the same ignorance of human nature that contributed to the boys' undoing. Commanding his cruiser, the officer will direct a maritime search-and-destroy mission identical to the island hunt. *Lord of the Flies* ends with the officer gazing at the cruiser, preparing to reenact the age-old saga of man's inhumanity to man.

Just as the naval officer cannot measure up to Euripides' Athena, so Ralph falls short of Sartre's Orestes. Orestes strides into the sunlight of his own morality to live Sartre's dictum that existence precedes essence. Creating himself anew with each action, he will become his own god. Ralph can only weep for the loss of innocence from the world; he shows no particular signs of coping with his newfound knowledge. To understand one's nature is not to alter it. Morally diseased, mired in original sin, fallen man can rise only by the apparently impossible means of transcending his very nature. In man's apparent inability to re-create himself lies the tragedy of *Lord of the Flies*. The futility of Simon's sacrificial death, the failure of adult morality, and the final absence of God creates the spiritual vacuum of Golding's novel. For Sartre the denial of the gods is the necessary prelude to human freedom. But for Golding, God's absence leads only to despair and human freedom is but license. "The theme of *Lord of the Flies* is grief, sheer grief, grief, grief."[11]

NOTES

1. William Golding, the title essay in *A Moving Target*, p. 163.

2. Golding, "Fable," p. 88.

3. E. M. Forster, introduction, in William Golding, *Lord of the Flies* (New York: Coward-McCann, 1962), p. xiii.

4. Orson Welles, *Mr. Arkadin*, 1955. Welles, in the title role of a wealthy and powerful tycoon, relates this story at one of his sophisticated soirees. Written and directed by Welles, the film depicts Arkadin hunting down and killing former friends who might expose his shady past.

5. Golding, "Fable," pp. 97–98.

6. James R. Baker, *William Golding* (New York: St. Martin's Press, 1965), p. 13.

7. Jean-Paul Sartre, *The Flies*, in *"No Exit" and Three Other Plays*, tr. Stuart Gilbert (New York: Vintage, 1955), p. 51.

8. Biles, *Talk: Conversations with William Golding*, p. 106.

9. Bernard F. Dick, *William Golding* (New York: Twayne, 1967), p. 30.

10. Ibid., p. 31.

11. Golding, "A Moving Target," p. 163.

STEFAN HAWLIN

The Savages in the Forest: Decolonising William Golding

1

*L*ord of the Flies has for a long time been a book set for children and young adults, and this status will be reinforced by its recommendation last year by the National Curriculum Council as advised reading for the 14–16 age group. It is well written, unusual and frightening, and it seems to advance a thesis, all these qualities making it ideal for classroom discussion. Such discussion tends to take place in a characteristically liberal framework; I want to suggest other ways of reading the novel by setting it within the history of decolonisation, and hence to show how the novel reflects a profoundly conservative ethos.

Lord of the Flies was published in 1954, in the middle of the period when Britain was beginning to give up Empire in a confused and reluctant way. 'Great' Britain's feelings of superiority were under threat, ruthlessly guarded in psychological and emotional terms but actually undermined by the pressure of nationalist movements and anti-colonial feeling. Later the official view was that Britain was engaged in 'the difficult and delicate politics of bringing new states to birth',[1] graciously withdrawing having helped to enlighten the dark places of the world. The ambivalence of feeling involved in the decolonisation process lies at the heart of *Lord of the Flies*, for the novel is defensive about the surrender of Empire, and makes an attempt to restate the old Empire misrepresentations of white enlightenment and black savagery. Under a thin

From *Critical Survey* 7, no. 2 (1995), pp. 125–135. © 1995 by *Critical Survey*.

disguise it presents the cliché about the bestiality and savagery of natives, the 'painted niggers' in the forest, ready at a whim to tear each other to pieces in tribal conflict unless the white 'grown-ups' come to rescue them from themselves. It is, in its odd way, a defence of colonialism.

The way the context of the 1950s has been largely ignored explains why the pattern above has gone unobserved, even though it exists on the surface of the text.[2] *Lord of the Flies* seems to make an eternally relevant point about human depravity, against progressivist views of humankind, but this point is well contained within the liberal consensus, and should hardly be shocking after Auschwitz and Hiroshima. This is Golding's own stated rationale. At first sight it seems so fair-minded that we need hardly see the problem involved:

> *Lord of the Flies* was simply what it seemed sensible for me to write after the war, when everybody was thanking God they weren't Nazis. And I'd seen enough and thought enough to realize that every single one of us could be Nazis. . . . Nazi Germany was a particular kind of boil which burst in 1939. That was only the same kind of inflamed spot we all of us suffer from, and so I took English boys and said, 'Look. This could be you.' This is really what that book comes to.[3]

This seems unexceptionable, but there is a hint of naïvety: whoever really doubted that one nation was as capable of evil as another? Another account of the novel to the same interviewer reveals the implicit chauvinism. The discussion has come to centre on how a good arrangement of society— constitutionally, legally, and so forth—can help to create a good people. This is implicitly a celebration of the long evolution of the British constitution. What emerges is Golding's Empire-orientated view of the world, with England, America and a few other countries as places of light, and much of the rest of the world, particularly Africa, as below the level of civilisation. (Notice in the quotation the one-line caricature of 'savagery'.) From the nature of the remarks it is evident that Golding knows nothing substantial about Indian, African or Chinese culture, yet this does not stop him placing Britain—the centre of Empire, the centre of light!—at the top of a hierarchy of societies:

> Aren't we giving too narrow a definition for society? I have been talking about the Western world. There are head-hunters still. There was Nazi Germany. There was Stalin's Russia. I don't know anything about China, but I'm prepared to believe anything you tell me about it. There are societies in India which do this, that, and t'other, and in Africa, et cetera, et cetera. I suppose what we are getting round to, finally, is the hopeless admission, in

> the middle of the twentieth century, that there is a hierarchy of
> society. The hierarchy of society must be based ultimately on a
> hierarchy of people. One can say that it is only by desperate efforts
> in one or two fortunate, or perhaps unfortunate, places on the
> surface of the globe that the bright side of man has been enabled
> to emerge even as dimly as it has, and this must be because of the
> nature of the people who built that society . . .[4]

This perspective is not unusual for its time, but it is nonetheless strikingly expressed. Looking down from the top of the hierarchies of people (Britain), Golding does a quick survey of the dark realms of the earth—the realms to which, in the official ideology, the Empire sought to bring comfort and civilisation. As he looks out from this centre of light, many of the caricatures of Empire, of 'savages', unnatural cultural practices, tribal warfare, and so forth, float through his mind.

The English boys in *Lord of the Flies*, deposited on a desert island some time in the 1950s, descend slowly into depravity and atrocity—they become, in the loaded and often-repeated word of the text, 'savages'. Golding believes that he is showing us that the veneer of civilisation is very thin, that even (!) English boys might become little Nazis. The problem is that in discussing this Eurocentric revelation, this European-evolved evil, he takes his image of 'savagery' from the classic cultural misrepresentation (Empire-evolved) of white civilisation and black/African barbarity. The text shows us white, respectable, middle-class boys—whose fathers, incidentally, were the kind that governed the Empire centrally and locally—becoming like tribesmen, 'savages', or to put it in overtly racist terms, 'no better than blacks'. In depicting his primitives, Golding knows nothing serious about African mores and civilisation. His knowledge is at the level expressed in the remark 'there are head-hunters still'. He paints his savages from out of the paint-box of Empire myths, from pretty much the same paint-box as popular racist literature— Rider Haggard, John Buchan, Nicholas Monsarrat, for instance—literature which, as the Kenyan novelist Ngugi has expressed it, 'glorified imperialism and the deeds of its British actors while vilifying those of its opponents be they from rival imperialisms or from the native resistance'.[5] Another way of expressing this is to say that *Lord of the Flies* is a faint rewriting of Conrad's *Heart of Darkness*.

2

The Nigerian novelist Chinua Achebe has shown the ways in which *Heart of Darkness* is a racist text; his criticism is not simplistic: he is not denying it literary distinction, or even a place in the canon, but he is refusing to value it as the very highest kind of art because it embodies 'that large desire in Western psychology to set Africa up as a foil to Europe, as a place of negations at once remote and vaguely familiar, in comparison with which Europe's own state of spiritual grace will be manifest':

> *Heart of Darkness* projects the image of Africa as 'the other world', the antithesis of Europe and therefore of civilization, a place where man's vaunted intelligence and refinement are finally mocked by triumphant bestiality.... For reasons which can certainly use close psychological inquiry the West seems to suffer deep anxieties about the precariousness of its civilization and to have a need for constant reassurance by comparison with Africa.[6]

One fictional counterpoint to *Heart of Darkness* is Achebe's *Things Fall Apart* (1958). The titles provide a revealing opposition. Africa, for Conrad, is the sinister and mysterious continent where the veneer of civilisation cracks and where the European mind goes mad; for Achebe it is a world of traditional tribal communities going about ancient ways of life, a world gradually and profoundly disturbed by the encounter of colonisation. *Heart of Darkness* may not be a naïvely racist text, and it is certainly aware of some of the depredations of colonialism, but it does not transcend 'the other world' image of Africa. It is a Eurocentric novel, something that *Things Fall Apart* naturally and simply shows up.

The island in *Lord of the Flies* is another version of Conrad's Africa (the quotations above from Achebe could equally well be applied to it), though in this case the meaning of place is partly internalised in the psychological and emotional changes happening to the children. In *Heart of Darkness*, says Achebe, Africa is portrayed as the place where the European may discover that the 'dark impulses and unspeakable appetites he has suppressed and forgotten through ages of civilization' may spring into life again in answer to Africa's 'free and triumphant savagery'.[7] In *Heart of Darkness* and *Lord of the Flies* the white, comfortable, European mentality is brought into touch with 'the other world'—in the case of *Lord of the Flies*, the interiorised other world—of savagery. In both cases the hearts of darkness are opened out, the terrifying world of Mr Kurtz on the one hand, and the group of children descending into savagery on the other. Neither work fully understands either the imperialist framework on which it is predicated, or the image of colonialism that it evokes. *Lord of the Flies* is more culpable in this respect; it may be that the phase of colonialism it evokes is less palatable because its myths are on the brink of dissolution. *Lord of the Flies* very nearly decodes itself in what it has to say about colonialism, its worries about insurgent nationalism, and its fears about the ending of confident white rule.

When they arrive on the island the British children are representatives of Empire and of Empire mores. In thin disguise, they are Oxford and Cambridge graduates newly arrived as administrators in a colony. The pervasive image is of whites bringing light, order and culture into 'the other world'. The boys set up a legislative council or parliament. They refer coolly to 'Gib. and Addis' (p. 28).[8] 'We're explorers', says Jack (p. 33); 'We ought to draw a map', says Ralph (p. 35). They survey their land and enjoy 'the right of domination' (p. 39). Their take-over corresponds in miniature with the way their great-grandfathers took over Africa.

The conch is in part a symbol of white constitutionalism, and is set against, later, the dark images of tribalism. As enacted through the novel, it beautifully conveys the authority and fragility of this constitutionalism when viewed in relation to white fears of the black man. In case we had forgotten— in the 1950s few schoolchildren could have forgotten—we are reminded how much of the globe was shaded in British colours:

> 'My father's in the navy. He said there aren't any unknown islands left. He says the Queen has a big room full of maps and all the islands in the world are drawn there. So the Queen's got a picture of this island' (p. 49)

. . . and of all her other colonial realms. The children also struggle to acclimatise themselves to the 'new rhythm' required by the tropical day (p. 74). Located in the 'other world' of the island, the boys begin to set up civilisation and good government in accord with all they know of imperial ways. They set a fire burning—almost literally, in the total context, 'the light of civilization'. The fire is associated with the first world that they wish to return to, and is a cipher for all that is rational and ordered. The boys are determined, like all good colonisers before them, to maintain standards of Englishness and to distinguish themselves from the natives. Golding's ironic stance almost backfires, for he indicates that the proprieties being set up are fragile and liable to break up, but he is not fully aware of the extent to which the boys appear as little colonisers, even to the inflections of their accents. Take, for example, the following statement by Jack; we are expected to see it as naïve, but there is a whole dimension of irony that is unintended, for what Jack says only reflects Golding's views:

> 'I agree with Ralph. We've got to have rules and obey them. After all, we're not savages. We're English; and the English are best at everything. So we've got to do the right things.' (p. 55)

The naïvety does not fully cover the implied understanding of Africa. Jack is only conscious, like Golding (and to use Golding's own words), that he comes from one of those rare, 'fortunate' places on the surface of the globe where 'by desperate efforts ... the bright side of man has been enabled to emerge', and at this point he is intent on keeping this bright side in the ascendant.

Jack's formulation of the threat is repeated at various points, and as the situation becomes more desperate the chauvinist and racist implications become more overt. The veneer of colonist civilisation is cracking and the nice white children are turning into black 'savages'. The blacks are taking over, coming into their element, and so the novel echoes fears of insurgent nationalism. To put it most simply, whiteness is converting to blackness:

> They heard him [Piggy] stamp.
> 'What are we? Humans? Or animals? Or savages? What's grown-ups going to think? Going off—hunting pigs—letting fires out—and now!' (p. 113)

In its context, the implications of this remark are clear. It occurs while the boys are debating about ghosts. 'Savages' would believe in ghosts: the remark conflates Africanness and bestiality and also sets up a contrast between white science and black superstition.

In Chapter 11 the climactic scene brings these oppositions into focus. Ralph, abetted by Piggy, stands as a last bastion of whiteness. The scene quite clearly echoes a mass of popular racist literature that sets the white hero before the pack of natives thirsting for his blood. It is also emblematic in contrasting the dark passions of tribalism with the fragile shell of constitutionalism. It is hard to read this scene without seeing it as a reflection of white fears about the fate of Empire:

> The booing rose and died again as Piggy lifted the white, magic shell.
> 'Which is better—to be a pack of painted niggers like you are, or to be sensible like Ralph is?'
> A great clamour rose among the savages. Piggy shouted again.
> 'Which is better—to have rules and agree, or to hunt and kill?'
> Again the clamour and again—'Zup!'
> Ralph shouted against the noise.
> 'Which is better, law and rescue, or hunting and breaking things up?'
> Now Jack was yelling too and Ralph could no longer make himself heard. Jack had backed right against the tribe and they were a solid mass of menace that bristled with spears. The intention of a charge was forming among them; they were working up to it and the neck would be swept clear. Ralph stood facing

them, a little to one side, his spear ready. By him stood Piggy still holding out the talisman, the fragile, shining beauty of the shell. The storm of sound beat at them, an incantation of hatred. High overhead, Roger, with a sense of delirious abandonment, leaned all his weight on the lever. . . . The rock struck Piggy a glancing blow from chin to knee; the conch exploded into a thousand white fragments and ceased to exist. (pp. 221–2)

3

Body-painting and masks are a developing symbol of the boys' fall from civilisation into savagery, and they provide one of the simplest ways in which we can analyse the racist/imperialist attitude. Golding does not see body-painting and masks as symbolisms functioning within a total social context, no more or less exotic and fearful than the uniforms of grenadier guards or the rituals of trooping the colour; for him they are intrinsically evil. In Chapter 4, 'Painted Faces and Long Hair', Jack defects to blackness: 'He made one cheek and one eye-socket white, then he rubbed red over the other half of his face and slashed a black bar of charcoal across from right ear to left jaw. He looked in the mere for his reflection, but his breathing troubled the mirror' (p. 79). Fearful indeed! more fearful, implicitly, than any of the historic oddities of British social fashion or military uniform. Later, Ralph states the alternatives: the light of fire (white enlightenment and civilisation) or African body-painting (the heart of darkness): 'I'd like to put on war-paint and be a savage. But we must keep the fire burning' (p. 175). It is almost as if he said '. . . But we must keep being British'!

The picture of tribalism, weapons, ululation, and body-paint is set against Ralph's legislative assembly, with its emblem of authority, the fragile white conch—almost, in the total context, the ruling sceptre of Empire. We are expected to be fearful of the anonymity and Africanness of Jack's tribe because in Golding's terms the boys have stepped down the 'hierarchies' of societies and peoples:

> The chief was sitting there, naked to the waist, his face blocked out in white and red. The tribe lay in a semicircle before him. . . . 'To-morrow,' went on the Chief, 'we shall hunt again.'
>
> He pointed at this savage and that with his spear. . . . A savage raised his hand and the chief turned a bleak, painted face towards him. (p. 197)

The gathering is intimidatory, irrational, and mysterious, the opposite of Ralph's assembly. The contrast gives us colonialism seen from the imperialist viewpoint:

white constitutionalism holding up the light of example to black tribalism. The children 'understood only too well the liberation into savagery that the concealing paint brought' (p. 212); their history books will have helped them. 'We won't be painted,' says Ralph, 'because we aren't savages' (p. 212). He is holding out against the heart of darkness. When, as symbolically the last white man, Ralph is on the run, his fear is that 'these painted savages would go further and further. . . . There was no solemn assembly for debate nor dignity of the conch'. The British legislature has been overrun and African savagery is in full cry (pp. 226, 241).

Chinua Achebe's *Things Fall Apart* (1958) and *Arrow of God* (1964) are good counterpoints to these views, though we have to be careful in reading them because of our imperialist heritage. They give us history and vision the other way round, the colonised peoples' view of the coloniser, and they show us the reality of ritual and custom. Achebe, writing in the period when Nigeria won independence, is rewriting the 'other world' of Africa, overturning the slow history of depreciation and imposed inferiority, the denigrating mental image, that was one aspect of colonialism. Instead of the 'other world', Achebe gives us the Igbo, an ordinary people going about their lives in a perfectly recognisable and dignified way. He decodes our caricatures: drums, masks, ululation, face- and body-paint, and so forth, are shown in context as part of the inherited rituals, codes and organisation of society, as part of a total way of life that it is impossible to grade in hierarchy on Golding's model.

Behind that model lies the equation of cultural misrepresentation linking blackness, childishness and savagery. The rationale of colonialism was that the colonised were children, and the developing rationale of decolonisation was that they were children being trained for independence. These ideas were commonplace when Golding was writing, and they can be found in liberal and apparently enlightened textbooks, even in contexts which show some awareness of the strength of nationalist pressure. In 1955, one writer could ask: 'What if the African child, resisting tutelage, wants to get rid of his British parent before he is fully grown up?'[9] When decolonisation was more advanced, in 1960, another writer could suggest that 'watching Africa deciding its fate has the same kind of fascination as watching schoolboys after they have been liberated from school'.[10] It is important to emphasise that these quotations are not from overtly racist sources, and that the attitude they show was a cliché. Achebe has described Kipling as the 'great imperialist poet',[11] and Kipling called the African 'half devil, half child', a phrase that might give us pause in the present context.

4

So far we have shown how the novel subscribes to an idea of hierarchy in relation to peoples and societies, and we have suggested some of the ways in which it can be read in relation to decolonisation as perceived from the imperialist perspective. We can go further by addressing the fact that at the very time when Golding was drawing together these images of tribalism, hierarchy, childishness and savagery—'painted niggers' in a forest—there were, as far as the British public were aware, real savages in the forest, dangerous and primitive ones, the Mau Mau guerrillas in Kenya (as presented by the Western media). One senior colonial official described the Mau Mau as 'debased creatures of the forest'.[12] One term for them in Kenya was *Ihii cia mutitu*, 'Freedom Boys of the Forest'. From the time of the State of Emergency declared in Kenya late in 1952, the British public had the impression that Mau Mau (the very name was fearful) were irrational rebels against the colonial regime who were out to murder white settlers in terrible ways, murder and mutilate black 'loyalists' and collaborators, and even kill and torture livestock and animals. It also appeared that they had ghastly systems of secret oathing that involved primitive rites, a potent way of binding members to the movement. In fact these emphases, and the way they were reported, represented a campaign of criminalisation on the part of the colonial regime in Kenya (and the British government behind them), one that covered over the fact that the Mau Mau had overwhelmingly legitimate grievances and aims. The paradigm is the old one of terrorist/freedom-fighter, only in this case aspects of 'tribal savagery' were being brought to the fore.

The Mau Mau were drawn mainly from the Kikuyu people of central Kenya, and the real reasons for their emergence are now well documented. It was essentially a movement drawing its support from the people and not from middle-class nationalism, and its causes lay in the oppressive and racist structuring of the colonial regime, and in the sufferings of the Kikuyu people under it: enforced landlessness and poverty, gross economic insecurity, the exploitation of the squatter farmers, aggressive racism and the complete denial of civil rights. The Mau Mau struggle was for land, independence, and freedom from internal social oppression and from foreign control. Their most common name for themselves was 'Land and Freedom Army' (*Kiama Kia Muingi*). This side of things was minimised by colonial and British propaganda, so effectively that, as several historians have complained, the wrong kinds of emphases in the analysis of Mau Mau have persisted well into the post-independence period.[13] In the immediate wake of the Emergency, emphasis was laid on Kikuyu culture and religion, particularly on the rituals and oaths of the Mau Mau, this being one way of playing down the economic and political aspects of the movement. Mau Mau was presented as a terrible atavism on the part of the Kikuyu. It was argued that the Kikuyu were backward-looking, conservative and tribal, and that they had a 'forest psychology' that made them secretive, irrational, and predisposed towards barbarism. They were the people of Kenya who had most difficulty adapting to the progress of twentieth-century white civilisation. Mau Mau was indicative of this, a childish backlash into darkness. Perhaps also, as one official report explained in 1954, it was the result of a failure of images:

> Africans, and particularly the Kikuyu, have been misled and the Government and Europeans have been vilified. This has done much to encourage the growth of the obsession which has induced the Kikuyu to believe in the crazy notion that they could manage their own affairs without the European.[14]

Soon after the State of Emergency was declared the British army and airforce were called in to fight and bomb the guerrillas out of the forest. After 'Operation Anvil' in 1954, 17,000 convicts and over 50,000 detainees were held in a system of camps, most for no crime, but simply on suspicion of being sympathetic to Mau Mau.

We are dealing with history that is sensitive from the standpoint of imperialism and from the standpoint of those who eventually came to power in independent Kenya. Kenyans opposed to Kenyatta and Arap Moi, who see their regimes as neo-colonialist in economic and political terms, have looked back to the freedom struggle of Mau Mau as an essentially unfulfilled project, a project of the people. The political elite that took over the country at independence contained some who had prospered under colonialism, while Kenyans whose politics had been more radical, more associated with Mau Mau, were slowly squeezed out of government. Many Kenyans believe that false loyalist and imperialist interpretations have prevailed in the history of the 1950s. Maina wa Kinyatti, one Kenyan historian of Mau Mau, was in prison for his work from 1982 to 1989, and Ngugi wa Thiong'o, the Kenyan novelist, was detained without trial, in appalling conditions, in 1977, and now lives in exile.

From a British standpoint, the period brings us face to face with aspects of our imperial past. Opinion in England has happily condemned apartheid in South Africa while forgetting that in the 1950s we stepped in militarily to support a colonial regime at least as unjust and racist. The battle against Mau Mau involved the large-scale persecution of the Kikuyu. We can now read the facts of the huge detention-camps, the hangings (for no more than the possession of firearms), the torture and brutalisation, and the process of 'villagisation' whereby traditional villages were razed to the ground. If we want to understand these things imaginatively we may turn to Ngugi's two fine novels set in the 1950s, *Weep Not, Child* (1964) and *A Grain of Wheat* (1967). These are true imaginative counterweights to *Lord of the Flies*, for in the one powerful instance of Mau Mau, they show us the gross injustices under which ordinary Kikuyu laboured, and how and why they became 'savages' to reclaim their lands from the white man.

I am arguing that *Lord of the Flies* is a seriously imperialist text. This is not a matter of whether or not Golding was directly influenced by the reporting of Mau Mau, but something to do with the total atmosphere of thought that created its one-sided interpretations. Golding's remarks quoted earlier are a part of that atmosphere, and we can see it also in the imaginative patterns of the novel and in the unconscious ways that its images would have been received. The novel's first readers could turn from the picture of child savages to a similar phenomenon in the newspapers: the Kikuyu who had regressed from white civilisation to their natural and dangerous barbarism. As perceived through the eyes of Western media, the Mau Mau were like Golding's children: they had apparently fallen back down the hierarchy so carefully nurtured by the white man—the hierarchy of civilisation on which decolonisation was posited—until they were now committing atrocious deeds. Novel and propaganda foreground ideas of regression and savagery, covering over the idea that violence might be a struggle against hierarchy, a liberationist movement.

The ending of *Lord of the Flies* has been criticised as a 'trick', an effect not fully achieved, but in the context of this reading we can see its necessity and how it fits with what has gone before. The boys should have created white civilisation and constitutionalism, and instead they have fallen back down the hierarchies, regressed to Africanness, and become 'half devil, half child'. What happens to them is, in the mythology of imperialism, a mirror of what would happen to African peoples without their white colonisers. Without the white 'grown-up' presence, you slip back to the savage, since, as Golding has told us, civilisation is a precarious achievement limited to few parts of the world! The ending is a kind of fantasy. The white 'grown-ups' come back to take care of the African 'children'; the savages are cowed—they see themselves for what they are—and order is restored.

There are military hints in the situation. The naval personnel come on shore perhaps expecting something out of the heart of darkness for they are well armed. Ralph sees 'white drill, epaulettes, a revolver, a row of gilt buttons down the front of a uniform' (p. 246), and the ratings behind the officer have a sub-machine-gun. (Note especially that the details of the uniform are another hint of hierarchy. The regular, trim effect is supposed to reassure us after all the body-paint and loincloths.) If we wonder at all why the ending seems glib, we should recall that it is a direct mirror of that other cliché of cultural misrepresentation, the US cavalry bringing rescue from the Red Indians.

The whole fantastic drift of the novel is to set the savages, the subject peoples, the 'children', back in their place at the bottom of a hierarchy ruled by the white man. The famous ending of Achebe's *Things Fall Apart* ironises colonialism by suddenly giving us the coloniser's viewpoint: the whole story of the hero and his tribe becomes only a small episode in the District

Commissioner's book *The Pacification of the Primitive Tribes of the Lower Niger*. Writing from the imperialist side, Golding gives us the reverse of this joke: the primitive tribe of children saved and brought to heel by their white superior. It is sad how fully the clichés of cultural misrepresentation carry over even into the details:

> A semicircle of little boys, their bodies streaked with coloured clay, sharp sticks in their hands, were standing on the beach making no noise at all.... Other boys were appearing now, tiny tots some of them, brown, with the distended bellies of small savages. (pp. 246–7)

5

Various conclusions may result from this reading. Firstly, we should accept what some African writers are telling us: that literature written by African writers in European languages must often be considered as part of European literature and should be studied as such. (Ngugi would like to call such literature written in English 'Anglo-African literature' to distinguish it from *African Literature* proper.[15]) All divisions on national lines have limitations, but splitting off so-called 'African' literature (written in English) from 'English' literature— splitting imperial centre from colony—makes little sense, especially when the literature involved has been created, conditioned by, and is a response to, the experience of colonialism. What is taking place at the so-called periphery is part of what is taking place at the so-called centre. It is vital for us to read 'English' literature in *intimate* relation with the literature of our ex-colonies, and classifications like 'other literature' and 'new commonwealth' are confusing in this respect. The imaginative terrain of colonialism and decolonisation is an extended commentary on patterns and influences on the imagination back in England, and to ignore this potentially shuts off the full reading of 'English English' texts. Courses in twentieth-century literature should recognise the shaping history of decolonisation by *mingling* 'African' and 'English' texts, and at school level 'African' texts need not be marginalised in any way, for they can provide reading quite as vital as *Lord of the Flies*.

Notes

1. Margery Perham, *The Colonial Reckoning* (New York: Alfred Knopf, 1962), p. 24.

2. Even Alan Sinfield, in his brief discussion of Golding, seeing *Lord of the Flies* primarily in opposition to *The Coral Island*, only concludes that 'Golding's distinct post-colonial inflection is to attribute savagery, in principle, to the British ruling élite' (p. 142), but he does not begin to question this idea of savagery. See *Literature, Politics and Culture in Postwar Britain* (Oxford: Blackwell, 1989), pp. 141ff.

3. Jack I. Biles, *Talk: Conversations with William Golding* (New York: Harcourt Brace Jovanovich, 1970), pp. 3–4.

4. Ibid., p. 45.

5. Ngugi wa Thiong'o, *Moving the Centre: The Struggle for Cultural Freedoms* (London: James Currey, 1993), p. 140.

6. Chinua Achebe, 'An Image of Africa: Racism in Conrad's *Heart of Darkness*', in *Hopes and Impediments* (Oxford and Ibadan: Heinemann, 1988), pp. 1–13 (pp. 2, 12).

7. Quoted from *Chinua Achebe: A Celebration*, ed. K. H. Peterson and A. Rutherford (Oxford: Heinemann, 1990), p. 5.

8. All references are to William Golding, *Lord of the Flies* (London: Faber, 1954); subsequent impressions keep this pagination.

9. John Gunther, *Inside Africa* (London: Hamish Hamilton, 1955), p. 330.

10. Anthony Sampson, *Common Sense About Africa* (London: Gollancz, 1960), p. 13.

11. Quoted from *The African Reader*, ed. W. Cartey and M. Kilson (New York: Random House, 1970), p. 164.

12. See Robert B. Egerton, *Mau Mau* (London: Tauris, 1990), p. 107.

13. See Frank Furedi, *The Mau Mau in Perspective*, Eastern African Studies (London: James Currey, 1989), p. 140.

14. Quoted from Egerton, p. 336.

15. See for example Ngugi wa Thiong'o, 'The Language of African Literature', in *Decolonizing the Mind: The Politics of Language in African Literature* (London: James Currey, 1986), pp. 4–33; see esp. p. 33, n. 24.

JAMES R. BAKER

Golding and Huxley:
The Fables of Demonic Possession

Surely we have heard enough about William Golding's *Lord of the Flies*. Published in 1954, it rapidly gained popularity in England, then in America, then in translation throughout Europe, Russia, and Asia, until it became one of the most familiar and studied tales of the century. In the 1960s it was rated an instant classic in the literature of disillusionment that grew out of the latest great war, and we felt certain it was the perfect fable (more fable than fiction) that spelled out what had gone wrong in that dark and stormy time and what might devastate our future.

But in the postwar generation a new spirit was rising, a new wind blowing on campus, a new politics forming to oppose the old establishment and its failures. Golding, proclaimed "Lord of the Campus" by *Time* magazine (64) in 1962, was soon found wanting—an antique tragedian, a pessimist, a Christian moralist who would not let us transcend original sin and the disastrous history of the last 50 years. Many "activist" academics came to feel his gloomy allegory was better left to secondary or even primary schools, where a supposedly transparent text (now put down as lacking in intellectual sophistication and contemporary relevance) might serve to exercise apprentice readers. It remained appropriate to read Orwell, *Animal Farm* or *Nineteen Eighty-four*, because he was a political novelist writing in behalf of what he called political freedom, whereas Golding was apolitical and seemingly without faith in political means. The Nobel poet

From *Twentieth Century Literature* 46, no. 3 (Fall 2000), pp. 311–327. © 2001 by Hofstra University.

Wislawa Szymborska describes the fashionable attitude, the movement itself, in her "Children of Our Age" (1986):

> We are children of our age,
> it's a political age.
>
> All day long, all through the night,
> all affairs—yours, ours, theirs—
> are political affairs.
>
> Whether you like it or not,
> your genes have a political past,
> your skin, a political cast,
> your eyes, a political slant.
>
> Whatever you say reverberates,
> whatever you don't say speaks for itself,
> So either way you're talking politics.
>
> Even when you take to the woods,
> you're taking political steps
> on political grounds.
>
> Apolitical poems are also political,
> and above us shines a moon
> no longer purely lunar.
> To be or not to be, that is the question,
> And though it troubles the digestion
> it's a question, as always, of politics.
>
> To acquire a political meaning
> you don't even have to be human,
> Raw material will do,
> or protein feed, or crude oil,
>
> or a conference table whose shape
> was quarreled over for months:
> Should we arbitrate life and death at
> a round table or a square one.
>
> Meanwhile, people perished,
> animals died

houses burned,
and the fields ran wild
just as in times immemorial
and less political. (149–50)

The identity assigned to Golding during these years was not substantially altered by his later work. *The Inheritors* (1955) and *Pincher Martin* (1956), two more fables on the limitations of "rational man," confirmed the prevailing judgment; the later attempts at social comedy, *The Pyramid* (1967) and *The Paper Men* (1984), or the long holiday from contemporary reality in the eighteenth-century sea trilogy, *Rites of Passage* (1980), *Close Quarters* (1987), *Fire Down Below* (1989), failed to efface the original image. He remained the man who wrote *Lord of the Flies*, the man who felt he had to protest his designation as pessimist even in his Nobel speech of 1983 (Nobel Lecture 149–50). Have we been entirely fair? Golding's reputation, like that of any artist, was created not simply by what he wrote or intended but also by the prevailing mentality of his readership, and often a single work will be selected by that readership as characteristic or definitive. Writer and reader conspire to sketch a portrait of the artist that may or may not endure. In "Fable," a 1962 lecture at the University of California at Los Angeles, Golding acknowledged that in *Lord of the Flies* he was acting as fabulist and moralist, as one who might as well say he accepted the theology of original sin and fallen man; and on other occasions during his rise to fame he acknowledged that for a time after the war he read almost exclusively in Greek tragedy and history. Such statements contributed to his identity as philosophical antiquarian and served to condition his reception by critics and millions of readers. Yet something was lost, something important obscured that must be recovered—or discovered— to amend our reading of *Lord of the Flies* (in spite of the attention lavished upon it) and our estimate of Golding's total accomplishment. Most critical judgements on the famous fable are locked into the clichés established soon after its appearance.

In 1962 I began correspondence with Golding in preparation for a book on his work (*William Golding: A Critical Study*). My thesis, foreshadowed in an essay published in 1963 ("Why It's No Go"), was that the structure and spirit of *Lord of the Flies* were modeled on Euripidean tragedy, specifically *The Bacchae*, and that the later novels also borrowed character and structure from the ancient tragedians. Golding's response to the book was positive, kinder than I expected, but it carried a hint I did not immediately understand:

> With regard to Greek, you are quite right that I go to that literature for its profound engagement with first and last things. But though a few years ago it was true I'd read little but Greek

for twenty years, it's true no longer. The Greek is still there and I go back to it when I feel like that; now I must get in touch with the contemporary scene, and not necessarily the literary one; the scientific one perhaps. (Baker and Golding, letter 12 August 1965)

Science? What could he mean? *Lord of the Flies* and *The Inheritors*, as many readers recognized, had displayed a broad knowledge of anthropological literature. *Pincher Martin*, the third novel, was not such an obvious case, but it did focus on an arrogant rationalist who repudiated any belief in a god and claimed for himself the god-like power to create his own world, his own virtual reality. *Free Fall* (1959) had more obviously employed scientific metaphor—the state of free fall or freedom from gravitational law—to describe the moral drift and lawlessness of the narrator, Sammy Mountjoy; and his mentor, the science teacher Nick Shales, is found in Sammy's retrospective search for pattern in his life to be an incredibly one-sided and naïve man. And the little comic play, *The Brass Butterfly* (1958), satirized the ancient Greek scientist Phanocles, a brilliant but dangerously destructive inventor who specializes in explosive devices. Was Piggy, the precocious protoscientist of *Lord of the Flies*, first in this series of negative and satirical portraits? At the urging of his father, a devotee of science, Golding had gone up to Oxford in 1930 to study science, but after two years he threw it over to study literature. Some of the student poems written at Oxford, published in 1934, mock the rationalist's faith that order rules our experience, and these seem to evidence that turning point. Years later he wrote a humorous autobiographical sketch, "The Ladder and the Tree" (1965), recalling the conflict that had troubled him as he prepared to enter the university. The voice of his father joined with Einstein and Sir James Jeans (and no doubt the authors of all those scientific classics found in the household), while the voice of Edgar Allan Poe, advocate for darkness and mystery, urged him to choose the alternative path.

When I interviewed Golding in 1982 I was determined to question him about this early confrontation with the two cultures. Had there been a "classic revolt," I asked, against his father's scientific point of view? After some defense of the father's complexity of mind, the conclusion was clear: "But I do think that during the formative years I did feel myself to be in a sort of rationalist atmosphere against which I kicked" (130). I also asked whether he felt he belonged to the long line of English writers who, especially since Darwin, had taken scientist and the scientific account of things into their own work—a line running from Tennyson and including among others Hardy, Wells, Huxley, Snow, Durrell, and Fowles. And Golding? His reply was oblique, equivocal, and we hurried on to other matters. In 1988 I tried to sum up what had been achieved and what needed to be done:

We need more work on the role of science in Golding's fiction (perhaps beginning with the impact of Poe on the formation of his attitudes) and we need to reassess his accomplishment in the larger context made up of his contemporaries. ("William Golding" 11)

No scholar has responded. Since Golding's death in 1993 his work has gone into partial eclipse, as he himself predicted. While we wait for recovery, if it ever comes, we should adjust our accounts. We shall find that much of the fiction was oriented and directly influenced by his knowledge of science and that there is an evolution from the extreme negativism of *Lord of the Flies* toward greater respect for the scientist and scientific inquiry. The much discussed sources for the dark fable lie in Golding's experience of the war, in his connection with Lord Cherwell's research into explosives, in the use of the atomic bombs on Japan, in the postwar revelations of the Holocaust and the horrors of Stalinist Russia—quite enough to bring on the sense of tragic denouement and, as he said in "A Moving Target" (163), "grief, sheer grief" as inspiration, if that is the proper word.

Was there a contemporary literary source or precedent on which he could build his own account of the failure of humanity and the likelihood of atomic apocalypse? There have been a few unfruitful forays into this question. Craig Raine, for example, finds occasional stylistic parallels in Golding with Huxley (*Antic Hay, Eyeless in Gaza*) as well as Dostoyevsky, Henry James, and Kipling but concludes that these or others that might be hunted down are not "real sources" (108) worthy of serious attention. We get more specific guidance from Golding himself. In an address titled "Utopias and Antiutopias" he comes, inevitably, to Aldous Huxley:

> As the war clouds darkened over Europe he and some of our most notable poets removed themselves to the new world.... There Huxley continued to create what we may call antiutopias and utopias with the same gusto, apparently, for both kinds. One antiutopia is certainly a disgusting job and best forgotten.... Yet I owe his writings much myself, I've had much enjoyment from them—in particular release from a certain starry-eyed optimism which stemmed from the optimistic rationalism of the nineteenth century. The last utopia he attempted which was technically and strictly a utopia and ideal state, *Island* (1962), is one for which I have a considerable liking and respect. (181)

Huxley arrived in America in 1937, toured part of the country, then wrote most of *Ends and Means* (1937) at the Frieda Lawrence ranch in New Mexico, and settled in Los Angeles that fall. He wrote only two books in the genre Golding discusses before his death in 1963, *Island* and an earlier antiutopia—undoubtedly the "disgusting job . . . best forgotten"—*Ape and Essence* (1948). Golding's harsh judgment on this book (shared by several reviewers and critics) may reflect disappointment in a literary idol. Again there is talk of Huxley in one of the last interviews, "William Golding Talks to John Carey," when the interviewer asks about the four novels the apprentice Golding tried to write. He abandoned all of them (they have never come to light) because they were merely imitations, "examples of other people's work":

> JC. Huxley was one of the influences on the earlier attempts, wasn't he?
>
> WG. I took him very neat, you know. I was fascinated by him. And he was, I think superb—but *clever*; it was cleverness raised to a very high power indeed. Never what Lawrence can sometimes produce—never that mantic, inspired . . . I don't think Huxley was even inspired; almost too clear-sighted to be inspired. (189)

Huxley was the near-contemporary (17 years separated them) so much admired in the early stage of Golding's efforts, and he was quite like Golding—knowledgeable about science and scientists, yet dedicated to literature, intent upon spiritual experience and a search for an acceptable religious faith. Huxley's skeptical views were an update on H. G. Wells and his rather quaint "scientific humanism," a faith fading in Huxley's mind and lost to Golding and many of his generation.

The California years were often difficult for Huxley. After the war began he was privileged to find himself in the company of one of the most extraordinary gatherings of intellectuals ever assembled in the United States—including exiles Mann, Brecht, Stravinsky, Schoenberg, Isherwood, and Heard, and Americans Faulkner, Fitzgerald, Agee, and West—some of them writing for money at the studios as Huxley was to do. On the negative side, he was attacked by his countrymen for his pacifism, his eyesight failed further, he was often short of money, and the anxious quest for spiritual sustenance drove him constantly. These personal problems were intensified by the events of the war, the ugly alliance of the scientific and military communities, the bombing of Japan, the emergence of the cold war. Inevitably, he was subject to bouts of depression and despair over the behavior of men and nations. David King Dunaway sums up the effect of these burdens: "In the fall of 1946, Aldous Huxley turned a dark corner and found himself in a hallway of desperation; *Ape* was at the end of that long dark corridor" (214). Back in England, Golding had entered upon a similar period of doubt and reorientation; at the end of his trial he would write *Lord of the Files*.

We have long thought of Huxley as a "novelist of ideas"—and one who rarely effected a perfect marriage of art and idea. Some of the ideas in his mind as he began *Ape and Essence* are found in the long essay *Science, Liberty, and Peace* (1946), but the novel he planned was to be a darker affair altogether, with flashes of grotesque comedy serving only to enhance the power of darkness. Don't take this too seriously, it seems to suggest, but remember that you have already created in reality an obscene disaster which stands as preface to the future described in this fiction. Yet, experienced as he was, Huxley could not find the right narrative voice, so abandoned the novelistic plan and turned to film scenario, a form in which he had enjoyed some success, notably with *Pride and Prejudice* and *Jane Eyre*. Nevertheless, most of Huxley's critics speak of *Ape and Essence* as a novel and judge it as a novel, ignoring the fact that it is an odd pastiche of scenario, dialogue, narrative, and verse. The scenario is indeed set up or framed by a Huxley-like narrator who recounts the discovery of a film script by an unknown, rejected writer, William Tallis. The setting for this discovery is a studio lot on 30 January 1948—"the day of Gandhi's assassination." Two Hollywood writers walk through the studio lot, one intent upon his own trivial affairs, the more serious narrator meditating upon the newspaper headlines and the fate of the saint in politics. Gandhi's mistake, he thinks, had been to get himself involved in the sub-human mass-madness of nationalism, in the would-be superhuman, but actually diabolic, institutions of the nation state."[1] Alas, it is only from without "that the saint can cure our regimented insanity . . . our dream of Order" which always begets tyranny. He speaks to his companion of other martyred saints, some of them rejected candidates for film treatment, all of them participants in this repetitive tragic pattern. The headlines in the morning paper were "parables; the event they recorded, an allegory and a prophecy" (8–9). Here, in the abstract, is the outline for Golding's allegory of the boy saint, Simon, martyr to a "sub-human mass-madness." At this point the narrator stumbles upon the rejected manuscript. After reading it he goes in search of this strange man, Tallis, only to find that he had retreated from the world to the Mojave Desert, where he died six weeks before his scenario was rescued from the studio trash. The narrator decides to "print the text of 'Ape and Essence' as I found it, without change and without comment" (32).

The author takes his title from Shakespeare's *Measure for Measure* (2.2.118–23):

But man, proud man,
Dress'd in a little brief authority,
Most ignorant of what he's most assur'd—
His glassy essence—like an angry ape
Plays such fantastic tricks before high heaven
As makes the angels weep.

His method is to employ an omniscient narrator who introduces the dramatic scenes and follows them with moralizing or sardonic commentary. The setting is a ruined city, Los Angeles in the year 2108.[2] How did the city fall? We are given flash scenes of Einstein and Faraday, representatives of the great men of science we have so revered, enslaved by the ape king and made to serve in an apocalyptic bacteriological and atomic war which ends in "the ultimate and irremediable / Detumescence" (42) of modern civilization. The narrator comments on the ends and means that brought about this great fall:

> Surely it's obvious.
> Doesn't every schoolboy know it?
> Ends are ape-chosen; only the means are man's.
> Papio's[3] procurer, bursar to baboons,
> Reason comes running, eager to ratify;
> Comes, a catch-fart, with Philosophy,
>   truckling to tyrants;
> Comes, a Pimp for Prussia, with Hegel's
>   Patent History;
> Comes with Medicine to administer the
>   Ape-king's aphrodisiac;
> Comes, with rhyming and with Rhetoric,
>   to write his orations;
> Comes with the Calculus to aim his rockets
> Accurately at the orphanage across the ocean;
> Comes, having aimed, with incense to impetrate
> Our Lady devoutly for a direct hit.[4] (45)

Soulless reason provides a means to serve animal lusts, especially the lust for power; thus the man becomes the ape, the "beast."

In Golding's island society the man of reason, the scientist, is represented in the sickly, myopic child Piggy, the butt of schoolboy gibes, but unfortunately many readers and most critics have failed to understand his limitations and thus his function in the allegory. This may be explained, in part, by the uncritical adoration of the scientist in our society, but another factor is the misunderstanding found in the prestige introduction by E. M. Forster in the first American edition of *Lord of the Flies* and subsequently held before our eyes for 40 years. We are asked to "Meet three boys," Ralph, Jack, and Piggy. We do not meet Simon at all. Piggy is Forster's hero, he is "the brains of the party," "the wisdom of the heart," "the human spirit," and as for the author, "he is on the side of Piggy." In a final bit of advice we are admonished: "At the present moment (if I may speak personally) it is respect for Piggy that is most needed. I do not find it in our leaders" (ix–xii).

Actually, rightly understood, Piggy is respected all too much by our leaders, for he provides the means whereby they wield and extend their powers. Jack must steal Piggy's glasses to gain the power of fire. Forster, of course, was the arch-humanist of his day and apparently a subscriber to the "scientific humanism" Golding wished to demean. Contrast Golding's remarks to Jack Biles, a friendly interviewer: "Piggy isn't wise. Piggy is short-sighted. He is rationalist. My great curse, you understand, rationalism—and, well he's that. He's naïve, short-sighted and rationalist, like most scientists." Scientific advance, he continues, is useful, yet

> it doesn't touch the human problem. Piggy never gets anywhere near coping with anything on that island. He dismisses the beast ... says there aren't such things as ghosts, not understanding that the whole of society is riddled with ghosts. . . . Piggy understands society less than almost anyone there at all.

Finally, Piggy is dismissed as a type, a clownish caricature who "ought to wear a white coat . . . ending up at Los Alamos" (12–14). He is the soulless child who adores the science that blew up the cities and obliterated the technological society he idealizes.

Putting Forster aside, we have in Golding's Jack, the lusty hunter who instinctively pursues power, a diminutive version of Huxley's ape. In the silence of the forest Jack hunts but is momentarily frightened by the cry of a bird, "and for a minute became less a hunter than a furtive thing, ape-like among the trees" (62). He meets his adult counterpart when the boys find the dead airman on the mountaintop: "Before them, something like a great ape was sitting asleep with its head between its knees" (152). And, in his hour of triumph, he looks down from his castle rock on the defeated Ralph and Piggy: "Power lay in the brown swell of his forearms: authority sat on his shoulder and chattered in his ear like an ape" (185).

On a bright day in Huxley's February 2108, a sailing ship, the Canterbury, flying the flag of New Zealand and carrying the men and women of the "Re-discovery Expedition to North America," approaches the coastline near the ruined city of Los Angeles. New Zealand has been spared, and now radiation has diminished enough to allow this shipload of scientists of all kinds to explore the remains of civilization. It is a ship of fools rediscovering America from the west, and the biggest fool aboard is our antihero, "Dr. Alfred Poole, D.Sc." Poole is a parody figure of a man entirely removed from his bodily functions and his very soul, but he is the man to watch because Huxley (unlike Golding) builds into his dismal story a parable of redemption. But there is no redemption awaiting the city of fallen men and women. These survivors are deformed, regressive, bestial, and held in check by a repressive dictatorship that combines the authority of church and state. The gamma rays have effected a reversal or devolution in which humans, like the beasts, mate only in season and are incapable of enduring love. Dr. Poole is taken prisoner by these decadent Angelenos. Throughout his scenario, the narrator (Tallis) juxtaposes lyrical description of the sublimity of nature—the dawn, the sunset, the stars, each an "emblem of eternity"—with scenes from the fallen "City of the Angels," now only a "ghost town," a mass of "ruins in a wasteland" (62) inhabited by a desperate and savage race. This second discovery of America is black irony in which we see the ruination of a "promised land," the paradise given at the outset to the bold pioneers. One recalls the tropical enchantments given to Golding's castaways and the burning island "discovered" by the naïve naval captain who is incapable of rescuing the ragged survivors. The two fictional societies have much in common, and even the history leading to their downfall is strikingly similar: parliaments fail, a third world war devastates the earth, and a new religion forms to recognize and honor the seemingly mysterious power manifested in this sequence.

The religion in Huxley's fable emerges with what its followers call "the Thing." This is not simply a reference to the bioatomic catastrophe but also to the psychopolitical dialectics that led to violent climax and apocalypse. The Chief, a rude master of the work crews that dig the graves of Hollywood Cemetery in search of manufactured goods, explains to his prisoner, Dr. Poole: "*The* Thing. You know—when He took over. . . . He won the battle and took possession of everybody. That was when they did all this" (71). There's no need to struggle for recognition here, since the future will resurrect a familiar idol known generically as the devil, though it is capable of assuming an interesting variety of forms. In a catechism offered by a "Satanic Science Practitioner" the children respond:

> "Belial has perverted and corrupted us in all the parts of our being. Therefore, we are, merely on account of that corruption, deservedly condemned by Belial."
>
> Their teacher nods approvingly.
>
> "Such," he squeaks unctuously, "is the inscrutable justice of the Lord of Flies." (94–95)

As the lessons continue we learn that woman is the "vessel of the Unholy Spirit," the source of deformities and therefore "the enemy of the race" (98). Annually, on Belial Day, mothers are publicly humiliated, punished, and their deformed babies killed. The purpose of this blood sacrifice is, of course, a vain attempt to purify the race, but more broadly the catechism reveals, "The chief end of man is to propitiate Belial, depreciate His enmity, and avoid destruction as long as possible" (93). Similarly, the little Christian boys on

Golding's island bow down before a ubiquitous fear and soon spontaneously invent a blood ritual to purge this fear ("*Kill the beast! Cut his throat! Spill his blood!*" [187]) and a rite of propitiation to ensure their survival. The pig's head on the stick becomes a "gift" for the beast and an idol, an incarnation of ancient Beelzebub, Lord of Flies. Like Huxley's devotees they invert and parody the lost and more hopeful religion given to them by a forgotten savior.

On the day of propitiation in 2108 crowds mass in the Los Angeles Coliseum and we witness "the groundless faith, the sub-human excitement, the collective insanity which are the products of ceremonial religion" (108) as the ritual unfolds and chanting is heard from a great altar. The chorus mourns that all have fallen "Into the hands of living Evil, the Enemy of Man":

Semichorus I
Of the rebel against the Order of Things

Semichorus II
And we have conspired with him against ourselves

Semichorus I
Of the great Blowfly who is the Lord of Flies
Crawling in the heart . . . (109)

The chorus curses woman, the mother, as "breeder of all deformities who is driven by the Blowfly," goaded "Like the soiled fitchew / Like the sow in her season" (112–13).

We know now that *Lord of the Flies* was not the title of the manuscript of a novel Golding sent to Faber in 1953. In a charming essay, Charles Monteith, who became editor of the manuscript, recalls the brief note attached: "I send you the typescript of my novel *Strangers from Within* which might be defined as an allegorical interpretation of a stock situation. I hope you will feel able to publish it" (57). Reader judgments were largely negative, much revision was demanded, the title was rejected, and a new one—*Lord of the Flies*—suggested by another editor at Faber. Golding readily agreed, as well he might have, for it was quite appropriate to give his devil a familiar name (Beelzebub, the fly lord, was present in the "buzz" of conflicting voices at the parliaments on the platform rock), and his theme of submission to evil remained intact. The original title, nevertheless, was no doubt deliberately chosen to reflect something built into the narrative progression—the gradual effacement of sane and civil behavior and the emergence of an alien power in the consciousness of the boys. The theme of demonic possession was most vital to Golding's purpose, and again it demonstrates the bond with Huxley.[5] When the Arch-Vicar delivers his talk on world history for Poole (all the while munching pig's trotters) he comes to a clear statement of his thesis on the downfall of civilization:

> [A]t a certain epoch, the overwhelming majority of human beings accepted beliefs and adopted courses of action that could not possibly result in anything but universal suffering, general degradation and wholesale destruction. The only plausible explanation is that they were inspired or possessed by an alien consciousness, a consciousness that willed their undoing and willed it more strongly than they were able to will their own happiness and survival. (128)

This "alien consciousness" signifies the presence of Belial and the defeat of "the Other" (god) in the minds of human beings. It is a form of psychological regression that brings the ape, the beast, into power. In Golding's manuscript metaphor, consciousness is invaded by "strangers from within."

In both fables of possession we see how ritual motion and corybantic chanting bring about the psychological birth of the aliens. Huxley captures this perfectly in the antiphonal chant of the priests on Belial Day hailing that brief period in which mating is spontaneous and allowed:

Semichorus I
This is the time,

Semichorus II
For Belial is in your blood,

Semichorus I
Time for the birth in you

Semichorus II
Of the Others, the Aliens

Semichorus I
Of Itch, of Tetter

Semichorus II
Of tumid worm.

Semichorus I
This is the time,

Semichorus II
For Belial hates you,

Semichorus I
Time for the soul's death

Semichorus II
For the Person to perish

Semichorus I
Sentenced by craving,

Semichorus II
And pleasure is the hangman;

Semichorus I
Time for the Enemy's

Semichorus II
Total triumph,

Semichorus I
For the Baboon to be master,

Semichorus II
That monsters may be begotten.

Semichorus I
Not your will, but His

Semichorus II
That you may all be lost forever. (142–44)

As individuals fall victim to collective hysteria, to possession, so too, the Arch-Vicar insists, do nations, entire civilizations. In his sketch of modern history (116–33), however, he offers some forceful arguments that go beyond theological platitude. He cites the failure of nations to curb population growth or to arrest environmental degradation (failures that would have resulted in world apocalypse even without "the Thing"), yet these and other negative policies were driven by the politics of "Progress and Nationalism" (125). The overarching myth of the age was "the theory that Utopia lies just ahead and that, since ideal ends justify the most abominable means" (125), ethical restraints collapse; in the scientific-technological society now defunct the "means" were extended beyond any power known to previous ages, the power to destroy the earth.

The growth of Alfred Poole, D.Sc. (known to his students and colleagues as "Stagnant Poole") to full manhood is the dubious subtext of Huxley's grim fantasy. Golding's harsh judgment on *Ape and Essence* in 1977 may be aimed primarily at this comedy of redemption. Young Alfred's psychological development has been stunted by a devoted and vampiric mother. It is tempting to compare this mother with Piggy's "auntie" and the life of self-indulgence she allowed, the diet of sweets and scientific fantasy. Poole is 38 when he arrives with the expedition in the company of a tweedy virgin, Miss Ethel Hook, "one of those amazingly efficient and intensely English girls" (57) who hopes to marry this incomplete man. His redemption begins when he is temporarily buried alive by the Chiefs crew of grave robbers and then, on the promise that he can help to produce more food, allowed to live; after all, he is an expert botanist. This symbolic resurrection is immediately followed by a liberating first-time drunken episode in the company of Loola—an 18-year-old girl who is blessed with an irresistible dimpled smile and burdened with an extra pair of nipples—who soon becomes the lover of this clownish scientist. Love touches his heart and the affective part of the man blossoms. The scenes with Loola provide incongruous low comedy or Hollywood romance (love among the ruins) in a story inspired by dismay for mankind. The love motif conflicts with the disaster scenario so that, in contrast, Golding appears wise to bar girls from boarding the plane that crashes on his coral island.

The third element of the man—his "glassy essence"—must be drawn from his depths to complete the classic triad of head, heart, and soul. It begins when Poole rescues "a charming little duodecimo Shelley" (91) from a pile of books used to fire the communal bread ovens. Here is the serious philosophical element in Poole's progress: glimpses into Shelley's *Epipsychidion* and *Adonais* furnish an inspired argument for the existence of a soul and a transcendent spiritual reality. Thus the admirably atheistic poet rationalized ubiquitous love incarnated in a multiplicity of female forms and immortalized fellow poet John Keats as an incarnation of the very spirit of beauty. As Poole flees the broken city (and the Arch-Vicar's invitation to eunuchhood) he is assured by lines from *Prometheus Unbound* (1: 152–58) which the narrator interprets:

> Love, Joy and Peace—these are the fruits of the spirit that is your essence and the essence of the world. But the fruits of the ape-mind, the fruits of the monkey's presumption and revolt are hate and unceasing restlessness and a chronic misery tempered only by frenzies more horrible than itself. (190)

Poole and Loola flee down into the Mojave as they journey to Fresno, there to join the minority community of Hots who are capable of enduring love and monogamy. In an incredible coincidence they camp at the site of William Tallis's grave. His monument reveals all that the lovers know of this man— that he died in profound grief for the world—but Poole cracks a (symbolic) hard-boiled egg over the grave before the lovers travel on to their new life. The infantile rationalist, who might have served out a destructive career *in nominee Babuini*, has been made whole.

In his last years Huxley came to a happier and more balanced view about the relation of science to the larger culture. His *Literature and Science*, published just before his death, is far more useful to writers on either side of that continuing debate than the heated exchanges of Snow and Leavis in the late 1950s and early 60s, and he avoids the overoptimistic prediction or projection of a "unity of knowledge" found in Edward O. Wilson's *Consilience* (1998). Though Huxley was mentor and guide for many of the ideas and devices that went into Golding's allegory, *Lord of the Flies* offers no real hope for redemption.[6] Golding kills off the only saint available (as history obliges him to do) and demonstrates the inadequacy of a decent leader (Ralph) who is at once too innocent and ignorant of the human heart to save the day from darkness. In later years Golding struggled toward a view in which science and the humanities might be linked in useful partnership, and he tried to believe, as Huxley surely did, that the visible world and its laws were the facade of a spiritual realm. He realized something of this effort in the moral thermodynamics of *Darkness Visible* (1974) and again, somewhat obscurely, in the posthumous novel *The Double Tongue* (1995). His Nobel speech asserts that the bridge between the visible and invisible worlds, one he failed to find in the earlier *Free Fall*, does in fact exist. Thus both novelists recovered to some degree from the trauma of disillusionment with scientific humanism suffered during the war, and both aspired to hope that humanity would somehow evolve beyond the old tragic flaws that assured the rebirth of the devil in every generation.

NOTES

1. Long before Gandhi's death Huxley had come to a "dismal conclusion" on those who attempt to mix politics and religion. See his letter to Kingsley Martin, 30 July 1939:

> So long as the majority of human beings choose to live like *homme moyen sensuel*, in an "unregenerate" state, society at large cannot do anything except stagger along from catastrophe to catastrophe. Religious people who think they can go into politics and transform the world always end by going into politics and being transformed by the world. (E.g. the Jesuits, Père Joseph,

the Oxford Group.) Religion can have no politics except the creation of small-scale societies of chosen individuals outside and on the margin of the essentially unviable large-scale societies, whose nature dooms them to self-frustration and suicide. (*Letters* 443–44)

2. Los Angeles has been destroyed in literature and film by every means imaginable. An enumeration and discussion appears in Davis, notably chapter 6, "The Literary Destruction of Los Angeles," in which he names *Ape and Essence* "the first and greatest of the many 'survivor's tales' situated in Southern California" (345).

3. The genus Papio: large African and Asian primates, including baboons.

4. Huxley quotes some of these lines in his *Literature and Science*, noting that they are still relevant in the ongoing "civil war" between reason and unreason (56–57).

5. Both novelists concluded that the late war demonstrated a psychological state that could legitimately be termed possession. See Huxley's theory in his letter to John Middleton Murry, 19 June 1946 (*Letters* 546–47). The depth of his interest in the subject is evidenced not only in *Ape and Essence* but in his study of a real case of sexual hysteria or possession in a seventeenth-century French nunnery, *The Devils of Loudon* (1952). Golding pursues the matter in *The Inheritors* and again in a contemporary setting in *Darkness Visible*.

6. In a letter to his brother, Sir Julian Huxley, 9 June 1952, Huxley counters the idea that there can be no redemption for fallen man:

Everything seems to point to the fact that, as one goes down through the subliminal, one passes through a layer (with which psychologists commonly deal) predominantly evil and making for evil—a layer of "Original Sin," if one likes to call it so—into a deeper layer of "Original Virtue," which is one of peace, illumination, and insight, which seems to be on the fringes of Pure Ego or Atman. (*Letters* 635–36)

WORKS CITED

Baker, James R., ed. *Critical Essays on William Golding*. Boston: Hall, 1988.

———. "Interview with William Golding." *Twentieth Century Literature* 28 (1982): 130–70.

———. "Why It's No Go: A Study of William Golding's *Lord of the Flies*." *Arizona Quarterly* 19 (1963): 393–405.

———. *William Golding: A Critical Study*. New York: St. Martin's, 1965.

———. "William Golding: Two Decades of Criticism." *Critical Essays* 1–11.

Baker, James R., and William Golding. *Correspondence 1962–1993*. Harry Ransom Humanities Research Center. University of Texas at Austin.

Biles, Jack I. *Talk: Conversations with William Golding*. New York: Harcourt, 1970.

Carey, John, ed. *William Golding: The Man and His Books*. London: Faber, 1986.

———. "William Golding Talks to John Carey." 1965. *William Golding: The Man and His Books* 171–89.

Davis, Mike. *Ecology of Fear: Los Angeles and the Imagination of Disaster*. New York: Holt, 1998.

Dunaway, David King. *Huxley in Hollywood*. New York: Harper, 1989.

Forster, E. M. Introduction. *Lord of the Flies*. New York: Coward, 1962. ix–xiii.

Golding, William. "Fable." 1962. *The Hot Gates* 85–101.

———. *The Hot Gates*. London: Faber, 1965.

———. "The Ladder and the Tree." *The Hot Gates* 166–75.

———. *Lord of the Flies*. London: Faber, 1954.

———. "A Moving Target." *A Moving Target* 154–70.

———. *A Moving Target*. New York: Farrar, 1982.

———. Nobel Lecture. 1983. Baker, *Critical Essays* 149–57.

———. *Poems*. London: Macmillan, 1934.

———. "Utopias and Antiutopias." 1977. *A Moving Target* 171–84.

Huxley, Aldous. *Ape and Essence*. 1948. Chicago: Dee, 1992.

———. *Letters of Aldous Huxley*. Ed. Grover Smith. London: Chatto, 1969.

———. *Literature and Science*. New York: Harper, 1963.

Monteith, Charles. "Strangers from Within." Carey, *William Golding: The Man and His Books* 57–63.

Raine, Craig. "Belly Without Blemish: Golding's Sources." Carey, *William Golding: The Man and His Books* 101–09.

Szymborska, Wislawa. *View with a Grain of Sand: Selected Poems*. Trans. Stanislaw Barabczak and Clare Cavanah. New York: Harcourt, 1995.

Time 22 June 1962.

PAUL CRAWFORD

Literature of Atrocity:
Lord of the Flies *and* The Inheritors

We are post-Auschwitz homo sapiens because the evidence, the
photographs of the sea of bones and gold fillings, of children's shoes and
hands leaving a black claw-mark on oven walls, have altered our sense
of possible enactments.

—George Steiner, *Language and Silence: Essays, 1958–1966*

Never shall I forget that night, the first night in camp, which has turned
my life into one long night. . . . Never shall I forget the little faces of
the children, whose bodies I saw turned into wreaths of smoke beneath
a silent blue sky. Never shall I forget those flames which consumed my
faith forever.

—Elie Wiesel, *Night*

In moving beyond the earlier critical recognition that Golding interrogates
English "immunity" from totalitarian violence and the institutionalization of
this brutality in its class structure, we need to show how this attack is achieved
through the use of fantastic and carnivalesque modes, modes that amount
to Juvenalian or noncelebratory satire in opposition to merely universal or
ahistoricist readings. As such, the fantastic is a technique of "literature of
atrocity," significant in terms of the Holocaust experience, and its theme
of demonization joins the noncelebratory carnivalesque in foregrounding

From *Politics and History in William Golding: The World Turned Upside Down*, pp. 50–80. ©
2002 by the Curators of the University of Missouri.

exclusionary gestures toward the Jews. Yet Golding's attack on English constructions of national identity in opposition to Nazism is obstructed by the fabular and hence indirect form of critique in both *Lord of the Flies* (1954) and *The Inheritors* (1955).

Contrary to those who claim the fantastic mode is escapist, Golding uses it in *Lord of the Flies* and *The Inheritors* to interrogate contemporary events and map out the violent superstition behind the exclusion and attempted extermination of the Jewish race that has been viewed historically as an outsider race.[1] In *Lord of the Flies*, fantastic hesitation breaks into the shocking natural explanation that the "Beast" is not an external, supernatural force of evil. The only "Beast" on the island is the fascist group of English adolescent males who kill or attempt to kill outsiders: Simon, Piggy, and Ralph. In their noncelebratory, violent, and fascistic carnivalesque behavior, we witness English schoolboys not only dressing but even acting like Nazis. Alan Sinfield, in his book *Society and Literature*, argues that "the British themselves (in spite of fighting against fascism in the war) were not immune from that very sickness [of regarding human beings as means rather than ends], diagnosed by the existentialists, which had given rise to fascist violence and totalitarianism. William Golding, in particular, challenged the notion that the British were, in some peculiar way, different or special." Sinfield asserts that "when Jack and Roger turn upon Piggy and Simon, they are, for Golding, simply making manifest the brutal and violent pattern of behaviour that underlies Britain's stratified and bullying social order." It is not insignificant that the boys who take up leadership roles, Ralph and Jack, appear to be from a privileged background, perhaps educated at public or boarding schools. In his essay "Schoolboys," Ian McEwan says: "As far as I was concerned, Golding's island was a thinly disguised boarding school." Certainly, as S. J. Boyd suggests, Golding's "deep bitterness at and hatred of the evils of class" are evident in *Lord of the Flies*, as in his later novels, *The Pyramid* and *Rites of Passage*. Boyd claims that there is a "middle-class ambience" to Ralph, who "is not slow to inform Piggy that his father is officer-class," and Jack, who has a "privileged choir-school background." He argues that Piggy himself is very much a "lower-class" outsider whose accent—a "mark of class"—is mocked. Indeed, Piggy's "main persecutor" is Jack who has strong notions of hierarchy because of his privileged education and previous status as head boy of his choir school. Sinfield's and Boyd's insights can be extended to reveal how Golding mixes his critique of the English class system with a critique of English fascism—a dual attack that is achieved through the deployment of fantastic and carnivalesque modes. If this is Golding's aim, we might wonder at the unfair nature of such a linkage, especially since being a member of the privileged classes does not necessarily make you right wing, as Auden, Spender, and Orwell can attest with their radicalism and Marxism during the

1920s and 1930s. In broad terms, however, Golding does seem to critique not just English complacency about being anti- or non-Nazi, but also the English class system that perpetuates so much division and exclusion of "outsiders." This suggests some link between Golding's work and what Blake Morrison calls the "token rebellion" against social privilege by "Movement" writers of the 1950s.[2]

In *The Inheritors*, the "shock tactic" of breaking fantastic hesitation brings a startling recognition that "civilized" human beings commit genocide against those they project as monstrous "ogres" or devils. The Cro-Magnon people, progenitors of Homo sapiens, exterminate a race that, Boyd argues, resembles the Jews. The fantastic tension between the real and unreal in all these novels is strongly evocative of the Holocaust experience and the kind of writing it provoked. This tension was not only a constituent of the Holocaust experience but also an aesthetic technique in "literature of atrocity" that portrayed horrors in a manner that went beyond documentary account.[3] *Lord of the Flies* and *The Inheritors* can be included in this tradition.

The carnivalesque in *Lord of the Flies* and *The Inheritors* is revealed in the suspension and shedding of the stable, ordered conformity of social life. Rules are forgotten for a period of time. In their place comes an enactment of desires and drives that have been repressed. But the carnivalesque behavior in these novels is presented as violently anti-Semitic. This noncelebratory aspect to carnival has been foregrounded by Peter Stallybrass and Allon White's argument that carnival "violently abuses and demonizes" outsiders such as the Jews, whose abjection is promoted by carnival practices such as the eating of pig flesh. The history of carnival's noncelebratory aspect was not lost on Golding in the light of the Jewish Holocaust. Indeed, *Lord of the Flies* is replete with violent carnival images of the pig. Thus, carnival is a site of violence against the weak, the marginalized. This was not missed in Golding's powerful evocation of English "Nazism." The carnivalesque, topsy-turvy world is widely represented in the violent, noncelebratory Dionysianism and scatology of *Lord of the Flies* and *The Inheritors*. This use of the carnivalesque cannot be understood within Mikhail Bakhtin's purely celebratory focus in *Rabelais and His World*.

Although *Lord of the Flies* is a strong attack on notions of English moral superiority vis-à-vis Nazism, such a critique is hampered somewhat by its fabular form. It subtilizes historical reference to Nazi-like group fascism. This obfuscation of historical reference continues in *The Inheritors*, which more generally attacks the notion of "civilization" rather than English moral superiority. However, we might see Golding's attack upon H. G. Wells's racial elitism and the comparison evoked between such views and Nazism as a general warning that the English have no grounds for complacency about their moral distance from atrocities carried out in the Holocaust. In

The Inheritors, the Holocaust is strongly evoked in the racial extermination of Neanderthal Man but is again hampered by Golding's use of fable. As I will demonstrate in the following chapter, this reference to contemporary atrocity and fascism is strengthened in *Pincher Martin* and *Free Fall*, novels that shift progressively from fabular to historical form and delineate more closely the totalitarian personality.

In *Lord of the Flies* particularly, and perhaps more tenuously in *The Inheritors*, Golding's *Vergangenheitsbewältigung*, or "coming to terms with the past," concludes that the English and Nazis are not so different as one might expect. It is this painful evocation of similitude that has been overlooked in earlier critical readings. Both novels should certainly be included in the wider European tradition of "literature of atrocity." That we know Golding himself to have been deeply involved in the war, on intimate terms with its horror, and exercised by expressions not just of Allied moral superiority to Nazis, but of racial violence that broke out in England after the war as well, is significant for a full understanding of his early novels.

In *A Moving Target*, Golding tells of the impact this loss of belief in the "perfectibility of social man" had on *Lord of the Flies*: "The years of my life that went into the book were not years of thinking but of feeling, years of wordless brooding that brought me not so much to an opinion as a stance. It was like lamenting the lost childhood of the world. The theme of *Lord of the Flies* is grief, sheer grief, grief, grief, grief" (*MT*, 163). Despite such commentary from Golding himself, the effect of the war and other social contexts such as racial violence on his writing has drawn scant attention from critics. This emphasis has tended to remain submerged.

Furthermore, there has been no consideration of how Golding, "punch drunk" on atrocity, uses fantastic and carnivalesque modes powerfully to register his grief about this context.[4] The following readings of *Lord of the Flies* and *The Inheritors* aim to redress this lack. These novels, which can be thought of as a pair, make an oblique response to the sociopolitical context of World War II and its aftermath. They provide an uneasy coexistence of the universal and historical.[5]

LORD OF THE FLIES

In *Lord of the Flies*, fantastic and carnivalesque modes are used to subvert postwar English complacency about the deeds of Nazism, particularly the Holocaust. Although oblique, Golding effects an integration between literature and cultural context. This interpretation renegotiates previous critical paradigms that have, for the most part, centered on the timeless or perennial concerns of this novel about a group of English schoolboys, deserted on a South Pacific island following a nuclear third world war, and their descent into ritual savagery and violence.[6] As most critics attest, the characters replicate those in R. M. Ballantyne's *Coral Island* (1858), who in similar straits pull together and overcome external dangers from natives and pirates. Ballantyne's schoolboys exemplify cultural assumptions of imperial superiority and conversely the inferiority of the "fuzzy-wuzzies" or "savages," the indigenous race feared for its cannibalistic practices. For Ballantyne's boys, evil and degenerative nature is outside of them, and the suggestion is that imperial colonialism is beneficent, that the savage can be "saved" by the civilized, Christian Western man. Such inherent and dominant racial elitism is extended in Ballantyne's *Gorilla Hunters* (1861), in which older versions of the same schoolboys, on a scientific expedition in Africa, hardly differentiate between the gorillas and the natives.

Golding subverts these notions of racial and cultural superiority, of scientific progress, notions casting long shadows over atrocities against the Jews carried out in World War II.[7] He draws a parallel between the violent history of English imperialist adolescent masculine culture and the extermination of the Jews. He broaches the grim fact that English colonial warfare against "inferior" races, modeled on hunting and pig sticking, was not a million miles away from the extermination of the Jews. Pig sticking, of course, was at the heart of R. S. S. Baden-Powell's scouting repertoire. Indeed, in 1924 he published *Pig Sticking or Hog Hunting*, a guide for scouts on that very art. Given the whole setting of *Lord of the Flies*, with its reference to Ballantyne and empire boys, Golding appears to have the imperial scouting ethic in his sights. John M. MacKenzie alerts us to the greater reach of such an ethic:

> Africans swiftly became the human substitute for the usual animal prey. Baden-Powell constantly stressed that the scouting and stalking techniques of the Hunt could immediately be transferred to human quarry in times of war. Hunting was also ... a preparation for the violence and brutalities of war. By brutalising themselves in the blood of the chase, the military prepared themselves for an easy adjustment to human warfare, particularly in an age so strongly conditioned by social Darwinian ideas on race.[8]

Golding's critique is not directed exclusively at Nazi war criminality but at the postwar complacency of the English who too readily distanced themselves from what the Nazis did. He reminds them of their long infatuation with social Darwinism. Graham Dawson maps the trajectory of the "soldier hero," an "idealized," militaristic masculinity at the symbolic heart of English national identity and British imperialism. He argues that this "imagining of masculinities" in terms of warfare and adventure pervades the national culture, swamps boyhood fantasies, and, in particular, promotes rigid gendering, xenophobia, and racial violence.[9] In *Lord of the Flies*, Golding's critique of British imperial, proto-fascist history is powerfully registered by the Nazification of English schoolboys: "Shorts, shirts, and different garments they carried in their hands: but each boy wore a square black cap with a silver badge in it. Their bodies, from throat to ankle, were hidden by black cloaks which bore a long silver cross on the left breast and each neck was finished off with a hambone frill" (*LF*, 20–21).

James Gindin insists that Golding's description of Jack's gang— who are English—"deliberately suggests the Nazis." Despite a preference for the universal aspects of Golding's fiction, Leighton Hodson suggests Piggy might represent the "democrat and intellectual," Jack "Hitler," and Roger a "potential concentration camp guard." L. L. Dickson identifies the novel as political allegory, referring to World War II atrocities, particularly those inflicted upon the Jews. Suzie Mackenzie refers to Jack's gang as a "fascist coup" and sees the opposition between democracy and totalitarianism as one of the novel's themes. The "black" garments and caps are, indeed, highly suggestive of the Nazi *Schutzstaffeln*, or SS—the "Black Angels" responsible for the Final Solution. Certainly, Golding's candid comments to John Haffenden suggest this: "I think it's broadly true to say that in *Lord of the Flies* I was saying, 'had I been in Germany I would have been at most a member of the SS, because I would have liked the uniform and so on.'" They also suggest Oswald Mosley's Blackshirts. The silver cross may obliquely bring to mind both the Iron Cross (*Eisernen Kreuz*) and the anti-Semitic swastika. The reference to "hambone" may suggest the skull and crossbones or Death's Head (*Totenkopf*) insignia of the SS. Certainly, the "black cap with a silver badge in it" resembles the black ski caps decorated with the skull and crossbones worn by Hitler's early group of bodyguards, the *Stabswache*. Like Hitler's *Stabswache*, which was made up of twelve bodyguards, Jack's gang or squad is small in number. Nazification of Jack's gang is further amplified by its delight in parades and pageantry, which together with "the unshackling of primitive instincts" and "the denial of reason" is all part of what psychoanalytical theories categorize under the "style and methods of fascism," according to Ernst Nolte.[10] This mingling of Nazism and Englishness is not to be overlooked. Of course, it is the violence of Jack's gang that most powerfully suggests links between them and the Nazis.

The centrality of violence to fascism can be charted, for example, in the appeal that Georges Sorel's apparent valorization of direct violent action in *Reflections on Violence* had for fascist ideologues. Adolescent male aggression, like that of Baden-Powell's pig sticking, is central to Nazism and other versions of fascism or totalitarianism.[11] Silke Hesse contends that because adolescents are "unattached," "mobile," impressionable, physically strong, and easily "directed towards ideals and heroes" on account of unfocused sexuality, the adolescent gang is seen as "a most efficient tool in the hands of a dictator." She concludes: "Of course, Fascism cannot be exhaustively explained with reference to male adolescence. Yet most of the major theories of fascism emphasize the youthful nature of the movement and, even more, its masculinity, in terms both of participation and of traditionally masculine values." Hitler himself has been called "an eternal adolescent" by Saul Friedlander. We may see Jack's gang as an English version of the *Hitlerjugend*, or Hitler Youth, who grew into the Jackboots of the SS, or, indeed, Mosley's New Party (NUPA) Youth Movement. Nicholas Mosley notes that Christopher Hobhouse, of Mosley's New Party, "said he saw the NUPA Youth Movement turning into something like the Nazi SS." Again, Robert Skidelsky argues that as with fascism in general, "the most striking thing about active blackshirts was their youth." In an early review, V. S. Pritchett links *Lord of the Flies* to "the modern political nightmare," and hoped that it was being read in Germany.[12] I would rather suggest that Golding hoped it was being read in Britain and other Allied nations.

For Golding, the dominant and prevalent cultural assumptions found in Ballantyne's stories support the projection of evil onto external objects or beings, such as savages, and in Nazi Germany's case the Jews.[13] But Golding maintains that the darkness or evil that humans fear, and consequently attempt to annihilate, is within the "civilized" English subject. Importantly, Golding appears to have a specific continuity in mind concerning an evil that is not overcome or displaced by English civilization, but is, in effect, a potential that comes hand in hand with it. He connects adolescent English schoolboys from privileged backgrounds, the imperial scouting ethos, and fascism. Thus, whereas in Germany fascism actually sprouted, while in England it did not, there is nonetheless the possibility that the English ethos could easily tip over into fascism (as it does on the island) since privileged education and scouting ideology have much in common with fascism. In order to rebut Ballantyne's projection of evil onto savages, and to draw attention to the ability of the English—with their schooling in fascistic behavior—to mirror Nazism, Golding uses the combined forces of fantastic and carnival modes.

In *Lord of the Flies*, the world of the island is apprehended from the viewpoint of the schoolboys. Initially, they appear to be all-around empire boys, characters in the island adventure tradition that stretches back to Daniel Defoe's *Robinson Crusoe* (1719), Robert Louis Stevenson's *Treasure Island* (1883), and Ballantyne's *Coral Island*. But their preoccupation with natural phenomena and survival rapidly changes to a preoccupation with the unknown and inexplicable. They face beasts and phantoms in a succession of apparently supernatural events. Uncertain and fearful, the boys are subjected to unexplained phenomena. Suspense and hesitation as to the nature of the "beast" follow, and their fear increases accordingly. Although at first it is only the "littluns" that appear affected by this fear, the circle widens until all the boys, including Ralph and Jack, believe in the "Beast." The term *beastie* (*LF*, 39) quickly matures into "beast" (*LF*, 40). Initially, Ralph and Jack hedge their bets by stating that even if there was a beast, they would hunt and kill it. The mysterious disappearance of the boy who had seen the "snake-thing" compounds with the fall of snakelike creepers from an exploding tree and adds fuel to fear. In their beach huts the "littluns" are plagued with nightmares. And in pace with the growing sense of strangeness, the island environment itself becomes equivocal and menacing: "Strange things happened at midday. The glittering sea rose up, moving apart in planes of blatant impossibility; the coral reef and the few, stunted palms that clung to the more elevated parts would float up into the sky, would quiver, be plucked apart, run like raindrops on a wire or be repeated as in an odd succession of mirrors. Sometimes land loomed where there was no land and flicked out like a bubble as the children watched" (*LF*, 63).

Yet this strange transformation of the natural fabric of the coral reef is rationally explained by Piggy as a mirage. But such is the general uncertainty now of what is real and unreal that the fall of darkness is unwelcome. The equivocal nature of familiar things is constantly in view: "If faces were different when lit from above or below—what was a face? What was anything?" (*LF*, 85). The "littluns" are constantly attacked for their fearfulness. Jack calls them "babies and sissies" (*LF*, 90). Piggy proclaims that if these fears continue, they'll be "talking about ghosts and such things next" (*LF*, 91).

But no sooner has Piggy subdued his own and everyone else's doubts by advancing a scientific approach to reality than Phil, another "littlun," speaks of seeing "something big and horrid" in the trees (*LF*, 93). Although Ralph insists that he was experiencing a nightmare, Phil maintains that he was fully awake at the time. Then Percival says he has seen the Beast and that "it comes out of the sea" (*LF*, 96). Thus, doubt and hesitation increase. Maurice says: "'I don't believe in the beast of course. As Piggy says, life's scientific, but we don't know, do we? Not certainly, I mean—'" (*LF*, 96). Then Simon amazes the older boys by admitting that "'maybe there is a beast'" (*LF*, 97). Here, Simon elliptically hints that the Beast might be them: "'We could be sort of . . .' Simon became inarticulate in his effort to express mankind's essential illness" (*LF*, 97). The boys even vote on the issue of whether ghosts inhabit the island. Only Piggy fails to lift his hand. Yet Piggy's claim that ghosts and suchlike do not make sense brings its own fearful counter: "'But s'pose they don't make sense? Not here, on this island? Supposing things are watching us and waiting?' Ralph shuddered violently and moved closer to Piggy, so that they bumped frighteningly" (*LF*, 101).

Schoolboy nerves are further jangled by what follows: "A thin wail out of the darkness chilled them and set them grabbing for each other. Then the wail rose, remote and unearthly, and turned to an inarticulate gibbering" (*LF*, 103). But this noise turns out to be Percival reliving his own personal nightmare. For the moment there is the relief of natural explanation. The Beast from Air we know to be a dead parachutist, shot down over the island while all but Sam and Eric are asleep. This figure is uncannily animate, moving in the wind:

> Here the breeze was fitful and allowed the strings of the parachute to tangle and festoon; and the figure sat, its helmeted head between its knees, held by a complication of lines. When the breeze blew the lines would strain taut and some accident of this pull lifted the head and chest upright so that the figure seemed to peer across the brow of the mountain. Then, each time the wind dropped, the lines would slacken and the figure bow forward again, sinking its head between its knees. (*LF*, 105)

Sam and Eric who are guarding the fire on the mountain hear the strange popping noise of the chute fabric in the wind. Here, hesitation between a supernatural and a natural explanation to the Beast from Air belongs only to the characters. They return and tell the others of the beast on the mountain. Despite a natural though uncanny explanation being available to us, we cannot fail to empathize with the subsequent fear and hesitation experienced by the characters: "Soon the darkness was full of claws, full of the awful unknown and menace" (*LF*, 108). However, the disturbing fact that the only beasts on the island are the boys themselves begins to gain ground: "Simon, walking in front of Ralph, felt a flicker of incredulity—a beast with claws that scratched, that sat on a mountain top, that left no tracks and yet was not fast enough to catch Samneric. Howsoever Simon thought of the beast, there rose before his inward sight the picture of a human at once heroic and sick" (*LF*, 113).

Our own hesitation and uncertainty as readers has begun to shift more clearly toward a natural yet uncanny explanation that the boys are their own monsters. But the breaking of this central hesitation, as to the nature of the Beast, does not exclude further peripheral uncertainty between natural and supernatural events. Apart from the fact that we participate vicariously in the hesitation of Ralph and Jack as they hunt down the figure on the mountain, a "great ape . . . sitting with its head between its knees" (*LF*, 136), the pig's head or "Lord of the Flies" remains on the border between reality and unreality. It is animated: "the Lord of the Flies hung on his stick and grinned" (*LF*, 152). It appears to be a focal point of something supernatural—Evil, the Devil, Satan. Here, peripheral uncertainty is maintained. We hesitate between formulating natural or supernatural explanations. There is a definite sense of the "Lord of the Flies" as a possessed object, and this possession is registered through the visionary viewpoint of Simon. Though Simon has repeatedly been described as mad, hesitation remains as to whether the strange conversation he has with the "Lord of the Flies" is a fit-induced psychosis or not; indeed, we hesitate to ascertain whether psychosis disallows vision. This threshold between Simon's sanity or insanity—a hazy world of split personality, psychosis, and dreams—magnifies fantastic uncertainty, as does, in a more marginal way, the "doubling" of the twins, Samneric. Simon's "madness" has its base in both Todorovian "themes of the self" and carnival foolery. Ironically, it is the death of the equivocal and mysteriously spiritual Simon that erodes fantastic hesitation. His "madness" may also mark the beginnings of Golding's perennial questioning of religious authority throughout his work, a critique most powerfully achieved in *The Spire*.

A final break of the core hesitation concerning the nature of the "Beast" occurs when in Simon's eagerness to explain the human nature of the phenomenon, he unwittingly becomes the "Beast" and is murdered. An exchange of beasts occurs. At this point, we become fully aware of the boys as beasts, in their vicious murder of Simon. This most poignant and telling delivery of an uncanny explanation breaks fantastic hesitation most completely. Then, by way of contrast, the harmless, dead Beast from Air exits the island, though, for the characters, its exit remains a supernatural phenomenon.

The shift, then, is from a predominant hesitation about the nature of the Beast to an uncanny explanation that the boys, and humans in general, project fear onto other groups, individuals, or objects. Even so, the uncanny resolution of who or what really is the Beast on the island remains somewhat equivocal. We are still unsure of a background supernatural activity or influence. The natural and the supernatural seem to coexist, a realm perhaps more akin to Todorov's "fantastic uncanny." Supernaturality is still registered, for example, in the description of Simon's body, which, like that of Lycaon in Homer's *Iliad*, is devoured by "sea monsters."[14]

The characters continue to fear an external beast, with Jack's gang having already tried to propitiate the Beast by making an offering of the pig's head, deciding to "keep on the right side of him" (*LF*, 177). Even rational, scientific Piggy ends up thinking strange sounds outside his hut are made by the Beast: "A voice whispered horribly outside. 'Piggy—Piggy—' 'It's come,' gasped Piggy. 'It's real'" (*LF*, 184). Of course, the sounds are those of Jack and members of his gang stealing the remains of Piggy's glasses. Again, the shift from character hesitation to uncanny natural explanation is effective. Notions of "beast" are transposed onto Jack's gang.

With Piggy's murder, and the "pig hunt" of Ralph under way, clarification of the human nature of the Beast is intensified. The natural as opposed to supernatural interpretation of events is given its final and fullest exposition.

Yet, even so, the uncanny does not completely override the supernatural. The pig's head remains strangely animated, as when the hunted Ralph strays upon it: "[T]he pig's skull grinned at him from the top of a stick. He walked slowly into the middle of the clearing and looked steadily at the skull that gleamed as white as ever the conch had done and seemed to jeer at him cynically. An inquisitive ant was busy in one of the eye sockets but otherwise the thing was lifeless. Or was it?" (*LF*, 204).

Effectively, the fantastic elements in *Lord of the Flies* operate in tandem with those of carnival: they combine to disturb us and subvert dominant cultural notions of the superiority of civilized English behavior. These are the kind of assumptions that buoyed the complacency of England, and indeed other Allied nations, namely, that the atrocities perpetrated by the Nazis were an exclusively German phenomenon. Within the fantastic framework, it is the break from potential supernatural explanation to the chilling and uncanny reality of natural explanation that disturbs us: that the Beast is human, Nazi-like, and English. We participate in the shock that this shift in perspective brings. Instead of externalizing and projecting evil onto objects, phantoms, and supernatural beasts, we confront the reality of human destructiveness. This is registered in both a universal or "perennial" frame and a specific "contemporary" frame, polemicizing the English capacity for Nazism, especially in the light of its exclusionary class system. Although the novel is set in the future, the surface detail, as discussed by earlier critics such as James Gindin, corresponds to World War II. In effect, the fantastic interrogates the postwar "reality" of Britain and its Allies. Yet it does not do so alone.

The shift from the fantastic to the uncanny amplifies carnivalesque elements in the text that symbolically subvert, turn upside down, the vision of civilized, ordered, English behavior. In combination, these elements are the structures through which *Lord of the Flies* disturbs. Yet such is the inherent irreversibility of the narrative structure—its dependence upon hesitation or suspense of explanation—that we cannot read *Lord of the Flies* and register the peculiar shock it delivers a second time.[15] Indeed, there is something particularly "evanescent" about the pure fantastic, not as a genre, but as an element.[16] Ultimately, the shock recognition of the negative, transgressive, "evil" side of not simply human behavior but the behavior of English boys is what is disturbing about *Lord of the Flies*. Such shock recognition is effected by the combination of fantastic and carnival elements. Because of the fantastic's evanescence, we need to recall our first reading when we reexamine *Lord of the Flies*: we must remember our initial shock. We find no relief in the novel's coda at the end of the book when the boys are "saved" by an English naval officer. Our unease shifts from the carnival square of the island to the wider adult world—a world at war for a third time, a world in which the theater of war greatly resembles, in its detail of a paramilitary fascist group, machine-gunning and, in its dead parachutist, the familiar Second World War. It is a world of continuing inhumanity. This open ending is typical of "the satirist's representation of evil as a present and continuing danger."[17] The naval officer marks the gap between ideal British behavior and reality: " 'I should have thought that a pack of British boys—you're all British aren't you?— would have been able to put up a better show than that—I mean—' " (*LF*, 222). The substantiation of the children as British subjects is not superfluous to the novel's meaning. It is fundamental to this novel's ethical interrogation of England, Britain, and its Allies at a specific juncture in history.

One of the most powerful carnivalesque elements in *Lord of the Flies* is that of the pig, which Golding uses symbolically to subvert dominant racial assumptions, in particular toward the Jews, and, universally, toward those humans considered alien or foreign to any grouping. This has alarming relevance to the atrocities committed against the Jews in World War II, yet has been overlooked by Golding critics who have not interpreted Golding's merging of the pig hunt with the human hunt, and the racial significance of eating pig flesh at carnival time.

The pig symbol is developed in *Lord of the Flies* as the pig of carnival time. It is a major motif: as locus of projected evil; as food for the schoolboys; as propitiation to the Beast; but more than anything, as the meat the Jews do not eat. This link between pig flesh and the Jews is reinforced by Golding's choice of the novel's Hebraic title. "Lord of the Flies," or "Lord of Dung," as John Whitley renders it, comes from the Hebrew word *Beelzebub*. As I noted earlier, Peter Stallybrass and Allon White argue that the eating of pig meat during carnival time is an anti-Semitic practice. It is an act of contempt toward the Jews for bringing about the Lenten fast. White asserts: "Meat, especially, pig meat, was of course the symbolic centre of carnival (*carne levare* probably derives from the taking up of meat as both food and sex)." That the pig becomes human and the human being becomes pig in the frenzied, carnivalistic debauchery of Jack and his totalitarian regime is important. The shadowing of pig hunt and human hunt, ending with Simon's and Piggy's deaths, and almost with Ralph's, signifies the link between the pig symbol and the extermination of those considered alien or outsiders. The name "Piggy" does not merely imply obesity. It is the lower-class Piggy who is always on the periphery of the group of schoolboys, always mocked, never quite belonging. As Virginia Tiger points out, "Piggy is killed ... because he is an alien, a pseudo-species."[18] Piggy is alien or foreign, and, as such, he is a focus for violence based on the sort of racial assumptions found in Ballantyne's writing, but it is important to clarify the precise nature of his outsider status. The character name "Piggy" does not, unlike that of Ralph and Jack, feature in Ballantyne's *Coral Island*. Piggy is Golding's creation—a creation that suggests a Jew-like figure: "There had grown tacitly among the biguns the opinion that Piggy was an outsider, not only by accent, which did not matter, but by fat, and ass-mar, and specs, and a certain disinclination for manual labour" (*LF*, 70). We find something of the Jewish intellectual in this description of the bespectacled Piggy, with his different accent and physical feebleness. The stereotype of Jewish feebleness has been a stock in trade of anti-Semites and peddlers of degeneration theories.[19] It is here that we witness the anti-Semitism of carnival. In essence, Golding utilizes the imperial tradition of pig sticking to suggest a continuum between English imperialism and fascism.

Jack's gang persecutes Jew-like Piggy and those it considers outsiders. As a carnival mob they break the normal rules of authority with a willful, transgressive violence that marks a shift from liberal democracy to fascism and anti-Semitism. We witness the demise of Ralph's parliament and the ascendancy of Jack's totalitarian, primitive regime based on savagery, hunting, and primal drives. There follows aggressive sexual debasement and frenzy in the killing of the carnival pig, mimicking anal rape by sticking the spear "'Right up her ass'" (*LF*, 150):

> [T]he sow staggered her way ahead of them, bleeding and mad, and the hunters followed, wedded to her in lust, excited by the long chase and the dropped blood. . . . [S]he squealed and bucked and the air was full of sweat and noise and blood and terror. Roger ran round the heap, prodding with his spear whenever pigflesh appeared. Jack was on top of the sow, stabbing downward with his knife. Roger found a lodgement for his point and began to push till he was leaning with his whole weight. The spear moved forward inch by inch and the terrified squealing became a high pitched scream. Then Jack found the throat and the hot blood spouted over his hands. The sow collapsed under them and they were heavy and fulfilled upon her. (*LF*, 149)[20]

The transgressive connotations of this act are amplified by Robert and Maurice's mimicry of the event. In effect, the whole scene is one of a carnivalesque focus on the lower body parts, particularly that "low" orifice, the anus. As Allon White points out: "Orifices, particularly the gaping mouth, emphasize the open, unfinished, receptive nature of the body at carnival, its daily proximity to flesh and to dung." We may further note scatological details of the "littluns'" toilet habits or Jack's orgasmic fart. Later we witness the "befouled bodies" (*LF*, 172) of Piggy and Ralph. The orifice as mouth or anus is found in several descriptions in *Lord of the Flies*. Arnold Johnston considers that Golding's Swiftian scatology strengthens an accusation that the contemporary world evades home truths about human nature such as the killing of six million Jews.[21] We have the foul breath from the mouth of the dead parachutist and the vast gaping mouth of the pig: "Simon found he was looking into a vast mouth. There was blackness within, a blackness that spread" (*LF*, 159). The theme of "lower body parts," symbolic of misrule, is replicated elsewhere in the novel, as in Ralph's derision of Piggy's asthma: "'Sucks to your ass-mar'" (*LF*, 156). Here, we find the connotations of anal damage or marring and "sucking ass." In the mock pig killing that follows, Robert ends up with a sore backside. The transgression of sodomy is further evidenced in the likely spear rape of Simon on the beach implied by the kind of elliptical references expected of sexual taboo. Although no explicit reference is made to such actions, we must bear in mind previous pig-killing ritual and play:

> "Don't you understand, Piggy? The things we did—"
> "He may still be—"
> "No."
> "P'raps he was only pretending—"
> Piggy's voice tailed off at the sight of Ralph's face.
> "You were outside. Outside the circle. You never really came in. Didn't you see what we—what they did?"
> There was loathing, and at the same time a kind of feverish excitement in his voice.
> "Didn't you see, Piggy?" (*LF*, 173)

We must read this transgressive violence in political terms. Golding is explicitly linking extreme violence with anti-Semitism and the kind of "sadomasochistic homosexuality" that Wilhelm Reich and Erich Fromm considered integral to fascism.[22] Of course, we might argue that Reich and Fromm's analysis is misplaced or erroneous, yet Golding adopts this kind of popularized image. As Roger Eatwell notes: "Images of fascism are part of our culture. For most people, the word 'fascism' conjures up visions of nihilistic violence, war and *Götterdämmerung*. 'Fascism' has a sexual side too: but it is the world of Germanic uniforms and discipline, of bondage and sadomasochism, rather than love."[23] Whether or not "sadomasochistic homosexuality" is a definitive aspect or style of fascism, Golding certainly appears to have drawn on such popularized theories and images, even though such an analysis is ultimately contradictory in terms of the Nazis' exclusionary acts toward homosexuals. Yet it makes sense in that what is feared is persecuted in others.

Jack's gang descends into a meat and sex society, rejecting the liberal democracy of the conch-invoked meetings. Their carnival is filled with dance, chanting, fire, "fun," and irresponsibility—of general festivity. Those routines that reflect responsible society, such as keeping a fire going on the mountain, are neglected. They wear masks and painted faces. They dress and present themselves as a choir, an oxymoronic combination in light of their actions. The rules are challenged, turned upside down—as we have noted, Jack cries "Bollocks" to the rules. They are the "painted fools" of carnival, part of a masquerade (*LF*, 197). Of course, such imagery may equally apply to the imperialist notion of descent into savagery, both carnival "painted fool" and "savage" being "low domains." Golding provides a dystopian representation of carnival that dwells on the pessimistic, violent, and racist seam that has had its place in the history of carnival crowd behavior. He makes a strong connection between this history and contemporary fascism. This aspect of the carnivalesque cannot be appreciated by those "critics who remain purely within the celebratory terms of Bakhtin's formulation," nor those who universalize transgression.[24]

Golding's dystopian representation incorporates noncelebratory carnival decrowning, where a king figure is parodied and derided as the played-out subversion of hierarchical society. This is evident in Jack's thrusting of a pig's decapitated head on a double-pointed spear, as propitiation to the Beast. Such an oxymoronic symbol, referred to in the title of the novel as "Lord of the Flies," reflects the enactment of misrule, the turning upside down of order and authority, of what is crowned. What is "lord" is lord only to flies—those insects of the scatological. This symbol is both fitting to the overall dark or dystopian misrule of carnival in *Lord of the Flies* and the etymological base of "Lord of the Flies" as meaning Beelzebub or Devil.

We may view Golding's use of carnival in *Lord of the Flies* as registering his deeply felt unease about the nature of English "civilization" in light of the events of World War II—of totalitarianism and genocide: a "civilization," among others, that is primed for the total wipeout of nuclear apocalypse. The misrule of carnival in contemporary history is presented as integral not simply to Nazis or other totalitarian regimes but also to England with its divisive and cruel class system. Golding lays bare an alternative view to civilized English behavior, one that counters accepted, familiar, erroneous complacencies. In the isolated focus, in the "carnival square" of Golding's island, carnival affirms that everything exists on the threshold or border of its opposite.[25] In effect, Golding explodes a Nazi–English or them–us opposition.

So, to summarize, noncelebratory or Juvenalian satire with its combined fantastic and carnivalesque in *Lord of the Flies* subverts the view that the "civilized" English are incapable of the kind of atrocities carried out by the Nazis during World War II. These modes are deployed in the novel as an attack on what Golding deems to be a complacent English democracy, and its masculinity and classist attitudes in particular, in relation to the rise of National Socialism.

THE INHERITORS

The Inheritors is Golding's second published novel and is in many ways thematically coextensive with *Lord of the Flies*. Like *Lord of the Flies*, it evokes a carnivalesque world with the violent actions of the Cro-Magnon people, the supposed progenitors of Homo sapiens, who annihilate the last of the Neanderthal race. As in his first novel, Golding explodes the myth of cultured, civilized humankind. From the distant "past" (*The Inheritors*) and "future" (*Lord of the Flies*), the two novels carry a similar message: humankind is damaged and flawed; it is predisposed toward violence to "outsiders" and transgression. Carnival, then, is not simply a ritual phenomenon or an immanent literary form; it is rooted in the consciousness of humans. It is through the use of carnivalesque elements that Golding symbolically subverts those assumptions that mark humankind as civilized and constructive, not simply in a universal or "perennial" sense, but also in the specific and powerful sense of the context of "present conditions"—those of World War II events.

In *The Inheritors*, as other critics have noted, Golding subverts certain cultural assumptions evident in H. G. Wells's *Outline of History* (1920) and "Grizzly Folk" (1927).[26] In these writings, Wells projects a view of Neanderthal Man as an inferior wild beast and Cro-Magnon Man, his evolutionary supplanter (now questioned), as superior, intelligent, and civilizing. But again, Golding is concerned to highlight the destructive quality that comes with intelligence. Furthermore, he portrays the Neanderthals as sensitive and gentle and bound to their kin by a collective consciousness. In his book *The Neandertal Enigma*, James Shreeve argues that "it is not the triumph of a superior race that drives the plots" of *The Inheritors* and Jean Auel's later work *The Clan of the Cave Bear* (1980), but "the loss of an alternative one."[27]

This representation of the Neanderthals is in contrast to the aggressive intelligence of the Cro-Magnon, a race of people critically flawed, as Ted Hughes suggests, by the premature birth of their offspring. Here, Hughes refers to rather speculative anthropological theory that the skeleton of Cro-Magnon woman had a greatly reduced birthing canal resulting in premature births. Thus, before Cro-Magnon Man, hominids may well have had a longer gestation period. The suggestion is that Neanderthal Man's instinctive potential and collective consciousness, unlike Cro-Magnon, had time to fully develop. However, Hughes admits such a theory throws only oblique and speculative light upon the novel.[28]

The Inheritors responds more generally to World War II atrocities by attacking notions of Western rather than purely English "civilization." Lok and seven other Neanderthals, having survived the Great Fire, are on their way to higher ground for the duration of the summer. Ravaged by natural disasters on that journey, they fall foul of the Cro-Magnons, or New People, who kidnap and kill members of the tribe. The New People view their victims (in much the same way as H. G. Wells in *The Outline of History* or "The Grisly Folk") as devils or ogres. We witness both what Bernard Bergonzi calls "the original act of colonialist exploitation" by the West and an extermination or genocide that suggests the Jewish Holocaust. The production and publication of this novel, like *Lord of the Flies*, are contiguous to this "defining event of our time."[29] Although set in the distant past, and lacking the surface details specific to World War II found in *Lord of the Flies*, *The Inheritors* powerfully suggests the sociopolitical context of contemporary genocide.

Fantastic hesitation creates uncertainty as to what forces are behind the insidious extermination of Lok's Neanderthal tribe. Natural explanation that it is the New People, progenitors of Homo sapiens, who are "racially cleansing" the territory of "ogres" subverts the notion of evolutionary progress and evokes the Holocaust. Again, Golding links masculinity with violent extermination. The patriarchal New People wipe out the matriarchal Neanderthal tribe. S. J. Boyd is keen to link the New People's actions to Nazi genocide: "In this context we should remember how in our own century an attempt was made to exterminate the Jewish race, a race identified by Hitler, as so often before, as a threat to the progress of civilization and the all-round bogey men of history, the sort of role Wells gives to the Neanderthal men in the epigraph to the novel." Boyd finds Lok's tribe "reminiscent of the Jews" and locates Jewishness in Mal's account of their genealogy and Fa's mournful words that owe much to the Psalms or the Lamentations of Jeremiah: "'They have gone over us like a hollow log. They are like a winter'" (*IN*, 198). Here, Fa links the atrocities committed by the New People and the image of "a smear on the smoothed earth that had been a slug" (*IN*, 198). Again, Boyd says: "Though it deals with prehistory, *The Inheritors* shares with *Lord of the Flies* a post-nuclear colouring" in its evocation of the Holocaust. Jack's gang destroys its island world by fire. The New People resemble "'a fire in the forest'" (*IN*, 197).[30]

The Inheritors, then, reiterates the theme of racial extermination found in *Lord of the Flies*. The carnivalesque practices of the New People mark the exclusionary, orgiastic violence of an advanced race toward those it considers inferior or "alien." This is powerfully demonstrated in the death of the child Liku who is roasted and eaten by the New People. She becomes a trace presence in the smoky air. Here, Golding appears to gesture toward those furnaces of the Holocaust that consumed great numbers of children. We also witness the kind of disbelief the Jews felt concerning their fate in Lok's failure to comprehend the New People's destructive intentions.

Golding's use of the fantastic takes a sophisticated turn in *The Inheritors*. It is manifest in the limited, equivocal point of view of the protagonist focalizer, Lok. We look over the shoulder, as it were, of a limited, unformed consciousness and are barely allowed the comfort of omniscient narration.

This equivocating process ensures that hesitation follows. Like Lok and his people, we build up uncertain, provisional pictures about events taking place:

> "I have a picture."
> He freed a hand and put it flat on his head as if confining the images that flickered there.
> "Mal is not old but clinging to his mother's back. There is more water not only here but along the trail where we came. A man is wise. He makes men take a tree that has fallen and—"
> His eyes deep in their hollows turned to the people imploring them to share a picture with him. He coughed again, softly. The old woman carefully lifted her burden.
> At last Ha spoke.
> "I do not see this picture." (*IN*, 15–16)

Through an uncertain terrain, Lok and his people make their way, struggling to piece concepts and ideas together, often given to elliptical, anthropomorphic, and protoreligious identification of objects. For example, a collection of icicles is viewed as an "'ice woman'" (*IN*, 27). Virginia Tiger notes: "Both Lok's primitive perspective and the omniscient authorial descriptions deliberately limit any formulation or deduction or interpretation of events . . . concealing familiar elements in anthropomorphic images. Thus the cliff is described as leaning out 'looking for its own feet in the water,' the island 'rearing' against the fall is a 'seated giant' . . ."[31]

We face constant equivocation of natural phenomena and explanation. It is difficult to ascertain exactly what Lok and the others see and experience. We constantly face the uncertainty of sharing pictures to explain events. Ha disappears mysteriously and Lok's people refer to the "other men." Who these "other men" are we do not know. Still everything remains difficult to decode. Lok goes in search of Ha and comes across a strange rock that changes shape:

> As he watched, one of the farther rocks began to change shape. At one side a small bump elongated then disappeared quickly. The top of the rock swelled, the hump fined off at the base and elongated again then halved its height. Then it was gone. . . . He screwed up his eyes and peered at the rock to see if it would change again. There was a single birch tree that overtopped the other trees on the island, and was now picked out against the moon-drenched sky. It was very thick at the base, unduly thick, and as Lok watched, impossibly thick. The blob of darkness seemed to coagulate round the stem like a drop of blood on a stick. It lengthened, thickened again, lengthened. It moved up

the birch tree with slothlike deliberation, it hung in the air high above the island and the fall. It made no noise and at last hung motionless. Lok cried out at the top of his voice; but either the creature was deaf or the ponderous fall erased the words that he said. (*IN*, 79–80)

Only gradually do we focalize through Lok's limited consciousness and recognize that the mysterious "other" is early humankind, and suffer the uncanny realization that the strange disappearance of Ha and death of Mal are due to these "other men." Like Lok, we suddenly stand before intelligent, violent humankind—ourselves made unfamiliar. Indeed, both Lok and Fa can see the smoke on the island, evidence of the "other" presence. Lok moves close to the water in the hope of seeing the "new man or the new people" (*IN*, 99). Our gradual shift from a supernatural explanation to events that are uncanny is stark as, in Lok's absence, actions unfold at the overhang. The "other" have crossed the water and plundered the tribe, killing the old woman and Nil, and kidnapping Liku and the newborn. Lok hears the strange sounds of the "other": "He could hear their speech and it made him laugh. The sounds made a picture in his head of interlacing shapes, thin and complex, voluble and silly, not like the long curve of a hawk's cry, but tangles like line weed on the beach after a storm, muddied as water. This laugh-sound advanced through the trees towards the river" (*IN*, 104).

We suddenly, like Lok, stand before intelligent, violent humankind—the New People. We half-recognize them as ourselves. Yet also like Lok, we fail to comprehend fully the events witnessed. As we do, our shock and disturbance are intense:

The bushes twitched again. Lok steadied by the tree and gazed. A head and a chest faced him, half-hidden. There were white bone things behind the leaves and hair. The man had white bone things above his eyes and under the mouth so that his face was longer than a face should be. The man turned sideways in the bushes and looked at Lok along his shoulder. A stick rose upright and there was a lump of bone in the middle. Lok peered at the stick and the lump of bone and the small eyes in the bone things over the face. Suddenly Lok understood that the man was holding the stick out to him but neither he nor Lok could reach across the river. He would have laughed if it were not for the echo of the screaming in his head. The stick began to grow shorter at both ends. Then it shot out to full length again.

The dead tree by Lok's ear acquired a voice.

"Clop." (*IN*, 106)

When Lok pursues the kidnapped Liku and New One across the river by climbing into the trees, he is delivered into a topsy-turvy world where he sees "random flashes of the sun below and above" (*IN*, 107) and is literally turned upside down when the branches give way: "They swayed outwards and down so that his head was lower than his feet" (*IN*, 107). In this inverted world he sees his reflected "double" and experiences "Lok, upside down" (*IN*, 108). In a fantastic "dreamlike slowness," he spies the horrific remains of the murdered old woman floating up to the surface and disappearing (*IN*, 109).

Like Lok, our view of events is turned upside down. By gradual recognition of natural phenomena, over the shoulder of Lok's limited consciousness, we shift from a fantastic world, where there is hesitation between explanations, where things are half-apprehended, barely ordered, to an increasingly clear resolution that we have been viewing this world through the eyes of Neanderthal Man—that the "others" are indeed the original colonists, our own progenitors, Cro-Magnon Man, and that these New People, like ourselves, are powerful, intelligent, and violent. It is this shift that, again, is mutually amplified with the carnivalesque elements that follow, and in combination renders unease and shock recognition as to the destructive nature of this first example of human civilization, and indeed the irony of intellectual evolution when a full account of humankind's history of violence, war, and destruction is made.[32]

The novel, then, presents a topsy-turvy account of human nature and registers a symbolic subversion of dominant cultural assumptions of humankind as superior, as morally progressive, beneficent, cultured colonizer. The disturbing nature of this discovery is further amplified by a description of Lok as a beastlike creature from a perspective similar to that of Wells in "The Grisly Folk" or *The Outline of History*. It is a perspective we cannot but reject as limited and prejudiced:

> The red creature began to sniff round by the fire. Its weight was on the knuckles and it worked with its nose lowered almost to the ground. . . . It was a strange creature, smallish, and bowed. The legs and thighs were bent and there was a whole thatch of curls on the outside of the legs and arms. The back was high, and covered over the shoulders with curly hair. Its feet and hands were broad, and flat, the great toe projecting inwards to grip. The square hands swung down to the knees. (*IN*, 218–19)

Golding effects a decrowning of the sacred assumption that one race is superior to another, a view that has proved useful to imperial colonialism and those wishing to carry out genocide. This decrowning is powerfully wrought in the ironic title to the novel: *The Inheritors*. The notion of inheritance is made topsy-turvy by what Tiger describes as the "violence, rapaciousness, and corruption" of the New People. She continues: "From the point of view of innocence, the biological evolution is a moral devolution, as ironic as the Wells epigraph or the Beatitude referred to in the title that the 'meek shall inherit the world.'"[33]

Constantly thwarted by their stumbling intelligence, Lok and Fa search for Liku and the New One who have been kidnapped by the New People. From the summit of a dead tree they study the behavior of the Cro-Magnon people, who have formed a camp below. From this unusual, catascopic viewpoint or vantage point—a feature of Bakhtin's inventory of Menippean satire—they witness a "violent celebration of the body, dirt, eating, drinking, and sexuality."[34] Although Lok and Fa's position may resemble that of the Yahoos in Swift's *Gulliver's Travels* (1726), it is the New People below who perform the "lower body" rites of carnival.[35]

The New People gather around their fire, are caught up in stag mimicking and hunting, and are surrounded by darkness: "Their Promethean fire itself metamorphoses darkness, makes the island so impenetrably dark that the night sight of Lok and Fa is temporarily lost."[36] As with *Lord of the Flies*, *The Inheritors* incorporates the carnivalesque motif of transformative fire, hideous in its shadow casting: "The people drank and Lok could see how the bones of their throats moved in the firelight" (*IN*, 166).

In this carnivalesque firelight the New People are transformed: "They were shouting, laughing, singing, babbling in their bird speech, and the flames of their fire were leaping madly with them" (*IN*, 170). Furthermore, the New People "were like the fire, made of yellow and white, for they had thrown off their furs and wore nothing but the binding of skin round their waists and loins" (*IN*, 171). Thus, the New People descend into drunkenness with a fermented honey drink that smells like "decay" (*IN*, 160), and perform brutal, violent sex. The camp yields a stench of filth and sweat. Orifices are open. The fat woman's "head was back, throat curved, mouth open and laughing" (*IN*, 171).

The Bacchanalian orgy, as in *Lord of the Flies*, blurs meat eating and sex. We find Tuami's "mouth creeping, his fingers playing, moving up as though he were eating her flesh" (*IN*, 171). Again, we find a vantage point from the dead tree: "Lok peered through the leaves again for the meaning of the words and he was looking straight at the fat woman's mouth. She was coming towards the tree, holding on to Tuami, and she staggered and screeched with laughter so that he could see her teeth. They were not broad and useful for eating and grinding; they were small and two were longer than the others. They were teeth that remembered wolf" (*IN*, 173–74).

The New People's sexual orgy is drunken, violent, and wild: "A man and a woman were fighting and kissing and screeching and another man was crawling round and round the fire like a moth with a burnt wing. Round and round he went, crawling, and the other people took no notice of him but went on with their noise" (*IN*, 172). It is fierce and vampirish and cannibalistic: "Tuami was not only lying with the fat woman but eating her as well for there was black blood running from the lobe of her ear" (*IN*, 175). And later: "Their fierce and wolflike battle was ended. They had fought it seemed against each other, consumed each other rather than lain together so that there was blood on the woman's face and the man's shoulder" (*IN*, 176). This meat and sex orgy is most shocking when we realize, over the shoulder of Lok's limited intelligence, that Liku has been cooked and eaten. Lok can smell her around the campsite, but cannot grasp that smell's significance. Her presence is carried in the smoke: "There was no smell of Liku unless a sort of generalized smell in his nostrils so faint as to be nothing" (*IN*, 182).

Later at the deserted camp, Lok comes across the stag's head that "watched Lok inscrutably. . . . The whole haunch of a stag, raw but comparatively bloodless, hung from the top of the stake and an opened stone of honey-drink stood by the staring head" (*IN*, 199). The stag's head is reminiscent of the pig's head in *Lord of the Flies*. The sense of decrowning here is similar. The irony of the novel's title, *The Inheritors*, is further established in a scene of parodic drunkenness, where Lok and Fa inherit the honey drink from the New People and as a result suffer a similar sexual and aggressive incontinence, followed swiftly by a hangover. The *mésalliance* of the "savage" inheriting savagery from the progenitors of humankind is powerfully subversive. As in *Lord of the Flies*, Golding's carnival is a "carnival of hate."[37] In both novels, a less celebratory and more dystopian carnivalesque powerfully creates a topsy-turvy world that critiques the arrogant and culturally elitist discourses found in the texts of Ballantyne and Wells. Golding's intertextual strategy rebuts the texts of these writers. In effect, the combined force of carnivalesque and fantastic elements may be viewed as the engine house to Golding's early art—his attack on racial elitism.

My analysis of the subversive function of carnivalesque and fantastic elements offers a more radical reading of *Lord of the Flies* and *The Inheritors* than has previously been attempted. These novels undermine notions of racial superiority. They interrogate human civilization in the wake of World War II atrocities. Combined carnivalesque and fantastic elements amplify a shock recognition of humankind's transgressive nature. These elements are integral, pivotal structures through which these novels interrogate contemporary "reality," its ideologies and cultural assumptions. They supply the impact of reversal, of turning established ideologies and viewpoints on their heads.

It is important that these novels are not "ethnically cleansed" by timeless approaches to Golding's work. The violence and hatred that "civilized" cultures perpetrate against the "lower" domains, such as the Jews and homosexuals (of growing importance to Golding), define their "higher" forms of expression and organization. The foot on the Jewish head both raises and simultaneously exposes the "higher" cultural body as fueled by exploitation, cruelty, and even genocide. With Golding we are made painfully aware of a "not-so-jolly" relativity. We need to recognize how these texts "preserve the face of violence for the distant future," and add their symbolic friction, if we are optimistic, in the production of cultural knowledge.[38]

There is a clear parallel suggested between the Cro-Magnon Men's atrocities and those carried out by the Nazis. But in effect, Golding attacks the whole mask of Western "civilization" that covers a long history of racial violence. Golding exposes this racial violence in his satire. Such a process has been highlighted by Michael Seidel who, influenced by René Girard, argues that the satirist succeeds in "bringing violations to the surface" that otherwise would have been covered up by "civilization."[39]

Golding, then, is among those writers who concern themselves with contemporary history and its atrocities. As such, his early fiction warrants examination not simply in terms of its "perennial" status, its focus upon the human condition *sub specie aeternitatis*, but in terms of its "present" contemporary relevance as well. Whereas both frames or foci coexist in his work, critics have tended to avoid the latter. As a result, readings of Golding have lost a vitality that the novels themselves afford. The dominant critical focus on the fabular and mythic framing of Golding's fiction, on its timelessness, has robbed those dependent on critical guidance of a more energetic reading. It has delivered a hemiplegic Golding. It has performed a critical stroke that has enervated the fascinating political and historical side to his fiction. Here, I hope to have revivified this aspect of Golding's work and suggested that the current practice of reading his fiction needs to be changed. Golding should be considered part of a wider movement of writers in the tradition of atrocity writing.

His early novels attack the "civilized" English for divorcing themselves from the kind of violent, adolescent masculinity that has been so much a part of the phenomenon of fascism. The novels are rooted in the historical moment of their production. Golding, the noncelebratory satirist, exposes English Fascist Man in the aftermath of World War II and the Jewish Holocaust. This historicized and politicized reading of Golding's "literature of atrocity" brings a new, radical understanding of his fiction. The timelessness of his work is countered. We no longer suffer that old formalist exclusion of history from literature. We witness Golding's determination to "'chasten, chastise, reform, and warn'" the "civilized" English that the black cap not only fits, but they are as likely as anyone to wear it.[40]

The Holocaust, then, is central to Golding's early fiction, although he avoids spurious documentary and is skeptical about the possibility of rendering a detailed historical account. Of Belsen, Hiroshima, and other atrocities, he asserts: "These experiences are like the black holes in space. Nothing can get out to let us know what it was like inside. It was like what it was like and on the other hand it was like nothing else whatsoever. We stand before a gap in history. We have discovered a limit to literature" (*MT*, 102). He can offer, then, only a frail memorialization of such atrocity—pointing to it yet not able to describe it in any full way. There has been much debate about who has the right to represent the Holocaust, and indeed about the very notion of the possibility of speaking or writing about such an event. Early on in the debate about the dangers of aestheticizing the Holocaust, Theodor Adorno claimed that writing poetry after Auschwitz is barbaric. He later revised this notion in his *Negative Dialectics*: "Perennial suffering has as much right to expression as a tortured man has to scream; hence it may have been wrong to say that after Auschwitz you could no longer write poems."[41] But his early comment became the "best-known point of reference" for those attempting to negotiate the limits of representing the Holocaust or, rather, the appropriateness of silence as a response to it.[42] Silence was preferred by those, like George Steiner, Elie Wiesel, and Irving Howe, who considered that the aestheticization of the Holocaust, especially by "long-distance observers and second- or third-generation writers," might erode the historical facts.[43] Yet there was a great deal at stake in all of this. Opting for silence appeared to strengthen the arguments of deniers that the Holocaust ever happened. The whole issue of countering the deniers and moving beyond the difficulties of presenting the "unrepresentable" or speaking the "unspeakable" was taken up in several publications by Jean-François Lyotard. What is fascinating about Lyotard's contribution is how the Holocaust is both implicated in the advent of postmodernism and subjected to this era's arch-relativism, especially in relation to historical knowledge.[44]

Lyotard argues that the Holocaust art "does not say the unsayable, but says that it cannot say it."[45] In essence, we cannot know or represent the Holocaust. Despite the fact that it is "unsayable" and that, for Lyotard, verification that Jews were exterminated by Nazis in gas chambers is impossible, he says that "the silence imposed on knowledge does not impose the silence of forgetting." He likens the fate of Holocaust witnesses to people who survive an earthquake that has destroyed all the instruments capable of measuring it. They would still have "the idea of a very great seismic force" or a "complex feeling" about what had happened. The Holocaust left too great a seismic shudder in the feelings and accounts of those who survived to allow that complex event to be wished away. We can trace this shudder in the writings of Golding so as to counter those who would wish away this aspect to his work, even though Golding was not literally a "survivor" of the Holocaust.

For Lyotard, but of course not for positivist historians such as Pierre Vidal-Naquet and Lucy Dawidowich, "competence" of historical knowledge is "impugned" by the fact that the instruments to "measure" the Holocaust have been destroyed. He argues that historians should focus on the "metareality" of the destruction of reality and the "feeling" that remains when testimony is not available. Lyotard, of course, examines the problems of obtaining a definitive history of what occurred in "Auschwitz" as a means of demonstrating "the impossibility of any single, integrated discourse about history and politics." According to Dominick LaCapra, Lyotard enacts "a massive metalepsis [substitution] whereby the Shoah is transcoded into postmodernism." LaCapra himself situates the Holocaust as a "point of rupture" between modernism and postmodernism. Similarly, Golding's fiction shifts from early representations of the Holocaust that struggle to move out of fabular evasion and make a "frank encounter" with the subject matter to fiction that "encrypts" this trauma in postmodern concerns about the status of literature, language, and meaning.[46]

In *Lord of the Flies* and *The Inheritors*, it may be that Golding wished to avoid effecting any kind of representation of the Holocaust that might appear to be what Lawrence Langer calls an "unprincipled violation of a sacred shrine."[47] Or maybe Golding was aware of the difficulty of "presenting the unrepresentable." Hence, his reference is somewhat masked by a universal or fabular setting of these novels. He does, however, strengthen his reference to broad or popular conceptions of fascism and the totalitarian personality in *Pincher Martin*, *Free Fall*, and *Darkness Visible*, perhaps to compensate for making too oblique a reference in these early more fabular novels. Yet even so, as we shall see, the later novels only barely connect with the "Final Solution" as such.

In conclusion, then, Golding surely knew that his representations of the Holocaust, and indeed fascism, were necessarily limited and partial. Yet he obviously wanted to make some kind of intervention with what he perceived as complacency among the English in particular about their moral distance from Nazism. This focus on English complacency is evident in Nigel Williams's comment on Golding's view of *Lord of the Flies*: "He once said to me that one of the main aims of his book was to tell the story of the breakdown of English parliamentary democracy. 'Don't make them into little Americans, will you,' he added." Golding does not attempt to be comprehensive or detailed in his reference to the Holocaust as he needs only to suggest the conceptual territories of this genocide and fascism to effect his satire. Golding knew that, like himself, the postwar reader would have sufficient familiarity with German prison camps and the Holocaust through a plethora of accounts. Like Clamence in Albert Camus's *La Chute* (1956), Golding did not need to play the historian here: "We children of this half-century don't need a diagram to imagine such places."[48]

In terms of the Holocaust, Golding placed himself within what Langer calls the "culture of dread" as opposed to the "culture of consolation." We cannot accuse Golding of any sentimental aestheticization of the Holocaust or the Nazi "Final Solution." We may accuse him of being a "long-distance" writer like Sylvia Plath, D. M. Thomas, and William Styron, but not a barbaric one. Indeed, as Berel Lang admits rather reluctantly, there is some justification in the "barbarism" of imaginative writing about the Holocaust, even "bad" or "false" contributions, "as a defence against still greater barbarism—against denial, for example, or against forgetfulness."[49] Golding's early fiction offers a defense against this barbarity of amnesia and denial. His later fiction moves away from what may be thought of as a grief response and encrypts the Holocaust in his reflection on "post-Auschwitz" life and meaning. Having instantiated the massive "seismic" force of the Holocaust in his early fiction, he traces its aftershocks or aftermath as they threaten comforting epistemologies and rationality itself with further collapse and fragmentation. Indeed, the archrelativization of meaning we call postmodernism has spawned a concerted attack on the historicity of the Holocaust. The Holocaust is treated as merely textual, as something that can be deconstructed. Part of this effort involves the extreme claim by deniers of the Holocaust that the mass killing of Jews in World War II was a hoax. In this sense, we might consider the Holocaust as heavily influencing the postwar skepticism that eventually developed into what we broadly call postmodernism yet subsequently fell foul of its more hard-boiled deconstructive and antifoundationalist pronouncements. Or, in other words, the Holocaust intensified the climate for its denial.

NOTES

1. For a useful summary of critical positions that support or oppose the notion of "escape" in the fantastic, see Siebers, *The Romantic Fantastic*, 43–45.

2. Sinfield, *Society and Literature, 1945–1970*, 35–36; McEwan, "Schoolboys," 158; Boyd, *Novels of Golding*, 10–11; Morrison, *The Movement*, 77.

3. Boyd, *Novels of Golding*, 40–42. See Langer, *Literary Imagination*, 43–49. Langer asserts: "To establish an order of reality in which the unimaginable becomes imaginatively acceptable exceeds the capacities of an art devoted entirely to verisimilitude; some quality of the fantastic, whether stylistic or descriptive, becomes an essential ingredient of *l'univers concentrationnaire*. Indeed, those who recorded details painstakingly in an attempt to omit none of the horror may have been unwittingly guilty of ignoring precisely the chief source of that horror—existence in a middle realm between life and death with its ambiguous and inconsistent appeals to survival and extinction, which continuously undermined the logic of existence without offering any satisfactory alternative" (43).

4. Oldsey and Weintraub, *Art of Golding*, 173. Oldsey and Weintraub consider the branding of Golding's vision "by acts of superior whites in places like Belsen and Hiroshima" as the core unifying thesis behind his early novels (45). Dick suggests that Golding's focus on the evil side of humankind in *Lord of the Flies* resembles media presentations of Nazi atrocities that do not tell the whole story (*William Golding* [1967], 34–35).

5. On the paradox of timeless novels that remain contemporary, see Oldsey and Weintraub, *Art of Golding*, 11, 43–45, 173; and Josipovici, *World and Book*, 236. Dickson,

developing the work of Edwin Honig and Angus Fletcher, evaluates allegory along the lines of what Scholes has termed "modern fabulation," which "tends away from the representation of reality but returns toward actual life by way of ethically controlled fantasy" (see Dickson, *Modern Allegories*, 1; and Scholes, *The Fabulators*, 11–14).

6. According to Crompton: "The book originally began with a description of the atomic explosion [cut prior to publication] out of which the children escaped, an event recapitulated exactly but in miniature by the fire that is destroying the island at the end of the book" (*View from the Spire*, 96). This is ratified by Golding who told John Haffenden that the "picture of destruction" in the fire scene "was an Atomic one; the island had expanded to be the whole great globe" ("William Golding: An Interview," 10).

7. S. Laing argues that "the reversal of texts of high bourgeois optimism" in Golding's early work, and focus on the irrational, follows Golding's participation in and reflection on World War II. He refers to Golding's revelation of "history as nightmare" ("Novels and the Novel," 241).

8. MacKenzie, "The Imperial Pioneer and Hunter and the British Masculine Stereotype in Late Victorian and Edwardian Times," 188.

9. See Dawson, *Soldier Heroes: British Adventure, Empire, and the Imagining of Masculinities*.

10. Gindin, *William Golding*, 22; Hodson, *William Golding*, 32. See also Medcalf, *William Golding*, 10, 13. Dickson, *Modern Allegories*, 24–25. McCarron has written that the novel "would not have been written had Belsen and Auschwitz never existed, or indeed had Dresden never been bombed by the Allies" (*William Golding*, 4). Mackenzie, "Return of the Natives," 40; see Rupert Butler, *The Black Angels*; Haffenden, "William Golding: An Interview," 11; see E. W. W. Fowler, *Nazi Regalia*, 150; Nolte, *Three Faces of Fascism*, 39.

11. The significance of male youth to fascist movements has been noted by historians and theorists of totalitarianism. See Hannah Arendt, *The Origins of Totalitarianism*, 227, 366, 377, 399; Renzo de Felice, *Interpretations of Fascism*, 179; Nolte, *Three Faces of Fascism*, 618; Noel O'Sullivan, *Fascism*, 74–75; and Alice Yaeger Kaplan, *Reproductions of Banality: Fascism, Literature, and French Intellectual Life*, 22. For a detailed examination of the importance of young male gangs to fascism, see Silke Hesse, "Fascism and the Hypertrophy of Male Adolescence," 157–75. She writes: "I would suggest that, rather than patriarchy, the very different structure of a gang of adolescent youths is the model of Fascist society" (172).

12. Hesse, "Fascism and Male Adolescence," 172, 175; Saul Friedlander quoted in Gerhard Rempel, *Hitler's Children: The Hitler Youth and the SS*, 1; Mosley, *Rules of the Game: Sir Oswald and Lady Cynthia Mosley, 1896–1933*, 211; Skidelsky, *Oswald Mosley*, 317; Pritchett, "Secret Parables," 37.

13. Hitler described the Jews as bloodsucking vampires (see *Mein Kampf*, 296).

14. See *The Iliad* 21.135–40: "Lie there, Lycaon! let the fish surround / Thy bloated corse, and suck thy gory wound: / There no sad mother shall thy funerals weep, / But swift Scamander roll thee to the deep, / Whose every wave some wat'ry monster brings, / To feast unpunish'd on the fat of kings" (in Pope, "The Dunciad," 466).

15. Todorov, *Fantastic*, 89.

16. Brooke-Rose, *Rhetoric of the Unreal*, 63.

17. Connery and Combe, *Theorizing Satire*, 5.

18. Whitley, *Golding: "Lord of the Flies,"* 43; see Stallybrass and White, *Politics of Transgression*, 54; White, *Carnival, Hysteria, and Writing*, 170; Tiger, *Dark Fields*, 63.

19. See Sander Gilman, *Franz Kafka: The Jewish Patient*. See also Gilman, *The Jew's Body*.

20. Stallybrass and White note that the Latin etymology of pig, *porcus* or *porcellus*, refers to female genitalia and that in Attic comedy, prostitutes were called pig merchants (*Politics of Transgression*, 44–45).

21. White, *Carnival, Hysteria, and Writing*, 170; see Johnston, *Of Earth and Darkness*, 38, 45.

22. See James A. Gregor, *Interpretations of Fascism*, 50, 55, 68, 74.

23. Eatwell, *Fascism: A History*, xix.

24. Stallybrass and White, *Politics of Transgression*, 191, 19. For early examples of crowd violence in carnival, see Ladurie, *Carnival in Romans*; Buchanan Sharp, *In Contempt of All Authority: Rural Artisans and Riot in the West of England, 1586–1660*; and Charles Tilly, *Charivaris, Repertoires, and Politics*. It is important to note the relevance of crowds or masses to theories on fascism. For a summary of the work of Gustave le Bon, José Ortega y Gasset, Emil Lederer, Sigmund Neumann, Eric Hoffer, Hannah Arendt, and William Kornhauser on the phenomenon of crowds or masses, see J. Gregor, *Interpretations of Fascism*, 78–127. See also Eatwell, *Fascism*, 4–10.

25. On the carnival square, see Bakhtin, *Problems of Dostoevsky's Poetics*, 128–29, 168–69.

26. See, for example, Hodson, *William Golding*, 39–42.

27. James Shreeve, *The Neandertal Enigma: Solving the Mystery of Modern Human Origins*, 6–7. Although Shreeve prefers to drop the *h* in *Neanderthal*, I keep the more familiar spelling.

28. Hughes, "Baboons and Neanderthals: A Re-Reading of *The Inheritors*," 162. See also *Pincher Martin*, where Golding describes man as follows: "He is a freak, an ejected foetus robbed of his natural development, thrown out in the world with a naked covering of parchment, with too little room for his teeth and a soft bulging skull like a bubble" (*PN*, 190).

29. Bergonzi, *The Situation of the Novel*, 179; John Banville, "Introduction: George Steiner's Fiction," viii.

30. Boyd, *Novels of Golding*, 41–42, 40. See also Dick, *William Golding* (1967), 38, 44.

31. Tiger, *Dark Fields*, 79.

32. Howard S. Babb locates "narrative mystification and shock" in *The Inheritors* (*The Novels of William Golding*, 47).

33. Tiger, *Dark Fields*, 72, 85.

34. White, *Carnival, Hysteria, and Writing*, 170.

35. See Hughes, "Baboons and Neanderthals," 161, 163. Richard Nash notes the liminal status of the "wild man" and the utility of this figure to satire's "border work" in "stripping away the civilized veneer of social respectability to reveal a bestial nature at the core" ("Satyrs and Satire in Augustan England," 98).

36. Tiger, *Dark Fields*, 85.

37. Milan Kundera, *The Unbearable Lightness of Being*, 26.

38. Ibid., 67.

39. Seidel, *Satiric Inheritance: Rabelais to Sterne*, 17 (see also 17–21).

40. Connery and Combe, *Theorizing Satire*, 5.

41. Adorno, *Negative Dialectics*, 362.

42. See Saul Friedlander, ed., *Probing the Limits of Representation: Nazism and "the Final Solution,"* 2. See also George Steiner, *Language and Silence: Essays, 1958–1966*.

43. Yael S. Feldman, "Whose Story Is It Anyway? Ideology and Psychology in the Representation of the Shoah in Israel's Literature," 228.

44. On the whole issue of presenting the "unpresentable," see Lyotard, *The Postmodern Condition: A Report on Knowledge*, 71–82. Lipstadt argues that those intellectuals who have promoted "deconstructionist history" (e.g., Fish, Rorty, de Man) have prepared the soil for deniers or so-called revisionist historians such as David Irving and Robert Faurrison. She maintains: "The deniers are plying their trade at a time when much of history seems up for grabs and attacks on the western rationalist tradition have become commonplace" (*Denying the Holocaust*, 17).

45. Lyotard, *Heidegger and "the Jews,"* 47.

46. Lyotard, *Differend*, 56–58; Friedlander, *Probing the Limits*, 5; LaCapra, *Representing the Holocaust*, 98, 222; Lawrence L. Langer, *Admitting the Holocaust: Collected Essays*, 11.

47. Langer, *Admitting the Holocaust*, 76.

48. N. Williams, *William Golding's "Lord of the Flies,"* ix; Camus, *The Fall*, 92.

49. Langer, *Admitting the Holocaust*, 9; Lang, "The Representations of Limits," 317.

VIRGINIA TIGER

Lord of the Flies

I

I would like to make a point about the writing of *Flies* and its position
in the world of scholarship. I said to Ann [Golding] in about 1953,
'Wouldn't it be a good idea to write a book about real boys on an island,
showing what a mess they'd make?' She said, 'That is a good idea!' So I
sat down and wrote it. You see, neither I nor she nor anyone else could
dream of the sheer critical firepower that was going to be levelled at this
mass of words scribbled in a school notebook. Then, carried away by the
reverence of exegetes, I made the great mistake of defending the thing
[. . .] It's astonishing that any of the book still stands up at all. It has
become painfully and wryly amusing to me when people throw things
like the Summa at my poor little boys. Of course, that trick works.
How not? Dialectic has always clobbered rhetoric, from Socrates down.
But—remembering the words scribbled in the school notebook—is the
journey really necessary? Isn't it cracking an opusculum with a critical
sledgehammer?

Golding, Letter, 1970

*L*ord of the Flies, the *Robinson Crusoe* of our time, still enjoys—like the
earlier island story of shipwreck and survival—a pre-eminent place in the

From *William Golding: The Unmoved Target*, pp. 22–56. © 1974, 1976, 2003 by Virginia
Tiger.

cultural climate of the West. Both cultural document and modern classic, the novel continues to provoke critical attention at the same time as it continues to prompt great general interest; over the past fifty years it has sold countless millions of copies. An obdurate and uncompromising story about how boys—very 1950s British boys—become beasts when the constraints of authority are withdrawn from their closed world, *Lord of the Flies* has proved to be a sustained literary and popular success.

Two feature films of the book have been produced, as well as a theatrical adaptation by the actor Nigel Williams—with performances in schools in England tied to an education programme which included interactive resource packs on the Internet—and ongoing productions in such venues as Canada's Stratford Festival in Ontario. Surf the Internet and one comes upon several sites referencing as well as simplistically analyzing the novel, including one that posts a (wholly concocted, unauthoritative, and unascribed) visual image of the novel's unnamed South Sea island. Regularly, and more painfully, the novel's title has been used to ponder the seeming rise in the United States and Great Britain of killings of children by children, from two-year-old James Bulger's murder in 1993 by two ten-year-old boys in Liverpool to the mass maiming and murder of children at Columbine High School in Utah by two teenage boys in April 1999.[1]

The book itself may well be one of the most internationally taught of twentieth-century novels. 'It's a great pleasure to meet you, Mr Golding,' remarked King Carl Gustaf XVI of Sweden on presenting the esteemed literary award in the 1983 Nobel ceremonies. 'I had to do *Lord of the Flies* at school.'[2] It has also, like its author, been 'endlessly discussed, analyzed, dissected, over-praised and over-faulted, victim of the characteristic twentieth-century mania for treating living artists as if they were dead,' as the novelist John Fowles once observed.[3] In fact, Golding's first novel is not nearly as long as the critical commentary it has spawned, with Golding himself contributing in no small degree to the phenomenon he once laconically described himself as having become: 'the raw material of an academic light industry'; 'the books that have been written about my books have made a statue of me.'[4]

Packets of pamphlets and articles on source, genre, meaning, archetype, symbolism, and casebooks and master guides for secondary school children have appeared over the years.[5] Unquestionably, the novel's teachability has fostered—as well as sustained—its reputation. Some would argue that this pedagogic feature, 'rather than any clearly established merit,' was 'responsible for the general acclaim with which it has been received'.[6] Others would more generously judge that the novel has 'an artfulness, even an air of demonstrating fictional possibilities, which make it eminently suitable for teaching and which must owe a lot to the well-trained critical habits of the author'.[7] Such is the critical position of a book-length volume, *Lord of the Flies: Fathers and*

Sons, devoted to solving the riddle of how the novel could be both 'a tract for the times … [and] a fable of timeless import, transcending its immediate occasion'.[8] Then there are the many doctoral dissertations taking as their point of departure *Time* magazine's 1962 quip that the novel was 'Lord of the Campus' in order to argue either the existence of a Golding vogue or the decline in popularity of a once generationally 'relevant fable', all of which can be put beside the many testimonials to the impact of the work on the untutored adolescent. Reading the novel when he was a thirteen-year-old, the novelist Ian McEwan apprehended immediately its applicability: 'As far as I was concerned, Golding's island was a thinly disguised boarding school.' And years later: 'When I came to write a novel myself, I could not resist the momentum of my childhood fantasies nor the power of Golding's model, for I found myself wanting to describe a closed world of children removed from the constraints of authority [in *The Cement Garden*, an urban *Lord of the Flies* …] Without realizing it at the time I named my main character after one of Golding's.'[9]

If the book can be situated in that tradition of narrative where the young reader is rewarded along with the individual whom Virginia Woolf called 'the common reader', *Lord of the Flies* is also expressive of, at the same time as located in, contemporary sensibility and historical context. Appearing in the years of drab austerity immediately following World War II, where, despite Britain's lost imperial power and the partial break-up of the class system, there was still a mixture of smug superiority and complacent Philistinism among the ruling establishment, the novel was written under the indirect presence of such great traumas as Belsen, Dachau, Hiroshima, Nagasaki, and the direct presence of the Cold War. Addressing more than the disillusioned pessimism of the 1950s, the work germinated from 'years of brooding that brought me not so much to an opinion as a stance. It was like lamenting the lost childhood of the world.'[10] Yet, as was the case with Doris Lessing's early fiction, readers seemed compelled to account for their initial astonishment and appalled recognition that a novelist was confirming what had previously only been privately understood about human behavior. For just as Lessing's *The Golden Notebook* in 1962 made public the private tone of female grievance, so Golding's *Lord of the Flies* tugged at private hunches that males—even small boys—enjoyed aggression, group hierarchies, and the savor of blood. So its appearance in 1954 and subsequent popularity in the 1960s did not so much coincide with as mirror emerging ethological/sociobiological investigations into male bonding, innate behavioral aggression, *Homo sapiens* as a hunting animal, and the evolutionary substratum of the male child's behavior.[11] Golding was 'typical of modern novelists in seeing his child characters as belonging to their own order of being',[12] a practice continued by Lessing in *The Fifth Child* as well as *Memoirs of a Survivor* and Marianne Wiggins in her declared female *Lord of the Flies*, *John Dollar*, in which a group of island-bound and unattended girls cannibalize a corpse. This conflation of 'savagery' and the brutality of children in the popular imagination was further fuelled by a kind of scopophilia: the noble savage negated.

II

> There are novelists who never make a mistake—a mistake, I mean, of fact. To them fact is sacrosanct, partly, it may be, because they suppose themselves capable of distinguishing between fact and fiction [...] The rest of us—sessile versions of the rogues and vagabonds who grace the stage—radiate from this central position to a circumference where it is fiction that is rock hard and history that is a dream or nightmare.
>
> Golding, *Foreword* 1994

The story itself is by now familiar. A group of schoolboys, educated by British public schools in a system still designed to control an empire, are dropped on an Edenic island in the Pacific Ocean. There they confront the task of survival. First the boys proceed to set up a pragmatic system based on a 'grown-up' model: government, laws, shelters, plumbing facilities, and food supplies. Quickly, however, the society disintegrates under the dual pressures of aggression and superstition. Signal fire becomes defensive hearth, then ritualistic spit: the darkness of night becomes a monstrous 'beast' to be propitiated by totemic pig heads. Hunting becomes killing as Jack's hunters break loose from Ralph's fire-keepers to form a tribal society with gods, rituals, and territory at the island's end. When two boys from the original group invade this territory they are killed, Simon ritually as a totemic beast and Piggy politically as an enemy. Finally a scapegoat, Ralph, is hunted down so as to offer his head to the Lord of the Flies. Then the adult world intervenes in the person of a naval officer, who has observed the dense clouds of smoke from the flaming fire: the scorched-earth strategy that Jack orders to ferret out the fleeing Ralph. The novel concludes with the pathetic image of the survivor, Ralph, crying for 'the end of innocence, the darkness of man's heart, and the fall through the air of the true, wise friend called Piggy'.

And yet, 'How romantically it starts,' wrote E. M. Forster in his 1962 introduction to *Lord of the Flies*, an essay that was influential in establishing Golding's early reputation as an unfashionable allegorist, writing from deep religious convictions about mankind's essential depravity. He 'believes in the Fall of Man [...] his attitude approach[ing] the Christian; we are all born in sin, or will all lapse into it.'[13]

Powerful thematic conceptions such as these seem to govern early readings of the narrative. As many of us now realize, the book's resonance comes only in part from its strong structural shape. While terms such as 'allegory', 'parable', 'fable', 'science fiction', 'romance', and 'speculative fiction' have been variously suggested to describe what was then felt to be the novel's chief characteristic, its element of arbitrary design, its form eluded easy categorization. Nevertheless, a consequence of such programmatic readings of the text was to fault the novel with reductive simplifications, rather than faulting its commentators. And Golding's complicity in this context must also be considered, for his lecture 'Fable' encouraged early on such interpretative methods. At the time, Golding's own preference was the term 'fable', which he once defined for me as 'allegory that has achieved passion'. This gnomic clue I took to imply the peculiar conjunction of contrived pattern and fictional freedom, which seemed a characteristic feature of not only *Lord of the Flies*, but *The Inheritors* and *Pincher Martin* alike. Gregor and Kinkead-Weekes put the matter rather cleanly in their 1962 introduction to Faber and Faber's school edition when they described *Lord of the Flies* as 'fable and fiction simultaneously'.

Another early and persistent classification was based on the book's intellectual schema—its affinity to neither romance nor realism, its definition as neither parable nor fable, but its relation to the Christian apologia. For just as the mid-century's New Criticism's allegiance to Christian belief shaped its approach to texts as containing authentic, stable meanings, so its method of close discussion of systems and structures facilitated the discussion of books like Golding's, which appeared to have levels of meanings entirely accessible to the authoritative interpreter. Frederick Karl's 1962 discussion in *A Reader's Guide to the Contemporary English Novel* was one of the first—but by no means the last[14]—to insist that Golding wrote 'religious allegories' whose conceptual machinery undermined the 'felt life' of the tale: 'the idea [. . .] invariably is superior to the performance itself'.[15] The notion that *Lord of the Flies* was somehow intellectually or philosophically contrived was to become the major critical assumption about the rest of his work. Ignoring the fictional landscape altogether, many early commentators constructed explications of 'meaning' more relevant to social, cultural, political, psychological, or anthropological history than the nature of the narrative itself. Later critics have adopted a comparable approach, although the terms of their critique have switched to colonialism and imperialism. Setting the work within the history of decolonization (in particular the 1952 liberation movement in Kenya where the Kikuyu people were balefully misrepresented by the colonial regime as savage 'Mau Mau' engaged in atavistic rituals), one critic has charged that *Lord of the Flies* amounts to 'a defence of colonialism', one which reinscribes 'the old Empire misrepresentation of white enlightenment and black savagery'.[16] If later skirmishes have charged the book with incipient racism, false essentialism, and immoderate misogyny, their denunciations are not unlike the teacup

controversies that early on raged in religious journals such as *Commonweal* and
America. A passage from one of these critics neatly sums up all the pertinent
critical attitudes of this type in one sentence. I quote it at length to underscore
the not insignificant fact that Golding's reputation was established on the
basis of *Lord of the Flies*. Against these hardened assumptions, judgements of
the other books—even the often ebullient *Rites of Passage*, the 1980 novel that
brought about a resurgence of interest in Golding's fiction—all too frequently
adopt the first novel as the single prototype for excellence or failure. That
1964 summary assessment reads:

> [*Lord of the Flies*] is, in fact, a cannily constructed—perhaps
> contrived—allegory for a twentieth-century doctrine of original
> sin and its social and political dynamics and it conforms essentially
> to a quite orthodox tradition not really more pessimistic than the
> Christian view of man.[17]

III

Original Sin. I've been rather lumbered with Original Sin.

Golding to Carey

That the text itself bears no such single or stable meaning is a matter made
evident by its susceptibility to a range of critical interpretations: religious,
philosophical, sociological, psychological, political, deconstructionist, post-
colonial, and the evidence that any literary text is mediated by way of its
readers' diverse subjectivities.[18] As moral fable, it can be construed as examining
individual (male) disintegration where the inadequacy, not the necessary
depravity, of human nature is emphasized; a legitimate abstraction from this
is that people are governable inasmuch as they can be the responsible authors
of their own actions. Simon is a 'saint'—Golding's extra-literary term for the
boy—because he tries to know comprehensively and inclusively. He possesses a
quality of imagination that forces an 'ancient inescapable recognition' (p. 171).
Before the obscene pig's head on the spike, Simon comes to acknowledge the
existence of his own capacity for evil and his own capacity to act on behalf
of others—thus his freeing of the tangled dead parachutist. In contrast,
Ralph, in what might be read as a failure of moral imagination, exhibits only
a 'fatal unreasoning *knowledge*' (p. 226, my italics) of his approaching death,
which is directed towards his own survival, not that of the community. Read
as a defensive imperialist fable, the novel's reiterative coding of hunters as
'savages'—Piggy's climactic charge before Jack's tribe at Castle Rock: 'Which
is better—to be a pack of painted niggers like you are, or to be sensible like
Ralph is' (p. 221)—the novel could be valorized as a Eurocentric racist text.

On the other hand, juxtaposing *Lord of the Flies* with one of its intertextual influences, *The Coral Island*, one could just as easily conclude that 'Golding's distinct post-colonial inflection is to attribute savagery, in principle, to the British ruling elite.'[19] Taken as a political fable, the text could be seen to explore social regression, where it is not so much the capabilities of the boys as their depravity, and by fabular extension humankind's inability to control aggression, within a workable social or political order.[20] While Piggy and Ralph do exercise good will and judgement, nevertheless they are inadequate politically, ultimately participating in the *Bacchae*-like murder of Simon, a murder effected by the tribal society that Jack leads.

From the perspective of mythic fable, the book could be viewed as offering an account of postlapsarian loss. As Adam unparadised, the boys cradle within themselves the beast of evil, 'Beelzebub' (the Hebraic original of the English translation, 'lord of the flies' [*Kings* 1.2]; 'the chief of the devils' in *Luke* 11.15). They turn the Edenic island into a fiery hell, although one must remember that on their arrival the island has been smeared by human intent, technology, and weaponry: the scar of the plane's discharged tail cutting across coconut trees and verdant jungle growth. Other readings have seemed equally pertinent. Using the lens of Freud's *Three Essays on Human Sexuality* or *Totem and Taboo* would open *Lord of the Flies* to a reading where the boys become representatives of various instincts or amoral forces. In anthropological terms the boys' society could be seen to mirror the societies of prehistoric man: theirs seems a genuinely primitive culture with its own gods, demons, myths, rituals, taboos. Seen from the vantage point of ethology, where, according to Lorenz's *On Aggression*, natural aggression which once enhanced survival has, with the advent of technological weaponry come to threaten that survival, the novel enacts on a small scale 'the pathological nature of contemporary aggression'.[21] One here recalls the nuclear warfare that initially occasioned the schoolchildren's evacuation and their ejection on to the island. Then again, viewed from the position developed by Hannah Arendt's *The Banality of Evil*, *Lord of the Flies* comes into focus as a dystopia, showing how 'intelligence (Piggy) and common sense (Ralph) will always be overthrown in society by sadism (Roger) and the lure of totalitarianism (Jack)'.[22]

Whatever the intellectual taxonomy in the wide range of explanations suggested, yet not wholly endorsed, by *Lord of the Flies*' rhetorical density, each could carry with it the critical error of magnifying into men what remain young boys. And English boys at that, stamped through with Britishness like seaside rock, educated by public schools in a system designed to rule an empire, stained, rung after pyramidal rung, by the class prejudices of a stratified society towards which Golding had a lifelong bitter antagonism. As he remarked to a *Guardian* interviewer, a quarter of a century after the writing of *Lord of the Flies*:

I think that the pyramidal structure of English society is present, and my awareness of it is indelibly imprinted in me, in my psyche, not merely in my intellect but very much in my emotional, almost my physical being. I am enraged by it and I am unable to escape it entirely [. . .] It dissolves but it doesn't disappear; it's fossilized in me.[23]

As one of the multiple chords playing through *Lord of the Flies*, social class contributes to the narrative's outcome as surely as does any other critique of conventional, civilized values. And the point is well made in one commentator's posing of the question as to how far the island group is a collection of boys (thus representative of human nature in a reductive state) or 'a collection of *English* boys'. Are they 'very much English boys responding to the island situation in an English way, so that what's true of them mightn't be true of a company of American, Chinese or Indian boys?'[24] Such is the position taken by Harold Bloom in a jaunty 1996 lambasting of a novel that he (presumably) thought highly enough of as 'a great literary work' to include in his study guide series on just such great works, when he asks: 'Do the boys [. . .] represent the human condition or do they reflect the traditions of British schools with their restrictive structures, sometimes brutal discipline, and not always benign visions of human nature?'[25] So another informative way to view the island-world would be to see it as a microcosm of *middle-class* wartime 1940s English society.[26] Thus, lower-middle-class Piggy—with his auntie's sweet shop as signifying the then despised tradesman class, as do the dropped aitches in the lad's speech—is derided because he's a social inferior. The fat boy with the short-sightedness of the caricature bookworm, Piggy's wounds—his asthma, his matronly body and his balding head—disqualify him as surely as his social class from any kind of resistance to the inbred insolence of a Jack Merridew. Instinctively sighting an inferior, Jack commands him to be quiet, and the boy obliges, instinctively knowing his place in the English class system: 'He was intimidated by this uniformed superiority and the offhand authority in Merridew's voice. He shrank to the other side of Ralph and busied himself with his glasses' (p. 32).

Middle-class Ralph, with his boy scout skills, fair complexion, and sense of fair play, is the son of a naval officer, thus is he closely linked to Britain's past magisterial powers on the seas. A demonstrable type of British schoolboy, his tolerant reasonableness is as much a product of breeding as schooling, but he is no match for the arrogance of the 'born leader', Jack Merridew. An elected leader only, Ralph cannot maintain the seat of power. 'We're English; and the English are best at everything; declares Jack' (p. 72), his complacent imperialism the love-child of a union between upper-middle-class chauvinism and an educational system designed to emphasize leadership, tradition, and the ingrained sense of superiority: indeed, all the requirements needed to reinforce social, racial, and colonial bigotry and maintain an empire—at any cost. Head boy at a cathedral school—'the most highly organized, civilized, disciplined group of children it's possible to find anywhere,' as Golding once observed[27]—Jack inhabits the upper-middle-class rung. From his first appearance on the island, Merridew (for so he announces himself, with that implicit social class signal) is in command, barking orders at the snake-line of black-cloaked choristers, their Canterbury caps topped by—what will all too soon become ironic—silver crosses.[28] If the semiotic of the choirboys' dress distinguishes them from the middle-class boys in their grammar school uniforms, the supercilious jingoism of Jack is the idiom of imperial rule. We will hear it balefully reiterated at the novel's conclusion in the naval officer's dismissive comment: 'You're all British aren't you?' (p. 248). In a story all the more striking because wonderfully real children are depicted—children who yank up socks, stamp feet, and quarrel over sandcastles—it is fitting that Jack's choir should march across the brilliant beach in tight military formation. It is also appropriate that, on being ordered to stand to attention, its most pacific chorister, Simon, should faint, the sun and the heavy costume overwhelming him. Perhaps one of the several reasons why Simon seems insufficiently drawn for many critics, a figure more symbolic than substantial, is because he is least connected to the web of social class and all that this is meant to imply in the novel's critique of 'the very roots of English society [...] how we have lived and how we ought to live'.[29] Unlike the other schoolboys, he never quite sheds the conceptual label assigned to his figure in the workings of the plot and his generalized significance. Epileptic, thus diseased by that strain which the ancients called sacred, he is the author's mouthpiece, given voice from the outside—as Virginia Woolf said of Brontë's *Jane Eyre* when its heroine declared a feminist manifesto—not giving voice from the inside. Piggy, by contrast, may well function as a kind of Augustan man of reason, easily able to prick illusion. His representativeness, however, diminishes to the human scale as the novel progresses: Piggy is no more and no less than a frightened boy, as he stands at the neck of Castle Rock, sightless, the beloved conch clutched in his hands. To appreciate the disparity in the depiction of these two characters is to see how literary a construction Simon is: garmented less in the chorister's signifying gown than the literary trappings of the holy fool, whose vatic insight, mystic unity with 'great creating nature', epilepsy, and illnesses are all traditional signs for holiness.

IV

I knew about *Lord of the Flies*. I planned that out very carefully.
William Golding to John Carey, 1986

Simon's symbolic function in the novel as the agent who provides the text's fibular message—that 'mankind is both heroic and sick'—has provoked the greatest negative criticism over the years, underscoring the charge that *Lord of the Flies* was thesis-ridden, facile in its didactic intent, an over-schematic allegory whose rhetorical effects were too rigidly patterned. 'Whether the psychological representations of *Lord of the Flies* remain altogether convincing seems to me rather questionable; the saintly Simon strains credibility as a naturalistic portrait. In many ways the book is remarkably tendentious, and too clearly has a program to urge upon us,' goes a late twentieth-century judgement.[30] Such an *idée reçue* can now be given the lie, informed as one is by the editorial revelations which appeared in 'Strangers from Within', Charles Monteith's page-turning account of the publisher's transformation of what Faber and Faber's first reader described as:

> An absurd and uninteresting fantasy about the explosion of an atomic bomb on the colonies and a group of children who land in jungle country near New Guinea. Rubbish and dull. Pointless.[31]

A sales director concurred, saying the manuscript (alternately titled *A Cry of Children, Nightmare Island, To Find an Island*) was 'unpublishable'. Monteith stuck with the novel despite this response; then there was an advance of £60, and the novel was published a full year to the day after first being submitted, its new title, *Lord of the Flies*. The now redolent and sumptuously evocative title was suggested by an editor, Alan Pringle, and, as Monteith observes: 'It has turned out to be the most memorable title given to any book since the end of the Second World War.'[32]

Those 365 days from September 17, 1953 to September 17, 1954 witnessed an editorial excision of the original novel's structure, with Golding being advised to abandon the tripart division of Prologue, Interlude, and Epilogue, all of which, evidently, described an atomic war being waged. Ralph's hair came to be cut; Simon was not permitted to lead 'Good Dances' on the lagoon side while the painted hunters began their sanguineous circling, high above on Castle Rock. As for what has appeared to his detractors to be further evidence of Golding as schematic fabulist, the chapter headings that, like 'Beast from Water' or 'Cry of the Hunters', pinpoint the symbolic momentum of their respective sections were proposed as absolutely necessary by the firm's production and design department.

That the manuscript's major flaw was a structural one in my judgement casts a new light on what one had assumed to be Golding's practice. The austerity of structure was not so much a Pallas Athene born from the head of an inspired Zeus as the work of very good, very mortal, editors. It also calls into question the veracity of several of Golding's comments on the writing of the novel. Alternately he has claimed that he thought of the last sentence first. That the draft of the novel, from first page to last, took from three to four months to complete, having been planned from the beginning to the end before the writing began.[33] That he had 'two pictures in his mind: one of a small boy waggling his feet in the air on an empty beach in sheer exuberance; the other, of the same boy crawling bloodstained through the undergrowth, being hunted to death.'[34] As with the contradictory explanations he has given for the origins of *Lord of the Flies*, the suggestion is that he no longer knew, or cared to know, how the story had evolved; the act of writing itself having been forged in the smithy of necessity at 'a time of great world grief.'[35]

V

A cluster of conventions determines the medium of a literary generation—the repertoire of possibilities that a writer has in common with his living rivals. Traditions involve the competition of writers with their ancestors. These collective co-ordinates do not merely permit or regulate the writing of a work. They enter the reading experience and affect its meaning.

Claudio Guillen

Conceptual accounts of origins and enhancements like the ones I have assembled above obscure—sometimes destroy—the primary strength of a novel. For *Lord of the Flies* is first and foremost a gripping story: 'It falls well within the mainstream of several English literary traditions. It is a "boys" book, as are *Treasure Island, The Wind in the Willows, High Wind in Jamaica* and other books primarily about juvenile characters which transcend juvenile appeal.'[36] In its dialogic relation to pre-existing literary patterns, it necessarily involves the reader as a party in that dialogue, the reader's response to the work being shaped by knowledge of previous literary conventions. Thus, in the intertextual relation of writings to other writings, survival narratives form a background to *Lord of the Flies*: *Robinson Crusoe, The Swiss Family Robinson*, and literature's pre-eminent island tale, *The Tempest*, with its repeated treacheries, knaves, fools, and insurrectionists, debates on the noble savage, and Gonzalo's fond conception of the ideal commonwealth.[37] The reader's expectations, arising from those associated with the pre-existing genre of shipwreck on tropical islands, are radically debunked in *Lord of the Flies'* transformation of that pattern in the context of its historical circumstances. For example, *Robinson Crusoe's* reinforcement of eighteenth-century ideals of individualism, progress, and imperialist rule are subverted and in their place are the mid-twentieth-century inversions of those conceptions: aggression, disorder, the child as predator. Indeed, the

Augustan man of reason here is the child Piggy, who suffers from asthma, diarrhoea, laziness, and abominable grammar.

Texts generate other texts, of course. Milton had his debt to Virgil, while Virgil and Joyce had theirs to Homer, just as Austen's *Northanger Abbey* parodically displaced Ann Radcliffe's *The Mysteries of Udolpho*. That *Lord of the Flies*, so explicit about its own forms, is patently dependent for its point on that of another novel links the work to this long-standing practice of intertextual mimesis. Readers are now more than familiar with the novel's ironic—indeed, subversive—recasting of R. M. Ballantyne's *The Coral Island* (1857), a Victorian boy's adventure that Golding admitted had 'a pretty big connection'.[38] *Lord of the Flies'* main characters are, like *The Coral Island's*, named Ralph and Jack—although Ballantyne's third character, Peterkin, is split into two boys: Peter and Simon. Shipwrecked on an uninhabited island, Ballantyne's boys lead prosperous lives, whereas Golding's boys progressively deteriorate. Explicit references to Ballantyne's title occur twice in the text: the intertextual allusion being more than ironic in the second instance when, at the end—surveying the hideous children before him—a naval officer remarks: 'I should have thought that a pack of British boys—you're all British aren't you?—would have able to put up a better show than that—I mean [. . .] Like *The Coral Island* (p. 248).

As embedded narrative, *The Coral Island* amounts to a revisionist strategy that recasts the nineteenth-century tale from a post–World War II perspective; the twentieth-century island is inhabited by English boys just as smug about their decency, just as complacent, and—except for Simon—just as ignorant. While Ballantyne showed unshakeable faith in the superiority of the white race—'White men always [rise to the top of affairs] in savage countries,' remarks a *Coral Island* empire-builder—Golding questions not just English chauvinism, but English civility itself. If in *The Coral Island* the natives' faces 'besides being tattooed were besmeared with red paint and streaked with white,' in *Lord of the Flies* it is the estimable choirboys who color their faces so their aggressive selves can be released from shame: 'Jack began to dance and his laughter became a bloodthirsty snarling [. . .] the mask was a thing of its own, behind which Jack hid, liberated from shame and self-consciousness' (p. 80). To debunk pastoral evocations of life on a tropical island where everything at first seems glamorous, *Lord of the Flies* stresses such physical realities as the diarrhoea of the 'littluns', who 'suffer untold terrors in the dark and huddle together for comfort' (p. 74); the densely hot and damp scratching heat of a real jungle; the remote and 'brute obtuseness of the ocean' (p. 137), which condemns the boys to the island; the filthy flies which drink at the pig's head; and the hair grown lank: 'With a convulsion of the mind, Ralph discovered dirt and decay; understood how much he disliked perpetually flicking the tangled hair out of his eyes'

(p. 96). And in a book that intended to tell a story 'about real boys on an island, showing what a mess they'd make',[39] that the boys grow frightened of the unknown demonstrates fictional realism as well as psychological verisimilitude. In fact, it is just this fear of the beast—and its ambiguous existence on the island—which forms the dramatic core of the novel.

VI

> Ralph found himself understanding the wearisomeness of this life, where every oath was an improvisation and a considerable part of one's waking life was spent watching one's feet. He stopped [...] and remembering that first enthusiastic exploration as though it were part of a brighter childhood, he smiled jeeringly.
>
> *Lord of the Flies* (p. 95)

Had *The Coral Island*'s morality simply been recast, *Lord of the Flies* might well have become a derivative fable along the lines of Richard Hughes' *High Wind in Jamaica*, demonstrating a mid-twentieth-century belief that, without the discipline of adults, children will deteriorate into savages. No such single account emerges, it seems to me; rather than finding one stable meaning residing in the text, I note its encouragement to create meanings. A structural reversal has been added to the initial source reversal and its revisionist strategy, making the text interrogate its own grounds by way of an ingenious coda, one that elevates *Lord of the Flies* above mere diagrammatic prescription. The text implies a correspondence between the schoolboys' island world and that of the adult: it is the operation of the text's structure—what I call its ideographic structure—that permits the reader to conclude that the children's experiment on the island has had a constant counterpart in the world outside. Hints are given—although never fully disclosed—in the children's comments about their aerial voyage from an apparent war zone; we come haltingly to surmise that the occasion of the boys' landing, like the mysterious arrival of a dead parachutist, may be unbenevolent gifts from the adult world. As the narrative progresses, the reader is lulled into the unguarded hope that adults may save the situation, while simultaneously decoding certain ironic clues, which the coda will confirm. Take the reiteration of motifs—for example, the schoolboy phrase 'Let's have fun', which Ralph as elected leader introduces and which the pig's head on a stick seems to throw obscenely back at Simon; finally, the phrase sits alarmingly easily on the tongue of the rescuing adult. The reader becomes entangled with these motifs, forcing a reconsideration of what seemed innocuous before. The heaving of logs by the twins Samneric, the rolling of larger and larger stones, the several donations to the sea, the several pig hunts, the two desperate races by Ralph: these sequences of repeated actions, placed at intervals during the story, intensify the ambiguous threat and give the illusion of a vastly speeded-up dénouement. The cumulative effect for the reader is to suffer from a vague yet familiar threat, a sense of doom that cannot be adequately located in the narrative's thrust until its confirmation in the coda.

The coda, with its reversed point of view on events contradicting initially established expectations, is a narrative feature of some subtlety, and not a 'gimmick'.[40] In *Lord of the Flies* the ideographic structure consists of two movements; in the first, the events are seen from the point of view of the childish protagonist, Ralph, as he gradually grows more and more aware of the island's disintegration, although his perspective is supplemented by austere narratorial commentary. In the second movement, the coda which concludes the text, the reader encounters events from a new point of view, that of the adult officer, who is completely unaware of and largely indifferent to the suffering. The coda, in conjunction with the parachutist, reveal that adulthood—what the boys have thought of as the 'majesty of adult life'— is also inadequate to prevent destruction: behind the epauletted officer a 'trim cruiser' floats, metonym for barbarism in ancient and contemporary civilizations alike. And although Golding once observed (extratextually) that the entangled, decaying corpse represents history,[41] textually it does haunt the boys, a haunting appropriately represented by its uncanny position and repetitive motion: 'the figure sat on the mountain-top and bowed and sank and bowed again' (p. 119). When the figure is released by Simon, this other metonym for the killing fields becomes the air combatant it once was as it 'trod with ungainly feet the tops of the high trees' and up, past the demented children, themselves engaged in Bacchae-like excess.

The children then should be read as behaving like the grown-ups, whose world Piggy and Ralph mistakenly believe can help theirs. But the child's world on the island is a painful microcosm of the adult world, and the ruin they bring upon themselves is widespread—recall again that it is atomic warfare in the air that brings about their initial descent to the island. The cruel irony of this matter is made all the stronger by the sudden switch in perspective. Here the officer's dismal failure to comprehend the 'semicircle of little boys, their bodies streaked with coloured clay, sharp sticks in their hands' (p. 246) is testimony to what the narrative voice describes as 'the infinite cynicism of adult life' (p. 170) and silent witness to the Lord of the Dung's general sway. It is as though the naval officer has sailed straight from the pages of *The Coral Island*, moments after we have suffered the consequences of that novel's banal optimism.

In fact, the story's riveting power comes precisely because the characters are children, children who belly-flop from trees, suck thumbs, suffer inestimable fears as the darkness falls, bully weaklings and grunt in then schoolboy slang:

'Wacko...Wizard...Smashing...Golly.'[42] 'I'm not going to play any longer. Not with you' (p. 132), a mutinous Jack mutters, the puerility of his words in incongruous contrast to his all too adult deeds. The arrival of the officer, with its sudden shift from Ralph's agonized eyes to the benign view of the adult, throws the story back into grotesque miniature. The children are dwarfed to children again. Here is how the officer sees Jack:

> A little boy who wore the remains of an extraordinary black cap on his red hair and who carried the remains of a pair of spectacles at his waist, started forward at the question [Who's boss?] then changed his mind and stood still. (pp. 247–48)

Throughout the narrative's first movement—and with appalling momentum—the children appear to be adults, dealing with adult problems. Now they are whining little boys, held in control by the presence of the adult. Yet the reader cannot forget the cruelty of what has gone before. For the conch of order has been smashed, the spectacles of reason and rescue have been used to destroy the island. An unnamed child with a mulberry mark has burned to death. Two individuals have been murdered. An aggressive tribal society has been hunting down another. Nor can the reader forget that Ralph's piteous weeping at the end transcends the smug cynicism of the rescuer, for Ralph attains awareness of the real nature of the 'pack of British boys' (p. 248).

Ralph is saved because the adult world has intervened, yet his rescuer is on the point of returning to an 'adult' war, which in numerical terms is infinitely more extravagant in its potential for disaster. Given the barbaric chaos the boys have been reduced to, the officer appears to them (to us) as order. It is only on a delayed decoding of the earlier clues that the reader comprehends that the officer is involved in a nuclear war and yet still represents 'order'.[43]

The resonances of *Lord of the Flies* are not allegorically simple but ideographically suggestive. 'Everything is twofold, every perspective provokes a competing alternative';[44] it is the reader's work to hold this sea-changing duality. The task undertaken by the reader, by way of the work's ideographic structure, is to make the apparent discordance of the two clashing patterns connect, to cross the child's educated view of things with the adult's uneducated view and by joining the two perspectives probe the rhetorical question: 'Who will rescue the adult and his cruiser?'

I write that *Lord of the Flies* is not allegorically simple, although readers have conferred social, political, moral, spiritual, and mythic universalities upon it, addressing readers' historical need for a universal text about aggression. Perhaps a useful elaboration on what I am suggesting about a contrast between an ideographic strategy and an allegorical one would be to examine one allegorical feature of the work upon which no doubt can be cast. In Golding's view, the innocence of the child is a crude fallacy. If 'there is a simplicity about human goodness, then it is just as true that there is a corresponding complexity about human evil,' Golding observed, some forty years after *Lord of the Flies*, in an essay on the murder of two-year-old James Bulger by two ten-year-old boys.[45] By nature—and given certain conditions, to whose recipe fear must be added—*Homo sapiens*, Golding argued, has a terrible potentiality for evil. And this potentiality cannot be eradicated by a humane political system, no matter how respectable. Thus in 'Beast from Water', one of the work's most contrived chapters, the fundamental inadequacy of parliamentary systems to deal with atavistic superstition is portrayed. In this episode, the scene's physical and psychological atmosphere is as schematically constructed as the major characters' different pronouncements on the 'beast'.

A parliamentary assembly begins at eventide; consequently, the chief, Ralph, is merely 'a darkish figure' (p. 96) to his group. Light is, at first, level. Only Ralph stares into the island's darkness; his assembly before him faces the lagoon's bright promise. But the light gradually vanishes, accompanied by increasing superstition and fear. The place of assembly on the beach is narratorially described as 'roughly a triangle; but irregular and sketchy, like everything they made'. The assembly's shape can be likened to that of a receding boat, a kind of mirror image of the island-boat. Ralph remarks at the outset that the island is 'roughly boat-shaped'; because of the tide's configuration, he feels that 'the boat was moving steadily astern' (p. 38).

Since Ralph sits on 'a dead tree' (p. 96) that forms the triangle's base, no captain occupies the boat's rightful apex, where 'the grass was thick again because no one sat there' (p. 97). Like the island that appears to move backward, the assembly-boat is pointed to the darkness of the jungle, not the brightness of the navigable lagoon behind. Hunters sit like hawks on the right of Ralph; to the left are placed the doves, mostly littluns who giggle whenever their assembly seat, 'an ill-balanced twister', capsizes. And Piggy stands outside the triangle, showing his moralizing ineffectuality. 'This indicated that he wished to listen but would not speak; and Piggy intended it as a gesture of disapproval,' as summarized by the narrative voice. The conch in his hands, a littlun says he's seen a snake thing, a beastie. Both Piggy and Jack emphatically deny its existence, but—to Ralph's astonishment—Simon agrees that it does exist, but that 'maybe it's only us'. Ludicrously, ineptly, damagingly, Ralph determines that a vote on its existence should be taken. Darkness descends on the shattered assembly and, for the first of many times, the 'beastie' is ritually appeased. Island boat, assembly boat, and what should be the ship of civilization itself, rational government, all drift bleakly into darkness. The wail of Percival Wemys Madison of the Vicarage, Harcourt St Anthony, turns into an inarticulate gibber, the 'dense black mass' (p. 115) of mock hunters swirls, and the 'three blind mice' (p. 116), Ralph, Piggy, and Simon, sit 'in the darkness, striving unsuccessfully to convey the majesty of adult life' (p. 117).

If theme in this episode is schematically stable, Golding's 'symbols are not in fact clear, or wholly articulate, they are always the incarnation of more than can be extracted or translated from them.'[46] Consider, for example, Simon's secret sanctuary with its perfumed candle-buds. Rendered in terms of the island/ship metaphor, Simon's canopied bower is likened to a captain's 'little cabin' (p. 72); its 'creepers dropped their ropes like the rigging of foundered ships' (p. 71), and its centre is occupied by a 'patch of rock' (p. 71) on which a foundering ship could strike. On this rock a demonology, not a church, will be built, one recalls; Jack has instructed his braves to '"ram one end of the stick in the earth. Oh—it's rock. Jam it in the crack"' (p. 169). The reverberations of this imagistic cluster are intensified when, with the advance of evening, Simon's cabin is submerged by the sea: 'Darkness poured out, submerging the ways between the trees till they were dim and strange as the bottom of the *sea*' (p. 72, my italics).

Consider as well the initial figuring of the island as a ship at sea; or is it not also a civilization threatened with submergence, a tooth in a sucking mouth, a body dissociated from nature, consciousness divorced from the brute passivity of the subconscious? On it, the boys are certainly islanded by the ineluctable sea to which they turn in awe and distaste. The trope is woven into the narrative texture at various places and, by a technique of clustering, suggestion engenders suggestion. By gathering to itself other metaphors, the island trope evolves a logic of association, the organizing principle being recurrence with variation. Thus Ralph's final isolation at the tail end of the island—'he was surrounded on all sides by chasms of empty air. There was nowhere to hide, even if one did not have to go on' (p. 130)—is the isolation of the despairing hero. And when a now blind Piggy is described as 'islanded in a sea of meaningless colour' (p. 91) while he embraces the rock with 'ludicrous care above the sucking sea' (p. 217), the microcosmic/macrocosmic resonances are rich. Since the dual clusters are associative rather than syntactical or logical, meaning hovers over several referents so that the reader experiences the text as dynamic, with shifting shapes like cells under a microscope or stars at the end of a telescope.

VII

What was that enemy? I cannot tell. He came with the darkness and he reduced me to a shuddering terror that was incurable because it was indescribable. In daylight I thought of the Roman remains that had been dug up under the church as the oldest things near, sane things from sane people like myself. But at night, the Norman door and pillar,

even the flint wall of our cellar, were older, far older, were rooted in the
darkness under the earth.

                    William Golding, 'The Ladder and the Tree'

In the passage above, drawn from an early essay about his childhood home
in Marlborough, Golding describes the autobiographical origins for an
atavistic quest through darkness that came to preoccupy much of his fiction.
Pondering over the church graveyard at the foot of his garden, the child Billy
grew terrified of some enemy he imagined was lurking there to harm him.
A comparable mythopoeia of a beast is interleaved through *Lord of the Flies*,
although its dimensions/implications are by no means as fully realized as
they come to be in *Pincher Martin*, *Darkness Visible*, or even *The Paper Men*.
Nevertheless, the hallucinatory process is depicted in crucial confrontation
scenes where two apparently irreconcilable views of one situation are brought
slap up against each other. Such scenes are a narrative feature characteristic
of Golding's subsequent fictional practice as well, the confrontation scene
bringing about a single crystallization of a work's total structure, bringing
together contradictory, yet complementary, concepts.

    And what is this enemy, this creature that haunts the children's
imaginations and which Jack hunts and tries to propitiate with a totemic
beast? In extratextual conversation, Golding may have called it 'one of the
conditions of existence, this awful thing', but how exactly does the novel
prompt the reader to create such a meaning? Through the presence, actions,
and transformational death of the strange visionary child, Simon? A stubborn
conception in the Golding mythopoeia is the figure of the holy fool; forerunner
to *Pincher Martin*'s Nat, *Darkness Visible*'s Matty, or *Rites of Passage*'s Parson
Colley, unsimple Simon comes to be wise. Sitting before the Lord of the Flies,
a stinking, fly-ridden pig's head on a stick, Simon is made to recognize the
human nature of the real beast: that he himself has the capacity for evil as
well as for good. 'Whenever Simon thought of the beast,' intones the narrative
voice, 'there arose before his inward sight the pictures of a human at once
heroic and sick' (p. 128). Motivated by the mythopoeic requirements of the
tale, Simon intuitively identifies the beast, which allows what is a narratorial
puppet to solve the problem terrifying all the other creatures in this imagined
world. Acting with the sheer simplicity of any agent of good, Simon ventures
arduously and alone to the mountain-top where he releases what he discovers
is a harmless but horrifying corpse; then he tries to tell the boys below about
'mankind's essential illness' (p. 111).

    At the heart of the developing mythopoeia in *Lord of the Flies* is the
trope of the severed head of the pig, to which Simon turns in distaste and
awe, and from which he at first tries to escape. Grinning cynically, its mouth
gaping and its eyes half closed, the head has been placed on a rock in a sea-

like clearing around Simon's secret sanctuary. As a trope, the Head also can be likened to an island surrounded by the sea, thus operating macrocosmically and microcosmically. A larger macrocosm, the Castle Rock at the island's end is like a severed head as well: another variant on the pig's head. Described as a 'rock, almost detached' (p. 38), this smaller landmass is separated—a point which the text makes repeatedly—from the island's main body by 'a narrow *neck*' (p. 130, my italics). 'Soon, in a matter of centuries' (p. 130) this head will be severed too, although the impersonal narratorial distancing invokes a nature as indifferent to the boys' rescue as geological time is to man's 'little life'. At the tale's conclusion, giggling black and green savages will swarm around and over the head of Castle Rock as the black and green flies swarmed around the Lord of the Dung's head.

As readers know, Piggy's death occurs at this rock head; Roger's releasing of the boulder re-enacts the slaughter of a pig, for Piggy is swiftly decapitated by 'a glancing blow from *chin* to knee' (p. 222, my italics). Traveling through the air, with a grunt he lands on the square red rock in the sea, a kind of grotesque refectory table. And the monster-sea sucks his body, which 'twitched like a pig's after it has been killed' (p. 223), the emblematic nature of the character's name being reasserted from objective narratorial distance, even narratorial indifference. Piggy's head has been smashed and Ralph, running along the rocky neck, jumps just in time to avoid the 'headless body of the [sacrificial] sow' (p. 223) the hunters are planning to roast. The preparation is clear; another head is needed.

A traditional reading would have the head—the centre of reason—destroyed at Piggy's death with the island society's regression cutting 'the bridge' (p. 134) between rationality and irrationality. But in the developing mythopoeia of *Lord of the Flies* rationality is a suspect concept just like the common sense of Piggy, who 'goes on believing in the power of reason to tame the beast'.[47] Nor is the severed head of the pig Beelzebub; it does not represent an evil external to the individual, but rather the corrupt and corrupting consciousness, that very human malaise—in Golding's construction—that objectifies evil rather than recognizing its subjectivity: the kind of moral distancing we understand to be committed by both the officer and Piggy alike, the latter believing that Jack alone is the cause for 'things break[ing] up'. Such is the intellectual complication that the severed head represents to Simon; it prospers on the island's head, Castle Rock. Three confrontation scenes formulate the mythopoeia: Simon before the head, Ralph before the skull of the pig, Ralph before a 'savage'.

It is Simon alone who is made to recognize the real beast and—like a Moses with tablets of law—bring the truth from the mountain: a truth he understands as he broods before the totemic sow's head, having witnessed its anal rape and decapitation. Then, in the only idiom a child of Simon's age could give to a hallucinatory authority, the pig's head begins to deliver 'something very much like a sermon to the boy', and this in the 'voice of a schoolmaster' (p. 178). It insists that the island is corrupt and all is lost: 'This is ridiculous,' the head, now named the Lord of the Flies, expostulates. 'You know perfectly well you'll only meet me down there—so don't try to escape!' Shifting by way of the ironic motif of 'fun' into schoolboy patois, the head assures: '*we* are going to have fun on this island' (p. 178, my italics), even though 'everything' is a 'bad business' (p. 170). Such counselling of the acceptance of evil amounts to 'the infinite cynicism of adult life': the cynicism of the conscious mind, the cynicism that can ignore even 'the indignity of being spiked on a stick', the cynicism that 'grins'—as does the pig's head—at the obscenities that even make the butterflies desert their beloved bower. For the reading of the encounter involves also the recollection that during the anal mistreatment of the sow and its bloody killing, the butterflies continued to 'dance preoccupied in the centre of the clearing' (p. 178). That they now leave suggests the head must represent something a great deal more obscene than blood savor or rape. Counselling acceptance amounts to the kind of cynicism and easy optimism of the naval officer—in all his meanings—who '*grinned* cheerfully at the obscene savages while muttering "fun and games"' (p. 247, my italics).[48]

The meaning that the reader is prompted to create in this confrontation scene is twofold. Not only does this pig's head 'weld together other aspects of the beast. It is the beast, the head of the beast, the offering to the beast, left by the boys whose bestiality is marked by the head on the stick,'[49] but also, and importantly, this Lord of the Dung is Simon. The Lord of the Flies that counsels acceptance is his own strategic consciousness. Myopically viewing the head as an objectification of evil, independent of consciousness, would be to repeat the same error as Jack makes in externalizing and objectifying his own evil. The identification of Simon and the head is worked out very carefully indeed. Consider the following similarities: speaking in schoolboy patois, the Lord's head has 'half-shut eyes' (p. 170), while Simon is described as keeping 'his eyes shut, then shelter[ing] them with his hand' (p. 171) so that vision is partial; he sees things 'without definition and illusively' (p. 171) behind a 'luminous veil'. Simon comprehends his own savagery: he 'licks his dry lips' and feels the weight of his hair. Later, after his epileptic fit, blood 'dries around his mouth and chin' (p. 180) in the manner of the 'blood-blackened' (p. 170) grinning mouth of the head. Detecting the shared identity, the flies—although sated—leave the pig guts 'alight by Simon's runnels of sweat' (p. 171) and drink at the boy's head. By a profound effort of will, Simon forces himself to penetrate his own loathing and break through his own consciousness: 'At last Simon gave up and looked back; saw the white teeth and dim eyes, the blood—and his gaze as held by that ancient, inescapable recognition' (p. 171).

Of course, the orchestration of this recognition is conducted through the narratorial voice, which positions the *two heads* opposite each other. It is Simon himself he is looking at. His double, the head, grins at the flies of corruption and Simon acknowledges it as himself. Like the boy before the Egyptian mummy in Golding's essay 'Egypt from My Inside', Simon prepares 'to penetrate mysteries' and 'go down and through in darkness'. Looking into a vast mouth, Simon submits to the terror of his own being. 'Simon found he was looking into a vast mouth. There was blackness within, a blackness that spread [. . .] He fell down and lost consciousness' (p. 178). Having penetrated here his own capacity for evil, he returns from non-being to awaken next to 'the dark earth close by his cheek' (p. 179) and to know that he must 'do something'. All alone he does what no other boy could dare to do: encounter the beast on the hill. There Simon discovers that 'this parody' (ringed as well by green flies) is nothing more 'harmless and horrible' (p. 181) than was the head. In releasing the figure 'from the rocks and [. . .] the wind's indignity' (p. 181), Simon demonstrates the heroism that has been posited as one side of humankind's dual nature.

Twice Ralph is confronted with just such a primal confrontation: face to face, eye to eye. Earlier we saw that he could not connect with the primal. For example, standing at the island's rock shore 'on a level with the sea' (p. 136), Ralph follows the waves' 'ceaseless, bulging passage' and feels 'clamped down', 'helpless', and 'condemned' (p. 137) by a 'leviathan' (p. 131) monster with 'arms of surf' and 'fingers of spray' (p. 137). Nor can he accept Simon's intuitive faith when the latter whispers 'you'll get back all right' (p. 137), that 'the brute obtuseness' (p. 137) of nature can be escaped from.

Much later, after the deaths of Simon and Piggy, Ralph stands in the clearing, confronted by the same offensive head, looking steadily at the skull that 'seemed to jeer at him cynically' (p. 227). The skull's 'empty sockets seemed to hold his gaze masterfully and without effort' (p. 228), as the narrative voice observes in its re-orchestration of Simon's earlier encounter. But, unlike Simon, Ralph turns away from acknowledging the identification to externalize the monstrous.

> A sick *fear* and *rage* swept him. Fiercely he hit out at the filthy thing in front of him that bobbed like a toy and came back, still grinning into his face, so that he lashed and cried out in loathing (p. 228)

Although he keeps 'his face to the skull that lay grinning at the sky', Ralph can no more recognize his own face than Jack can recognize his own image behind the 'awesome stranger' (p. 80) with his mask of war paint when he looks into the water-filled coconut.

But Ralph cannot penetrate this 'parody thing', which in its motion amalgamates the parachutist's bowing and the 'breathing' of the sea, whose movements are those of an ancient primal rhythm that does not so much 'progress' as endure 'a momentous rise and fall' (p. 137). Such a 'minute-long fall and rise and fall' (p. 131) is the rhythm that engulfs the parachutist's body on its way to sea: 'On the mountain-top the parachute filled and moved; the figure slid, rose to its feet, falling, still falling, it sank towards the beach' (p. 189), the rhythm that imparts to Piggy some serenity: the water became 'luminous round the rock forty feet below, where Piggy had fallen' (p. 234). It is especially this rhythm that transfigures Simon in death. I quote at length, so foregrounded in this benedictory requiem is the steadfast movement:

> Somewhere over the darkened curve of the world the sun and moon were pulling; and the film of water on the earth planet was held, bulging slightly on one side while the solid core turned. The great wave of the tide moved further along the island and the water lifted. Softly, surrounded by a fringe of inquisitive bright creatures, itself a silver shape beneath the steadfast constellations, Simon's dead body moved out towards the open sea. (p. 190)

Yet for Ralph it is a terrifying rhythm, 'the age-long nightmares of falling and death' (p. 235) that occur in darkness, intimating the 'horrors of death' (p. 228).

Ralph is given a second experience of this atavistic rhythm. In his last desperate race (depicted in the penultimate scene where many of the earlier motifs are recapitulated) Ralph hides himself in Simon's cell, which notably is now described as 'the darkest hole' (p. 242) on the island. Like Simon before him, Ralph connects in terror with the primal: 'He laid his cheek against the chocolate-coloured earth, licked his dry lips and closed his eyes' and feels the ancient rhythm: 'Under the thicket, the earth was vibrating very slightly' (p. 243). Jerking his head from the earth, he peers into the 'dulled light' and sees a body slowly approaching: waist, knee, two knees, two hands, a spear sharpened at both ends.

A head. Ralph and someone called a 'savage' peer through the obscurity at each other, repeating in their action Simon's scrutiny before the head. Just at the moment his eyes connect with those of the 'savage', Ralph repeats Simon's early admonition, 'you'll get back' (p. 245), and with this partial acknowledgement of his own darkness he breaks through the cell. Expecting nothing he strikes out, screaming: 'He forgot his wounds, his hunger and thirst, and became fear; hopeless fear on flying feet, rushing through the forest towards the open beach' (p. 245).

Rushing, screaming through the fire that is described as undulating 'forward like a tide' (p. 245), screaming and rushing and *'trying to cry for mercy'* (p. 246, my italics), he trips and—fallen on the ground—sees, before him, the officer. In a manner of speaking Ralph is saved; in a manner of speaking Ralph is given mercy.

VIII

> For I have shifted somewhat from the position I held when I wrote the book. I no longer believe that the author has a sort of *patriae potestas* over his brain-children [...] Once they are printed [...] the author has no more authority over them [...] perhaps knows less about them that the critic.
>
> Golding, 'Fable'

As Fredric Jameson remarked in *The Political Unconscious*, 'Genres are essentially literary [...] or social contracts between a writer and a specific public whose function it is to specify the proper use of a particular cultural artefact.'[50] And *Lord of the Flies* is no exception to the ways in which reading practices make meanings. From my perspective, a germinal eschatology of the scapegoat/sacrificial victim can be seen emerging here. Simon's recognition of humankind's complicity occasions his ritual death with him meeting the fate of those who remind society of its guilt: we prefer to destroy the objectification of our fears rather than recognize the dark terrors in ourselves. In 'Fable' Golding (extratextually) declared this strategy as a 'failure of human sympathy', one that amounts to 'the objectivizing of our own inadequacies so as to make a scapegoat.'[51] Of course the ritual enacts the confinement and destruction of the boys' own terrors. They kill Simon as a beast, a point underscored by the perspective employed so that the frenzied crowd first sees 'a thing [...] crawling out of the forest', which immediately becomes 'the beast [that] stumbled into the [empty] horseshoe'. Then that crowd itself becomes the ravenous beast: 'the mouth of the new circle crunched and screamed' as its 'teeth and claws tore flesh' (p. 188). No scapegoat, Piggy is killed because he is alien, a pseudo-species, his death marking the inadequacy of any rational, logical world, for the conch is smashed as a blind Piggy falls into the sea. But the mild and ordinary Ralph operates only within the community's pattern; such a figure could never exorcise its fears. With no way to release fully the fear in himself, he can only weep, as the mezzo voce of the narrative voice directs, 'for the end of innocence, the darkness of man's heart' (p. 248).

Implicit as this eschatology is in the narrative texture of *Lord of the Flies*, little is explicit in the plot itself. True, Simon's encounter with the airman brings about his death, while unravelling the mystery of the bobbing figure.

Likewise, Ralph's foray with the 'savage' does release the dénouement; the fire sweeps through the island thus signalling the naval ship—a not implausible arrival given the earlier ship—and the ultimate, ironic rescue. So are charges of 'gimmickry', manipulation, and allegorizing ill considered? Do such tonally weighted episodes as those before the head contribute to, or detract from, the narrative's authenticity? And does *Lord of the Flies* present a really rather simple dictum: mankind's evil?

My sense is that, experienced at the level of reader response, these confrontation episodes reverberate beyond the allegorizing mandate. By way of their density and ambiguity, and yet familiarity, these confrontation scenes draw the reader into the imaginative act the characters themselves are depicted as making. Which is to say that the confrontation scenes construct a parallel between the focusing of individual characters' vision and the focusing of the reader's vision. Point of view, having been so skilfully handled when Simon is made to recognize that he must affirm his face, puts the reader into just such a position of recognition. As with confrontation scene so with ideographic structure, the text's total structure bringing about a similar fusion in the readers' focusing of events. By means of this ideographic structure, *Lord of the Flies* permits the reader to create textual thematics that are generated again and again, depending on the context in which it is read.

Notes

1. In the short article Golding published on James Bulger's murder, he insisted that 'There is nothing the slightest bit simple about what happened to the two-year-old [. . .] after he was led out of a Liverpool area shopping centre by two older boys,' suggesting, however, that 'there are certain things about cruelty—and especially the cruelty of boys—which may be true and from which we can learn' in 'Why Boys Become Vicious' (*San Francisco Examiner*, February 28, 1992, B-1). No recent phenomenon, the killing of children by children has a concentrated horror. In 1983, a two-year-old pushed from a roof by a seven-year-old in an argument over a toy car; in 1989, a seven-year-old shot by a nine-year-old in an argument over a Nintendo game; in 1994, a fourteen-year-old shot by an eleven-year-old boy, himself shot by gang members worried he would tell authorities about the aborted plan to kill rivals; in 1994, a five-year-old thrown from a window by ten- and eleven-year-old boys; in 1994, a five-year-old beaten to death allegedly by two children, one of them nine; in 1994, an eleven-year-old girl raped and murdered by seven- and eight-year-old boys; in 1998, fellow students (five killed and ten wounded) shot by twelve- and fourteen-year-old boys outside Jonestown, Arkansas; in 2001, a Columbine copycat fatal shooting of schoolmates at Santana High School in California, the killers provoked by perceived mistreatment and ridicule by other students.

2. Charles Monteith, 'Strangers from Within' in John Carey (ed.), *William Golding, The Man and his Books: A Tribute on his 75th Birthday*, New York, Farrar, Straus & Giroux, 1986, p. 63.

3. John Fowles, 'Golding and "Golding"' in John Carey (ed.), *William Golding, The Man and his Books: A Tribute on his 75th Birthday*, ibid., p. 149.

4. Golding, *A Moving Target*, New York, Farrar, Straus & Giroux, 1982, p. 169. Bibliographic articles like Maurice McCullen's early 1978 survey of the critical reception since *Lord of the Flies'* first publication in 1954, '*Lord of the Flies*: The Critical Quest' from *William Golding: Some Critical Considerations*, Jack Bills and Robert O. Evans (eds.), Kentucky, The University Press of Kentucky 1975, pp. 203–236, Patrick Reilly's *Lord of the Flies: Fathers and Sons*, New York, Twayne Publishers, 1992, pp. 41–42, Virginia Tiger's *William Golding: The Dark Fields of Discovery*, London: Calder & Boyars, 1974, pp. 41–46, or the chapter in James Gindin's *William Golding*, New York, St Martin's Press, 1988, pp. 20–30, reviewing the popular and critical reception—indeed, a 1994 full-length book, *William Golding: A Bibliography 1934–1993* by R.A. Gekoski and P.A. Grogan, London, André Deutsch, 1994—all give witness to 'the sheer critical firepower' that Golding charged had been levelled at the novel, now over five decades of sometimes repetitive exegeses.

5. See here, for example, Harold Bloom, *William Golding's Lord of the Flies*, Broomall, PA, Chelsea House Publishers, 1996; Gillian Hanscombe, *William Golding: Lord of the Flies*, Penguin Passport, 1986; Raymond Wilson, *Macmillan Master Guides: Lord of the Flies by William Golding*, London, Macmillan, 1986; Brian Spring, *Lord of the Flies: Helicon Study Guide*, Dublin, Helicon, 1976, Clarice Swisher (ed.) *Readings on Lord of the Flies*, San Diego, Greenhaven Press, 1997; as well as the Pamphlet entry in the bibliography of Tiger's study, covering items from 1963–1977. That *Lord of the Flies* was eminently teachable in a period following 1945 where English literature came to dominate the curricula in universities and schools in Britain, North America, India, and Pakistan (indeed, the Anglophone world, at large) was never lost on the publishing industry.

6. A. C. Capey, 'Questioning the Literary Merit of *Lord of the Flies*' in Clarice Swisher (ed.), *Readings on Lord of the Flies*, ibid., p. 146.

7. Neil McEwan, 'Golding's *Lord of the Flies*, Ballantyne's *Coral Island* and the Critics', *The Survival of the Novel: British Fiction in the Later Twentieth Century*, London, Macmillan Press, 1981, p. 148.

8. Reilly, op. cit., p. 6.

9. Ian McEwan, 'Schoolboys' in John Carey (ed.), *William Golding The Man and His Books: A Tribute on his 75th Birthday*, ibid., p. 159.

10. William Golding, *A Moving Target*, New York, Farrar, Straus & Giroux, 1982, p. 163.

11. Such preoccupations were seen in the work of Konrad Lorenz, Lionel Tiger and Edward O. Wilson, who themselves built upon Freud's earlier discoveries about infant sexualities.

12. Ian McEwan, op. cit., p. 157.

13. E.M. Forster, 'Introduction', *Lord of the Flies*, New York, Coward McCann, 1962, p. x.

14. See L.L. Dickson's *The Modern Allegories of William Golding*, Gainsville, University of South Florida Press, 1990 and Lawrence S. Friedman's *William Golding*, New York, Continuum, 1993, the publication dates of which would seem to suggest the authors might have taken into account developments in literary theory, particularly the interrogation of textual symptoms of doubt and duplicity.

15. Frederick Karl, 'The Novel as Moral Allegory: The Fiction of William Golding', *A Readers Guide to the Contemporary English Novel*, New York, Noonday Press, 1962, p. 247.

16. Stefan Hawlin, 'The Savages in the Forest: Decolonizing William Golding', *Critical Survey* 7 (1995), p. 126.

17. George Herndl, 'Golding and Salinger, A Clear Choice', *Wiseman Review* (1964–1965), p. 310.

18. In this context see the concerns of late twentieth-century readers in Caitlin Quinn-Lang, 'Jets, Ships and Atom Bombs in Golding's *Lord of the Flies*' in Will Wright & Steven

Kaplan (eds), *The Image of Technology in literature, the Media and Society*, University of Southern Colorado Society for Interdisciplinary Study, Pueblo & Co, 1994, pp. 78–83, and Steven Connor, 'Rewriting Wrong: On the Ethics of Literary Reversion' in Theo D'haen (ed.), *Liminal Postmodernisms: The Post Modern, the (Post) Colonial and the Post Feminist*, Amsterdam-Atlanta, GA: Rodopi: B.V, 1994, pp. 79–97. One should be reminded, however, that in the fifty years of exegesis, never once has the question been asked as to what would have happened had girls been dropped on the island.

19. Alan Sinfield, *Literature, Politics and Culture in Postwar Britain*, Oxford, Blackwell, 1989, p. 141.

20. Quite diverse interpretations have emerged, even when there was the agreement that the novel should be read as a political fable. 'A population of interpretations', generated by some two hundred undergraduate students' responses to the novel, was the result of an experiment undertaken in a political theory course where such idiosyncratic views as the following appeared: 'The novel has Marxist overtones of the connections between economic conditions and social structure.' (Quoted in Steven Brown's 'Political Literature and the Response of the Reader: Experimental Studies of Interpretation, Imagery, and Criticism', *The American Political Science Review* 72, 1977, p. 569). Golding was at pains to make 'economic conditions' on the island so embracing that, literally and metaphorically, fruit was for the plucking; with physical hardship banished, the experiment in living could be tested on its own grounds.

21. Kathleen Woodward, 'On Aggression: William Golding's *Lord of the Flies*' in Martin H. Greenberg and Joseph D. Olander (eds), *No Place Else: Explorations in Utopian and Dystopian Fiction*, Southern Illinois University Press, 1983, p. 216.

22. C.B. Cox, '*Lord of the Flies*', *Critical Quarterly* 2 (1960), p. 112.

23. Golding to Webb, 'Interview with William Golding', W L. Webb, *Guardian* (October 11, 1980), p. 12.

24. Bergonzi, Bernard and John Whitley, *The English Novel: Questions in Literature*, London, Sussex Books, 1976, p. 176. The second film adaptation of the novel (Harry Hook, Director; Castle Rock Entertainment with Nelson Entertainment, 1990) changed the children from English preparatory school boys to American Naval cadets, thus damaging the movie's narrative specificity, for me at any rate.

25. Bloom, op. cit., p. 6.

26. That Golding chose 'a homogeneous group of middle-class white children, all of whom are boys' is not so much an omission which prevented the emergence of 'racial tension [. . .] sexual tension . . . [and] the tension of cultural difference' (Woodward, op. cit., p. 208) as one which included class acrimony, an abiding British malignancy and one which English authors, from Austen onwards, have castigated.

27. Adding that the choice of the cathedral school was deliberate, Golding explained that the intent was to intensify the narrative's peripatetic reversal of fortune: 'It's only because of that civilized height that the fall is a tragedy' (Golding in Douglas M. Davis, 'A Conversation with William Golding', *New Republic*, May 4, 1963, p. 29).

28. Many commentators have remarked upon Golding's unsentimental assessment of the culture of schoolboy society, with its bullying, and correctly ascribed that familiarity to his years as a master at Bishop Wordsworth School in Salisbury. However, to my knowledge, it has yet to be pointed out that (unlike his father before him, who taught at a grammar school in Marlborough, the town itself being dominated by Marlborough College, attended by the sons of the upper echelons of British society since 1843) Golding taught in a public school, adjacent to Salisbury Cathedral, with its choristers. The class disparity would not have gone unnoticed. The former lay vicar and adult singer in the choir of Salisbury Cathedral, Richard Shepard, observed that the cathedral's choristers corresponded quite

closely to Jack's in terms of their clothes. 'The boys used to march crocodile fashion across from the school to the cathedral [...] The head chorister would shout the words "Stand erect, by the left, quick march" and the procession would march off across the green into the cloisters and on into the cathedral. The shouted commands "LEFT! RIGHT!" were, for the sake of decency and decorum, silenced once the boys were inside the cathedral.' 'Programme Commentary', Nigel Williams, *Pilot Theatre Company Production of Lord of the Flies*, Lyric Theatre Hammersmith, July 1998.

29. Golding to Williams, ibid., p. 4.

30. Bloom, op. cit., p. 5.

31. Monteith, op. cit., p. 57.

32. Monteith, op. cit., p. 62.

33. Jack Biles, *Talk: Conversations with William Golding*, New York, Harcourt, Brace & Jovanovich, 1970, p. 53.

34. Ian Gregor, '"He Wondered": The Religious Imagination of William Golding' in John Carey (ed.), *William Golding The Man and his Books: A Tribute on his 75th Birthday*, New York: Farrar, Straus & Giroux, 1986, p. 99.

35. 'Interview with William Golding', Henry David Rosso, *Ann Arbor News* (December 1985) p. 5.

36. Bernard S. Oldsey and Stanley Weintraub, *The Art of William Golding*, New York, Harcourt, Brace and World, 1965, p. 16.

37. Indeed, '[t]here are echoes of *The Tempest* throughout *Lord of the Flies*: a shipwreck, transactions with evil, a final ambiguous rescue' (Reilly, op. cit., p. 119).

38. Kermode's analysis of the parodic features of the two books ('The Meaning of It All', *Books and Bookmen*, August 1959, pp. 10–16) was amplified by Carl Niemeyer in '*The Coral Island* Revisited' *College English* (1961), pp. 241–45, still a useful essay, although one that maximizes this dependence into a limitation. As a corrective, McEwan's 'Golding's *Lord of the Flies*, Ballantyne's *Coral Island* and the Critics' (op. cit.) makes the point that the academic community of the 1960s, 'eager to explain the "contemporary sensibility" [of *Lord of the Flies*]' rested its case 'on a mid-Victorian book for boys' (p. 151).

39. Golding to Kermode, op. cit., p. 12.

40. The term was James Gindin's in a 1960 essay, 'Gimmick and Metaphor in the Novels of William Golding', *Modern English Studies* 6 (1960), pp. 145–52, one which provided arms for attacks on the author's allegedly contrived and manipulative ('cheating') endings. This acrimonious, if influential, criticism, seems odd when one considers the following: Joyce's narrative shift was not seen as a gimmick when in *Ulysses* we move from Leopold Bloom to Molly; Euripides is nowhere described as cheating when a *deus ex machina* concludes the *Ion*. Golding has gone on record more than once in ascribing his own structures to the influence of the Greek dramatists; see Golding in conversation with Davis (op. cit.) and in conversation with Carey (op. cit.).

41. Problematic as authorial explications are, since they impose extra-literary 'meaning', in 'Fable' Golding wrote: 'What the grownups send them is a sign [...] [T]hat arbitrary sign stands for off campus history, the thing which threatens every child everywhere, the history of blood and intolerance, of ignorance and prejudice, the thing which is dead and won't he down [...] it falls on the very place where the children are making their one constructive attempt to get themselves helped. It dominates the mountaintop and so prevents them keeping a fire alight there as a signal' (pp. 95–96).

42. Waves of expletives roll from the schoolboy tongues in the 1990 American movie adaptation, presumably in an effort to update schoolboy slang. Is the mimetic change successful?

43. Golding's explication of the book's thematics is once again problematic, since authorial commentary tends to immobilize the play of meanings in a text, creating another potential text. As he explained: 'The whole book is symbolic in nature except the rescue in the end where adult life appears, dignified and capable, but in reality enmeshed in the same evil as the symbolic life of the children on the island. The officer, having interrupted a manhunt, prepares to take the children off the island in a cruiser, which will presently be hunting its enemy in the same implacable way. And who will rescue the adult and his cruiser?' (Golding to Epstein, E.L. Epstein, 'Notes on *Lord of the Flies*', *Lord of the Flies*, New York, Capricorn Books, 1959, pp. 191–92)

44. Patrick Reilly, op. cit. p. 102. Amplifying this doubleness, Reilly examines what he felicitously describes as the novel's 'competing narratologies': 'the two parallel texts, the first in a "low" style of schoolboy slang evocative of the world of Greyfriars and Billy Bunter, the other in the "high" style of the narrator's gloss and commentary, his reinterpretation of the action to reveal its underlying import' (p. 100). Reilly's point, that without the narratorial commentary the reader would be limited to the incomprehensible perceptions of the children, is well taken.

45. Golding, 'Why Boys Become Vicious', op. cit.

46. Ian Gregor and Mark Kinkead-Weekes, *William Golding*, London, Faber and Faber, 1967, p. 19.

47. Reilly, op. cit., p. 111.

48. In an essay entitled 'Digging for Pictures' there is a re-orchestration of these motifs; excavating for ruins in the chalk hills of Wiltshire, the Golding-persona discovers a victim of prehistoric murder in a 'dark quiet pit'; its 'jaws were wide open, *grinning* perhaps with *cynicism*' (p. 60, my italics).

49. John S. Whitley, *Golding: Lord of the Flies*, London, Edward Arnold, 1970, p.48.

50. Fredric Jameson, *The Political Unconscious*, Ithaca, Cornell University Press, 1981, p. 106.

51. Golding, 'Fable', p. 94 (my italics). In the many years that he had been compelled to 'explain' *Lord of the Flies*, this was the only occasion where he publicly uses this term.

Chronology

1911	Born in Cornwall on September 19, 1911, one of two sons of Alec Glolding, a math teacher and soon-to-be senior master of Marlborough Grammar School, and Mildred Golding, an activist for women's suffrage.
1930	Completes secondary education at the Marlborough School; can play several instruments. Enters Brasenose College, Oxford, to study science; soon switches to study English literature.
1934	A friend sends twenty-nine of Golding's poems to Macmillan; *Poems* is published in Contemporary Poets series.
1935	Receives bachelor's degree in English and diploma in education from Oxford. Writes, acts, and produces for a small, noncommercial theater in London.
1939	Marries Ann Brookfield, an analytical chemist; begins teaching English, Greek literature in translation, and philosophy at Bishop Wordsworth's School in Salisbury. Involved in adult education; teaches in army camps and Maidstone Gaol.
1940–45	Enlists in Royal Navy at start of World War II; works at secret scientific research center, is injured in an explosion, and recovers. Given command of small rocket-launching craft; involved in chase and sinking of the *Bismarck*; takes part in D-Day assault in 1944.

1945	Returns to teach at Bishop Wordsworth's School.
1954	*Lord of the Flies* is published by Faber and Faber after being rejected by twenty-one other publishers. Retires from teaching to write full time.
1955	*The Inheritors* is published. Golding becomes a fellow of the Royal Society of Literature.
1956	*Pincher Martin* is published; republished in the United States in 1957 as *The Two Lives of Christopher Martin*.
1958	A play, *The Brass Butterfly*, is performed at Oxford and in London.
1959	*Free Fall* is published.
1960–62	Becomes frequent contributor of essays and book reviews to the *Spectator*. From 1961 to 1962, spends year as writer in residence at Hollins College, Virginia, and tours as lecturer at other American colleges.
1960	On April 20, BBC radio script, *Miss Pulkinhorn*, is performed.
1961	Completes master of arts degree at Oxford. On March 19, BBC radio script, *Break My Heart*, is performed.
1963	*Lord of the Flies* is first produced for film.
1964	*The Spire* is published.
1965	Collection of essays, *The Hot Gates*, is published. Golding made a commander of the British Empire.
1967	*The Pyramid* is published.
1971	*The Scorpion God: Three Short Novels* is published.
1976	First visits Egypt.
1979	*Darkness Visible* is published.
1980	*Rites of Passage* is published; wins Booker Prize for fiction.
1982	A second collection of essays, *A Moving Target*, is published.
1983	Wins Nobel Prize for Literature.
1984	*The Paper Men* is published.
1985	*An Egyptian Journal* is published.
1987	*Close Quarters*, the second volume of the sea trilogy begun with *Rites of Passage*, is published.
1989	*Fire Down Below*, the conclusion to the sea trilogy, is published.
1993	Dies on June 19 in Cornwall.

Contributors

HAROLD BLOOM is Sterling Professor of the Humanities at Yale University. He is the author of 30 books, including *Shelley's Mythmaking, The Visionary Company, Blake's Apocalypse, Yeats, A Map of Misreading, Kabbalah and Criticism, Agon: Toward a Theory of Revisionism, The American Religion, The Western Canon,* and *Omens of Millennium: The Gnosis of Angels, Dreams, and Resurrection. The Anxiety of Influence* sets forth Professor Bloom's provocative theory of the literary relationships between the great writers and their predecessors. His most recent books include *Shakespeare: The Invention of the Human,* a 1998 National Book Award finalist, *How to Read and Why, Genius: A Mosaic of One Hundred Exemplary Creative Minds, Hamlet: Poem Unlimited, Where Shall Wisdom Be Found?,* and *Jesus and Yahweh: The Names Divine.* In 1999, Professor Bloom received the prestigious American Academy of Arts and Letters Gold Medal for Criticism. He has also received the International Prize of Catalonia, the Alfonso Reyes Prize of Mexico, and the Hans Christian Andersen Bicentennial Prize of Denmark.

K. CHELLAPPAN has been a professor and chairman of the English department at Bharathidasan University, Tiruchirapalli, India. He has authored titles such as *Bharathi: The Visionary Humanist.*

JAMES GINDIN is the author of several books, including *Postwar British Fiction; New Accents and Attitudes.*

S. J. BOYD has taught at the University of St. Andrews in Scotland and is the author of *The Novels of William Golding.*

L. L. DICKSON is the author of *The Modern Allegories of William Golding*.

LAWRENCE S. FRIEDMAN has published books on William Golding, Cynthia Ozick, and Isaac Bashevis Singer.

STEFAN HAWLIN is a senior lecturer at the University of Buckingham. He has published *The Complete Critical Guide to Robert Browning* and edited or co-edited other works as well. He is on the advisory panel for *Victorian Poetry*.

JAMES R. BAKER is the author of *William Golding: A Critical Study* and co-editor of the Casebook Edition of *Lord of the Flies*. He is one of the founders of the journal *Twentieth Century Literature*.

PAUL CRAWFORD has been a lecturer at the University of Nottingham, England. He is the author of *Politics and History in William Golding: The World Turned Upside Down* and also has published a novel.

VIRGINIA TIGER is a professor and chair of the English department at Rutgers University–Newark. She is the author of *William Golding: The Dark Fields of Discovery* and has published many pieces in journals and other texts.

Bibliography

Baker, James R., and Arthur P. Ziegler Jr., eds. *Lord of the Flies* (Casebook Edition). New York: Berkley Publishing Group, 1988.

Bay-Petersen, Ole. "Circular Imagery in *Lord of the Flies.*" *Studies in Language and Literature* 4 (October 1990): 103–19.

Boyd, S. J. *The Novels of William Golding.* Brighton: Harvester Press, 1988.

Carey, John, ed. *William Golding: The Man and His Books.* New York: Straus & Giroux, 1987.

Dick, Bernard F. *William Golding.* New York: Twayne, 1967. Rev. ed. 1987.

Fitzgerald, John F. and John R. Kayser. "Golding's *Lord of the Flies*: Pride as Original Sin." *Studies in the Novel* 24, no. 1 (Spring 1992): 78–88.

Hadomi, Leah. "Imagery as a Source of Irony in Golding's *Lord of the Flies.*" *Hebrew University Studies in Literature and the Arts* 9, no. 1 (1981): 126–138.

Hesling, Isabelle and Anne-Marie Carassou. "Cerebral Analysis of Rational and Emotional Traces in Literature." In *Impersonality and Emotion in Twentieth-Century British Literature*, edited by Christine Reynier and Jean-Michel Ganteau, 167–81. Montpellier, France: Université Montpellier III, 2005.

Hollindale, Peter. "*Lord of the Flies* in the Twenty-First Century." *Use of English* 53, no. 1 (Autumn 2001): 1–12.

Johnston, Arnold. "*Lord of the Flies*: Fable, Myth, and Fiction." In *Of Earth and Darkness: The Novels of William Golding.* Columbia: University of Missouri Press, 1980.

Kinkead-Weekes, Mark. "*Lord of the Flies*." In *William Golding, A Critical Study*, edited by Mark Kinkead-Weekes and Ian Gregor. London: Faber & Faber, 1967.

Kruger, Arnold. "Golding's *Lord of the Flies*." *Explicator* 57, no. 3 (Spring 1999): 167–69.

Macleod, Norman. "How to Talk about Prose Style: An Example from Golding's *Lord of the Flies*." *Revista Canaria de Estudios Ingleses* 10 (April 1985): 119–140.

Monteith, Charles. " 'Strangers from Within' into '*Lord of the Flies*.' " *(London) Times Literary Supplement* 4355 (September 19, 1986): 1030.

Niemeyer, Carl. "*The Coral Island* Revisited." *College English* 22, no. 4 (January 1961): 241–45.

Page, Norman. "*Lord of the Flies*: From Ballantyne to Conrad." In *Fingering Netsukes: Selected Papers from the First International William Golding Conference*, edited by Frédéric Regard, 25–29. Saint-Étienne: Univ. de Saint-Étienne, with Faber, 1995.

Redpath, Philip. "The Resolution of Antithesis in 'Lord of the Flies' and 'The Inheritors.'" *English: The Journal of the English Association* 33, no. 145 (Spring 1984): 43–52.

Regard, Frédéric. "The Obscenity of Writing: A Reappraisal of Golding's First Novel." In *Fingering Netsukes: Selected Papers from the First International William Golding Conference*, edited by Frédéric Regard, 31–47. Saint-Étienne: Univ. de Saint-Étienne, with Faber, 1995.

Roncace, Mark. "*The Bacchae* and *Lord of the Flies*: A Few Observations with the Help of E. R. Dodds." *Classical and Modern Literature: A Quarterly* 18, no. 1 (Fall 1997): 37–51.

Roy, Paula Alida. "Boys' Club—No Girls Allowed: Absence as Presence in William Golding's *Lord of the Flies* (1954)." In *Women in Literature: Reading through the Lens of Gender*, edited by Jerilyn Fisher and Ellen S. Silber, 175–77. Westport, Conn.: Greenwood, 2003.

Selby, Keith. "Golding's *Lord of the Flies*." *Explicator* 41, no. 3 (Spring 1983): 57–59.

Singh, Minnie. "The Government of Boys" Golding's *Lord of the Flies* and Ballantyne's *Coral Island*." *Children's Literature* 25 (1997): 205–13.

Swisher, Clarice, ed. *Readings on* Lord of the Flies. San Diego, Calif.: Greenhaven, 1997.

Tanzman, L. "The Mulberry in William Golding's Fiction: Emblematic Connotations." *Notes on Contemporary Literature* 21, no. 5 (November 1991): 7–8.

———. "The Murder of Simon in Golding's *Lord of the Flies.*" *Notes on Contemporary Literature* 17, no. 5 (November 1987): 2–3.

Whitley, John S. *Golding: Lord of the Flies.* London: Edward Arnold Ltd., 1970.

Woodward, Kathleen. "On Aggression: William Golding's *Lord of the Flies.*" In *No Place Else: Explorations in Utopian and Dystopian Fiction*, edited by Eric S. Rabkin, Martin H. Greenberg, and Joseph D. Olander, 199–224. Carbondale: Southern Illinois University Press, 1983.

Yoshida, Tetsuo. "The Reversal of Light and Dark in *Lord of the Flies.*" *Studies in English Language and Literature* 35 (March 1985): 63–84.

Acknowledgments

K. Chellappan, "Vision and Structure in *Lord of the Flies:* A Semiotic Approach," from *William Golding: An Indian Response.* © 1987 by Taqi Ali Mirza.

James Gindin, "The Fictional Explosion: *Lord of the Flies* and *The Inheritors,*" from *William Golding.* © 1988 by James Gindin.

S.J. Boyd, "The Nature of the Beast: *Lord of the Flies* (1954)," from *The Novels of William Golding,* St. Martin's Press, 1988. Reproduced with permission of Palgrave Macmillan.

L.L. Dickson, "*Lord of the Flies,*" from *The Modern Allegories of William Golding.* © 1990 by the Board of Regents of the State of Florida. Reprinted with permission of the University Press of Florida.

Lawrence S. Friedman, "Grief, Grief, Grief: *Lord of the Flies,*" from *William Golding,* Continuum. © 1993 by Lawrence S. Friedman.

Stefan Hawlin, "The Savages in the Forest: Decolonising William Golding," from *Critical Survey* 7, no. 2. © 1995 by *Critical Survey.*

James R. Baker, "Golding and Huxley: The Fables of Demonic Possession." Originally appeared in *Twentieth Century Literature's* Fall 2000 issue (vol. 46, no. 3). Reprinted by permission of the publisher.

Index